The Power and Limits of NGOs

The Power and Limits of NGOs

A CRITICAL LOOK AT BUILDING DEMOCRACY
IN EASTERN EUROPE AND EURASIA

Sarah E. Mendelson and John K. Glenn, Editors

COLUMBIA UNIVERSITY PRESS

NEW YORK

Columbia University Press
Publishers Since 1893
New York Chichester, West Sussex

Library of Congress Cataloging-in-Publication Data
The power and limits of NGOs : A critical look at building democracy in Eastern Europe
and Eurasia / Sarah E. Mendelson and John K. Glenn, editors.
   p. cm
   Includes bibliographical references and index.
   ISBN 0-231-12490-2 (alk. paper) — ISBN 0-231-12491-0 (pbk. : alk. paper)
    1. Democratization—Europe, Eastern. 2. Non-governmental organizations—Europe,
Eastern. 3. Europe, Eastern—Politics and government—1989— 4. Democratization—
Former Soviet republics. 5. Non-governmental organizations—Former Soviet republics.
6. Former Soviet republics—Politics and government—1991— I. Mendelson, Sarah
Elizabeth. II. Glen, John K.

JN96.A58 P69 2002
320.947—dc21   2002019245

∞

Columbia University Press books are printed on permanent and durable
acid-free paper.

Printed in the United States of America
c 10 9 8 7 6 5 4 3 2 1
p 10 9 8 7 6 5 4 3 2

To Jack Snyder, with appreciation

CONTENTS

TABLES

ACKNOWLEDGMENTS

A book like this one can be done only with the support of many different institutions and individuals. It was made possible by a grant from the Carnegie Corporation to Columbia University's Institute of War and Peace Studies and the Harriman Institute. On behalf of the project's participants, we would like to thank in particular Jack Snyder, Ingrid Gerstmann, Audrey Rosenblatt, and Annette Clear. We thank those who attended the May 1997 conference at Columbia University, in particular Jeanne Bourgault, Larry Diamond, Larry Garber, Michael McFaul, and Kathryn Sikkink. Thanks also to Mark Von Hagen, Raj Menon, Alex Motyl, Alex Cooley, Robin Bhatty, and Tibor Papp. For their efforts on the larger project we especially thank Jim Clem, Marta Dyczok, Tina Nelson, Anne Nivat, Sandra Pralong, Vello Pettai, and Sherrill Stroschein. We would also like to thank Teresa Lawson for her help in organizing and editing this volume. We would especially like to thank Tom Carothers and the Carnegie Endowment for International Peace for providing a home to this project in the early stages.

Sarah E. Mendelson is grateful to the Fletcher School of Law and Diplomacy at Tufts University for granting leave and supporting her work on this project. She particularly thanks Vigen Sargsyan and Anita Gambos for their research assistance.

John K. Glenn gratefully acknowledges the support during the research for the project and in the preparation of the manuscript given by the Institute for Human Sciences in Vienna, the European University Institute in Florence, New York University, and the Council for European Studies.

CONTRIBUTORS

Fiona B. Adamson is a postdoctoral fellow at the Belfer Center for Science and International Affairs, Harvard University.

Karen Ballentine is the research coordinator for the International Peace Academy in New York City.

V. P. Gagnon Jr. is an assistant professor of political science at Ithaca College and visiting research fellow in the Peace Studies Program at Cornell University.

John K. Glenn is executive director of the Council for European Studies and a visiting scholar at New York University.

Pauline Jones Luong is an assistant professor of political science at Yale University.

Patrice C. McMahon is an assistant professor of political science at the University of Nebraska at Lincoln.

Sarah E. Mendelson is an assistant professor of international politics at the Fletcher School of Law and Diplomacy, Tufts University, and a senior fellow at the Center for Strategic and International Studies, Washington, D.C.

Leslie Powell is a senior associate of the Eurasia Group in New York City.

James Richter is an associate professor of political science and chair of the Environmental Studies Program at Bates College.

Erika Weinthal is an assistant professor of political science at Tel Aviv University.

The Power and Limits of NGOs

Chapter 1

INTRODUCTION: TRANSNATIONAL NETWORKS AND NGOS IN POSTCOMMUNIST SOCIETIES

Sarah E. Mendelson and John K. Glenn

Since the end of the cold war, postcommunist states in Central and Eastern Europe and Eurasia have been host to a virtual army of international nongovernmental organizations (NGOs) from the United States, Britain, Germany, and elsewhere in Europe. These NGOs are working on various aspects of institutional development, such as helping to establish competitive political parties and elections, independent media, and civic advocacy groups, as well as trying to reduce ethnic conflict. A decade after the fall of the Berlin Wall and the collapse of the Soviet Union, policy makers and scholars had barely begun to assess the effect of international efforts to help build democratic institutions.[1] Although opinions are strong, little is truly known about the influence of this assistance, carried out on a transnational level with local political and social activists. This book, which grew out of a project based at Columbia University, was designed to address this gap by focusing on the strategies that the international NGOs used to help build institutions and support activists in these countries.[2]

Initial hopes and enthusiasm for a rapid and smooth transition toward democracy have long since given way to the reality that the process is incremental and uneven and that it will likely continue to be so for decades. The premise of this book is that a better understanding of the process, one that differentiates the strategies of international NGOs rather than treating them as if they are the same, could lead to more effective support for the development of democratic institutions. At the most basic level it could help in building healthier ties between international activists and those activists inside postcommunist societies who experience every day the chaotic, sometimes violent, usually nonlinear world of political and social transformations.

The political trajectory of these states and societies, especially Russia's, is central to peace and stability in Europe. A Russian descent into authoritarianism would, for example, affect not only its immediate neighbors but also Western Europe and the United States. However, the mechanisms behind these transitions are still poorly understood. Policy makers, scholars, donors, and especially activists working in the field need to understand to what extent these transitions are domestically determined and whether and to what extent international organizations and other outside groups, such as transnational networks, have affected them. What institutional designs common to Europe and North America have been transplanted to these regions in ways that are likely to be sustainable? What designs have been successfully adopted by existing indigenous organizations? Have international efforts helped, hurt, or been irrelevant to the transitions? Have these efforts been poor investments? What have been their unintended consequences?

To answer these questions the contributors to this book take a detailed look at efforts to support civil society in a number of the postcommunist Eastern European and Eurasian countries. The case studies presented here are part of a larger study that examined developments in several sectors of activity, including political parties, elections, media, and efforts at reducing ethnic conflict. Investigators interviewed activists from international NGOs and local activists, including those who had not directly received outside assistance, to assess the influence of international NGO strategies. They compared developments in a specific sector in the late 1990s with what the sector had looked like when the country's communist regime fell from power. Case selection included regions that are strategically important, such as Russia, parts of Central Europe widely viewed as successfully democratizing, and parts of Central Asia that are less so. The cases also address the types of institutions—such as civic advocacy groups—that are thought to be integral to democratic states and societies and that have therefore received considerable attention from international donors and NGOs. The project provides a portrait of the mechanisms by which ideas and practices commonly associated with democratic states have diffused to and evolved in formerly communist states and societies, revealing also some of the conditions that inhibit diffusion and development.

The cases show mixed outcomes. With relatively small amounts of money international donors and NGOs have played a large and important role in many formerly communist states, helping local activists to design and build institutions associated with democracy. However, they have done little as yet to affect how these institutions actually function. Political parties, regular elections, independent media, and local NGOs are all now part of the political landscape in many states across Eastern and Central Europe and Eurasia; their links with foreign groups are considerable and often robust. In nearly every one of our cases, however, these new institutions function poorly and have but weak links to their own societies. Such organizations have proliferated but often serve the interests of foreign donors more than those of the local population. In certain cases, such as environmental groups in Russia and Kazakhstan, their vigor and effectiveness have actually declined, even as environmental degradation and international engagement have increased.

Historical legacies of the decades of communist rule account in part for the poor functioning of fragile new institutions, but in this book we show that these results are also in part a consequence of the international NGOs' strategies. Western groups tended to rely on practitioners with little knowledge of the region, such as political activists from U.S. communities or British civic organizers, to implement strategies for building democratic institutions that were developed in Western capitals. These technicians often were poorly prepared to anticipate how local activists, given local historical legacies, were likely to receive recommendations.

Beyond an assessment of which international NGO strategies worked and how, the book addresses other reasons for variations in outcomes, pointing to the conditions that affect the diffusion of ideas and practices. The ways in which international NGOs engage or ignore local political entrepreneurs and local political and organizational cultures emerge as particularly important. Context and the degree to which new ideas and practices complement or compete with well-established customs and beliefs play a critical role.

Below we discuss the state of the debate about democracy assistance, surveying policy and scholarly concerns about transnationalism and international relations. We describe the project from which the case studies were written and highlight the methods of evaluation that our investigators used in researching and writing the case studies. We present synopses of the chapters, drawing out the lessons learned from each case study. We close by identifying the limits of this project and summarizing the main findings of the study.

THE STATE OF THE DEBATE

Neither champions nor critics of democracy assistance have systematically grounded their discussion in detailed analysis of contemporary efforts at promoting democracy. Because the trajectory of the formerly communist states of East-Central Europe and Eurasia is a high-stakes issue in international relations and international security, assessments of the scope and pace of democratization and

the influence of democracy promotion on their transition deserve detailed research. Instead, particularly in the United States, political and organizational interests drove assessments for much of the 1990s.

Officials from the Clinton administration, the U.S. Agency for International
Development (USAID), and American NGOs working in the regions tended to
overestimate the role that democracy assistance played in fostering positive
change and thus helped create expectations that contrasted negatively with
what was actually happening in the recipient countries. The administration and
the NGOs tended to talk only about success stories, because they feared losing
funding from a hostile Congress if they openly discussed the difficulties of democratization and the limited role that assistance often plays in the process.[3]
Democracy assistance, while growing in the 1990s, has been vulnerable to de-
clines in overall foreign aid budgets. It remains a small proportion of the total
amount of U.S. foreign assistance, averaging 16.5 percent of aid to Eastern Europe and 3.5 percent of total aid to the former Soviet Union from 1990 to 1999
(see table 1.1).[4]

Partly in response to this approach, there has been a backlash in policy journals, with critics arguing that assistance is a waste of money and could even be
dangerous. In an influential article Fareed Zakaria implies that assistance
helped to promote what he labels "illiberal democracy," where, although elections occur, rulers ignore constitutionally guaranteed freedoms.[5] Critics typically understand themselves not as ideological or partisan but as responding to
specific events. For example, Russia watchers' criticisms of assistance became
increasingly frequent following, among other manifestations of arbitrariness,
Boris Yeltsin's firing of several prime ministers, a second war in Chechnya, and
money-laundering scandals that appeared to involve both international assistance and the Kremlin.[6] Commentary on assistance became fodder for election
campaigns: In the United States "who lost Russia" was one of the few foreign
policy topics discussed in the 2000 presidential race.

Understanding the power and limits of external support for democratic development is important because of the changing, some say eroding, nature of
state sovereignty. Foreign policy increasingly involves nonstate actors. While
the promotion of democracy has been a central plank of U.S. foreign policy
since the end of the cold war, it has frequently been nongovernmental organizations (occasionally funded by USAID) that have implemented this policy in
the formerly communist countries. Similarly, while states have pursued such
foreign policy initiatives as enlargement of the North American Treaty Organization (NATO) and the expansion of the European Union, successful integration into the Euro-Atlantic community may depend at least as much on the degree to which organizations outside the governments embrace norms, rules,
and practices common in Western democracies. One way to understand the

TABLE 1.1 Western Governmental Assistance to Central
and Eastern Europe and Eurasia 1990–1999 (millions of U.S. $)

	1990–99	Democracy Assistance	% of total to Democracy Assistance
To Central and Eastern Europe:			
U.S.	3,640	599	16.5
EU[1] (other than PHARE)	4,568		
EU (PHARE)	4,550	891[2]	19.5
To Russia:			
U.S.[3]	4,471	133	2.8
EU	1,417	272	19
To Eurasia (not including Russia):[4]			
U.S.	5,807	222	3.8
EU	3,597	393	11
To Eurasia (total):[5]			
U.S.	10,278	355	3.5
EU	4,995	665	13

Sources: U.S. Department of State 1998 *Annual Report*; Support for East European Democracy (SEED) Act Implementation Report, 1998; TACIS; Kevin F.F. Quigley, *For Democracy's Sake: Foundations and Democracy Assistance in Central Europe* (Washington, D.C.: Woodrow Wilson Center Press, 1997); Janine Wedel, *Collision and Collusion: The Strange Case of Western Aid to Eastern Europe, 1989–1998* (New York: St. Martin's Press, 1998); Thomas Carothers, *Aiding Democracy Abroad: The Learning Curve* (Washington, D.C.: Carnegie Endowment for International Peace, 1999).

1. EU figures do not include 1998 assistance.
2. This is the minimum calculation, as provided by the PHARE program, based on the "Civil Society Democratization" subtitle figures: $231 million for "Administrative Reform" and $651 million for "Education, Training and Research." With these totals the "Democracy" spending would equal $891 million, that is, 19.5% of the total.
3. Totals of U.S. assistance to Russia and Eurasia include Freedom Support Act (FSA) funds and non-FSA funds, such as cooperative threat reduction. All "democratic assistance" programs are funded by FSA. From FSA, 6% for Russia went to democracy assistance (figures include percentage of funds expended for "Democratic Reform" and the "Eurasia Foundation"). About 7% of FSA funds for all of Eurasia were spent on democracy assistance.
4. Assistance to the countries of the former Soviet Union started in 1992. The figures here represent assistance expenditures in 1992–1998.
5. These figures do not include assistance distributed through the IMF, the World Bank, or the European Bank for Reconstruction and Development.

potential for successful integration is to examine behavior in the nongovernmental realm and the effect of external support.

This book concentrates on democracy assistance to support the development of "civil society." The argument that a robust civil society is the basis for sustainable democracy is heard widely in public debate, from Robert Putnam's writings on civic culture to the management guru Peter Drucker's declaration that the main global challenge is promoting "worldwide civil society, without which there can be neither political nor social stability."[7] By contrast, others have argued that international assistance is simply irrelevant. The problem centers on how civil society might emerge within countries that lack traditions of independent organization or volunteerism and lack a legal framework that recognizes and supports not-for-profit activity. Claus Offe has claimed starkly that "the rise of a robust 'civil society' cannot be initiated from the outside." He explains that

> while democratic institutions and economic resources can be "transplanted" from the outside world (or their introduction facilitated and their durability protected by a host of positive and negative sanctions designed to support and strengthen new democratic regimes), the civic "spirit" or "mental software" that is needed to drive the hardware of the new institutions is less easily influenced by external intervention.[8]

Paul Stubbs declares that most "civil society" assistance programs become merely troughs at which local elites feed.[9]

The term *civil society* requires careful use: Sometimes the term refers to democratic opposition to communist regimes in Eastern Europe.[10] In formerly communist countries independent advocacy groups—the core of civil society—emerged in opposition to regimes that sought to repress all activity outside the control of the ruling communist parties. The success of such repression varied, with results ranging from vibrant underground activity in Poland in the 1980s to its total absence in parts of the former Soviet Union. At other times, however, the term seems to refer to a normative model of an economic and political "third way" between socialism and capitalism.[11]

In light of the contested debate and multiplicity of meanings, we use the term to mean public interest advocacy organizations outside the control of the state that seek to influence it on behalf of public aims. In this sense of the term the development of civil society is essential to democracy; a "third sector" of nonprofit organizations can serve as advocates for the public good and as watchdogs of political power.[12] Thomas Carothers observes that advocacy-oriented groups are crucial to democracy because they "seek to influence governmental policy on some specific set of issues" and thus serve to articulate citizens' interests vis-à-vis the state.[13] But as several contributors to this volume point out, the mere existence of NGOs, as part of this third sector, does not necessarily reflect the strength of civil society. It merely points to its potential. Instead, we need to look closely at how NGOs actually function and their influence on both discourse and policy. To speak accurately about the vibrancy or weakness of civil society requires in-depth case studies.

Western support for the development of civil society and the ties that bind activists across borders is part of the larger debate in international relations scholarship on transnationalism.[14] This aspect of international life drew much attention from scholars in the 1990s. The main focus tended to be on human rights, on norms regulating behavior in the security realm such as those concerning the use of land mines or nuclear weapons, and on environmental policies.[15] Much international relations literature has focused on how the power of the norms explains various outcomes, such as changes in a state's human rights policy, prohibitions against using certain weapons, or the development of legislation to protect the environment. But scholars have begun to broaden their inquiries from the role of norms to the mechanisms by which norms diffuse (or do not diffuse) throughout the international system. In a groundbreaking book Margaret Keck and Kathryn Sikkink established the influence of transnational advocacy networks (networks of nonstate actors), state actors, and international organizations that are bound together "by the centrality of principled ideas or values."[16] Increasingly, such networks have begun to alter traditional conceptions of and practices relating to national sovereignty by making new resources available to domestic challengers and by transforming the behavior of international organizations.

The transnational democracy networks in this book, like the theoretical models discussed in the literature, have multiple nodes. Principal nodes include the local activists in postcommunist states; the international NGOs that usually operate both within these states and from home offices in Western capitals; the assistance officials in Western embassies; international organizations and other donors; and some policy makers. As with Keck and Sikkink's work, these networks are advocating on behalf of others or promoting and "defend(ing) a cause or proposition."[17] The principled ideas underpinning the networks concern a range of "fundamental freedoms." Many are laid out in international conventions such as the Universal Declaration of Human Rights (1948), the Organization for Security and Cooperation in Europe Final Act (1975), the International Covenant on Civil and Political Rights (1994), the U.N. Resolution on the Right to Democracy (1999), and the Warsaw Declaration (2000). The original rights outlined in the 1948 Declaration of Human Rights and repeated in the other documents include freedom from "arbitrary arrest, detention or exile" (article 9), the right to a "fair and public hearing" (article 10), the right to "freedom of opinion and expression," including the "freedom to . . . seek, receive and impart information and ideas through any media regardless of frontiers" (article 19), "the right to freedom of peaceful assembly and association" (article 20), the right to "periodic and genuine elections" (article 21), and "the right to form and to join trade unions" (article 23).[18]

The strategies that international NGOs have used for pursuing the institutionalization of various rights have been, with few exceptions, composed and carried out with relatively little interference or supervision from government bureaucracies or market interests, although the interests of donors, including foreign governments, have shaped NGO activities. In the postcommunist cases it makes sense to look closely at the work of NGOs, since they are the actors that provide much of the external support within the country.[19] By exploring the role of NGOs in these transnational networks, by examining what strategies have worked in helping to build institutions associated with democratic states, and by analyzing how best to coordinate efforts, we can add to a better understanding of the power and limits of NGOs in effecting change inside states. The lessons are not merely academic; they could help make Western engagement with the democratization process more effective and sustainable.

The work in this volume offers something of a corrective to the many uplifting stories that scholars (and policy makers) have focused on.[20] The closer one looks, the more one finds that developments in Eastern Europe and Eurasia, and the transnational influences on these developments, are extremely complex. The cases here should help scholars further specify the power as well as the limits of these advocacy networks. The work by the contributors to this volume should encourage close examination of the behavior of NGOs. Most important, the cases in this book suggest that the diffusion of norms and practices associated with democracy has more to do with their interaction with regional norms and practices than much of the literature acknowledges. Local context matters more than the robustness of democratic norms in the international community.[21]

ABOUT THE PROJECT

In May 1997 Jack Snyder, then the chair of Columbia University's political science department, invited a group of experts on formerly communist states, practitioners of democracy assistance, and other scholars to explore ways of assessing international efforts at helping to build democratic institutions in East-Central Europe and Eurasia.[22] Funded by the Carnegie Corporation of New York, Sarah E. Mendelson and John K. Glenn, the editors of this book, developed a comparative research design and convened a group of seventeen investigators to research and write the case studies.. The investigators had social science training and regional expertise; many had worked in or previously evaluated democracy assistance projects. They completed their case studies by the winter of 1999. Mendelson and Glenn then wrote a general report with a synopsis of each case study, which the Carnegie Endowment for International Peace published and distributed to the NGO and donor communities.[23]

METHOD OF ANALYSIS

Our project focuses on the strategies by which international NGOs sought to achieve their goals, emphasizes qualitative evaluation, and compares NGO strategies across different sectors of activity and regions. Recognizing that international NGOs often use multiple strategies at the same time, we distinguish four general types of strategies in terms of the targets of assistance and the terms of involvement. These include infrastructural assistance, or assistance to organizations to improve their administrative capacities by providing equipment or operating expenses; human capital development, or assistance to individuals intended to increase their skills, knowledge, or experience; proactive or imported strategies, in which Western groups advocate ideas and practices based on programs and projects designed outside the country; and responsive strategies, in which Western groups solicit requests from and respond to the requests of local representatives and potential grant recipients.

The investigators relied on the comparative social science method, which examines similarities and differences across contexts.[24] In most cases we asked the investigators to contrast either the same strategy in different contexts or different strategies within the same context. Three case studies in this book compare strategies in a specific sector in two different countries, such as assistance to media in the Czech Republic and Slovakia or to women's groups in Hungary and Poland. Five case studies analyze the influence of different international NGO strategies on a specific sector in one country, such as different approaches by international NGOs to rebuild civil society in Bosnia or to help support women's groups or the environment in Russia.

We asked our investigators to evaluate and describe a range of issues that would gauge the effects of international assistance. These included the emergence of local organizations that had not existed during the communist era; the professional development of activists and organizations, including their economic sustainability; national or international networking and access to technology such as the Internet; the ability to work with media to enhance public awareness of issues; new legislation resulting from NGO efforts; and the empowerment of new groups in society.

Our approach contrasts with standard quantitative methods of evaluation favored by the assistance community.[25] Quantitative methods do offer useful data: It is helpful to know, for instance, that at the end of the Soviet period, a state had one political party and no NGOs, while now it has many parties and thousands of NGOs. Important numbers also relate to assistance dollars spent, particularly in Russia, where at one point eight times as many U.S. dollars were spent on economic assistance as on democracy assistance, in stark contrast to policy makers' declarations of the importance of building democratic institutions.[26] However, numbers tell only a limited story. NGOs are engaged in a long-term incremental process of changing behavior and perceptions that is simply not linear or quantifiable. The number of dollars spent on assisting NGOs, for example, does not tell us about the behavior or effectiveness of advocacy groups. Similarly, the number of NGOs in a country does not tell us much about the nature of its civil society or its social capital, both of which are seen by funders as central to a democratic state and thus to funders' overall goals.[27]

This project instead pursued *qualitative* assessments of international NGO strategies. This type of evaluation is labor intensive and requires regional expertise, but it provides a more detailed picture of developments. Because the investigators are social scientists and had independent funding, they were free from many of the usual constraints on evaluators, such as discussing only the parts of society that assistance had targeted (e.g., the "democrats") or focusing only on "good news." While local NGOs may resist external evaluation, the international NGOs and funders were cooperative, because the investigators were primarily academics and because this study was not done on behalf of an NGO or a major donor to the region.[28]

We asked our investigators to analyze whether and in what ways local settings shape responses to international NGOs, whether some settings are more conducive to positive response than others. At the most general level we analyzed the degree to which a country's integration into the international community affected the work of international NGOs. By integration into the international community we mean the degree to which both the government and the citizens in these new states have tended, over time, to embrace norms, ideas, and practices common to the democratic states of Western Europe and North America. These include the rule of law, respect for human rights, and transparency in competitive elections. They encompass formal institutional structures such as the Organization for Cooperation and Security in Europe and less formal ones such as a free press. The inclination toward integration does not strictly follow geography: Although more states farther west tend to favor these ideas and practices, there are exceptions. Estonia, for example, has been more inclined toward integration than either Slovakia or Serbia.

We identified three general types of integration that affect and constrain the effect of international NGO strategies:

- *Thickly integrated states*, such as the Czech Republic, Poland, and Hungary, are those whose populations and governments have largely embraced the international, and specifically European, community.

Their political and social institutions, while still fragile, are developing in a relatively uncontested fashion. Their officials widely follow Western political rules of the game.

- *Thinly integrated states*, such as Slovakia under the Meciar regime and Russia, are those where national identity is still highly contested; integration into the European community is uneven; institutions remain incomplete and function poorly; and officials follow Western political rules only in an uneven and often superficial way.

- *Unintegrated states* are those such as Kazakhstan, Kyrgyzstan, and Uzbekistan where little or no integration into the international community has occurred and where one party or faction virtually rules the country without the participation of diverse groups.

- Bosnia makes up a fourth category, as a de facto international protectorate. It is unique in our study, but Kosovo since has become another example.

We expected that the more integrated the state and society within, the thicker the transnational democracy network would be. Conversely, in less integrated states and societies, such as those in the Central Asian cases, we expected to find a greater divide between the international donor community and the local population.

SUMMARY OF CASE STUDIES

The case studies follow a common research design and presentation. Each begins by outlining the historical legacy and political context of the country. It highlights what the international NGOs found when they began work, as a baseline against which to measure developments. Each case study then explores the strategies that international NGOs used to pursue their goals. For example, it specifies whether international NGOs focused on infrastructural assistance to grassroots organizations or to elites and what the basic organizational issues were, such as whether they relied upon local staff or foreigners in decision making. Investigators pursued a set of questions with international NGOs as well as with the local groups that the international NGOs had worked with. Where possible, to provide comparisons investigators also interviewed or observed groups and individuals that had not come directly into contact with foreign assistance.

The cases offer comparisons across countries in different issue areas, as well as assistance from different types of international NGOs. The chapters examine support for women's groups in Poland, Hungary, and Russia; for independent media in the Czech Republic and Slovakia; for environmental groups in Kazakhstan and Russia; for civil society in Uzbekistan and Kyrgyzstan; and, finally, for the reconstruction of civil society in Bosnia. The international NGOs studied

include private foundations such as the Soros, Ford, and MacArthur foundations, as well as NGOs that received funding from national governments, such
as the Initiative for Social Action and Renewal, the Network for East West
Women, the International Research and Exchanges Board (IREX), and the European Union–sponsored programs under Poland and Hungary: Action for the
Restructuring of the Economy (PHARE).[29]

WOMEN IN POLAND AND HUNGARY

In Poland and Hungary the Communist Party intervened in almost every aspect
of life until 1989. Women were able to establish mass organizations only under
the direction of the party. Ambitious communist rhetoric and the existence of
large and well-organized women's groups, however, did not mean that socialism's promise of gender equality had been fulfilled. As in other countries,
women were paid less than their male counterparts and were barely represented
in positions of power.

Since the fall of communism in 1989 the process of democratization has proceeded at a comparable rate in Poland and in Hungary, and women in both
countries have experienced similar challenges. Changes in the early 1990s exacerbated existing economic disparities between men and women, and to one degree or another women throughout the region suffered disproportionately from
political uncertainty and economic restructuring. Moreover, the anticommunist
paradigm engendered a patriarchal backlash as these societies struggled to
reestablish their traditional cultures. Yet despite their initial similarities, the diverse and fairly well developed landscape of women's NGOs in Poland looks dramatically different from the still fledgling and unorganized activities in Hungary.

In chapter 2 Patrice McMahon assesses the strategies of international foundations and NGOs for helping the women of Poland and Hungary respond to
the challenges posed by the transition to democracy and the market in the postcommunist period. She distinguishes strategies in terms of the identity of the
beneficiary (infrastructural assistance to organizations versus human capital development); the terms of involvement or method of transfer that the international NGO used (proactive or imposed strategies versus reactive or responsive
ones, and elite-centered versus mass-focused approaches); project-based strategies in terms of their orientation to process or to product; and short- versus long-
term involvement.

The effectiveness of international NGO strategies, McMahon finds, is constrained in these two countries by variations in governmental support for the
sector, the strength of indigenous NGO culture and traditions, and the different challenges facing women in these countries. Ten years after the fall of communism the landscape of women's organizations in Poland differs tremen-

dously from that in Hungary. In Poland infrastructural assistance has had a large influence on the number and the diversity of women's organizations that were established after 1989 and that continue to exist today. Hungary has attracted fewer international donors and international actors to the plight of women's advocacy. Polish women's NGOs, McMahon observes, appear to be better organized and are far more active outside the capital than their Hungarian counterparts.

Overall, while McMahon's chapter provides more evidence of the power of transnational networks than others in this book, it also illuminates many of its complexities. McMahon argues that international NGOs have been crucial to institution building and that the strongest women's NGOs in Poland and Hungary are those that have had support from international NGOs. However, international involvement has not been the sole driving force in the development of women's advocacy groups. Indeed, its effect has been paradoxical: While international involvement has sped up the process of building a nascent women's lobby and has promoted the development of a feminist consciousness, it has also resulted in the isolation and even ghettoization of women's NGOs that neither depend upon nor seek to support local women or national governments.

WOMEN IN RUSSIA

For most of the Soviet period there were no independent public associations in Russia. The Communist Party did create a number of social organizations that enjoyed nominal autonomy, but they depended on the regime for funding and personnel and served more as a means of social control than of empowerment. During perestroika in the late 1980s, while official women's organizations promoted an ideal of Soviet womanhood, a number of activists came together to form the first independent women's movement since the 1917 revolution.

Although Russian feminists often met with indifference and hostility at home throughout the Soviet period, they were able to forge ties with women in the United States and Western Europe. In chapter 3 James Richter analyzes the efforts of transnational feminist organizations and donors to support a network. Richter categorizes strategies according to the tasks that the organizations and donors sought to accomplish (building NGO infrastructure, public advocacy, or community outreach), the identity of their beneficiaries (individuals or organizations), and their terms of involvement (comparing, for instance, grants to individuals or organizations for a specific project with multidimensional grants to enable organizations to accomplish a range of services).

As in Poland and Hungary, international support of women's organizations in Russia has been, Richter argues, a mixed blessing for the construction of civil society. In many ways international engagement has made it possible for the women's movement simply to survive. Although some independent feminist organizations would have carried on without outside assistance — indeed, some have done so — they probably could not have remained sufficiently active and connected to be called a movement if Western money had not sustained a core of organizations. These core organizations have not only survived but become vigorous participants in Russia's growing third sector of professional nonprofit organizations that interact with state and market actors. Donors' efforts to encourage Moscow organizations to reach out to the regions have been particularly successful. The political successes of some organizations have also ensured that each of the three major power centers of the Russian government — the Duma, the Federation Council, and the presidential apparatus — has a committee or commission devoted to issues concerning women and families.

Yet by creating a cadre of professional activists involved in their own networks, norms, and practices, international assistance has in some ways widened the distance between the Russian women's movement and the rest of society. The nongovernmental sector may have been strengthened, but the effect on civil society is uncertain. As civic associations have become more institutionalized and professionalized, they have frequently been transformed into more hierarchical, centralized corporate entities that value their own survival more than their social mission. Their dependence on international assistance has often forced them to be more responsive to outside donors than to their internal constituencies. As in the case of Poland and Hungary, by selecting feminist organizations over other women's organizations, donors assisted organizations whose goals were, from the outset, more firmly based in the transnational network than in Russian society. Their dependence on that network has had the unintended consequence of removing incentives to mobilize new members and of fostering competition for grants, resulting in mistrust, bitterness, and secrecy between and within organizations.

MEDIA IN THE CZECH REPUBLIC AND SLOVAKIA

The Czech Republic and Slovakia share a common background, having been constituent republics of the Czechoslovak Federation from 1918 until the Velvet Divorce of 1993. They began the postcommunist transition in 1989 with similar legal and political environments and with comparable (albeit not identical) media cultures and structures. In both countries international democracy assistance — including projects designed to support the development of independent media — began at roughly the same time and with similar strategies. However, while the Czech Republic increased its integration with Western institutions by becoming a member of NATO and a first-round candidate for membership in the European Union, democratic consolidation in Slovakia took a different turn. When Vladimir Meciar was reelected prime minister in 1994, he instituted a semiauthoritarian regime characterized by harassment of the political opposition, independent media, and minorities. Subsequently, both NATO and the European Union refused to grant Slovakia membership until it elected a new government committed to Western integration in 1998. A comparison of the Czech Republic and Slovakia permits examination of how the same strategies work, or fail to work, in political environments both hospitable and inhospitable and how in some instances international assistance organizations have subsequently adapted to these different political conditions.

Karen Ballentine's analysis of media in the Czech Republic and Slovakia focuses on the strategies of several international NGOs and especially on variations in the targets of their assistance. In chapter 4 she compares human capital development aimed at individuals with infrastructural assistance aimed at media outlets and at development of the regulatory environment. Within these categories she compares product-oriented and process-oriented strategies: those that focus on the long-range, incremental development of media skills and infrastructure and those aimed at delivering a specific product for a specific need, such as consultation on a draft media law. She also describes assistance strategies as either selective—those that restrict assistance only to beneficiaries that meet specified criteria of eligibility—or nondiscriminatory, those that aim to spread the benefits of assistance to the media sector at large. Most commonly, this meant limiting assistance to the media that were not state run or, in some cases, to media that could demonstrate their potential commercial viability.

Ballentine finds that international support has had a positive influence in shaping the norms and practices of the postcommunist media in both the Czech Republic and Slovakia: It has enhanced their professionalism and their viability and has helped to integrate them into the larger transnational media community, which in many cases overlaps with the transnational democracy network. Contact with Western groups has also made a large difference for many individual journalists and has helped keep some nongovernmental media alive. But Ballentine finds that the relative importance of this support depends in large part on more general trends. Where the consolidation of democracy has been relatively unproblematic, assistance may facilitate the development of the independent media but not determine its existence. In contrast, where democratic transitions remain partial or are threatened by significant reversals, assistance may be necessary to ensure the material and financial basis necessary for independent media to operate.

Context looms large in Ballentine's findings. She argues that strategies should include responsiveness to the needs of the various local media; attention to building strong local partnerships; a focus on infrastructural needs as well as individuals' skill building; provision of long-term, specialized, skills-oriented training by local talent rather than short-term general training by outside advisers; and strategically limiting support to a small number of niche projects sustained for a longer period of time.

ENVIRONMENT IN RUSSIA

The environmental degradation in Russia as a result of the Soviet legacy is among the worst in the world. The controlling nature of the state aggravated the damage: Environmentalism in the Soviet Union was either an outright fiction or, at best, an effort by the Communist Party leadership to turn what could have been autonomous social organizations into state-sponsored and state-controlled entities. With Gorbachev's policies of perestroika in the late 1980s, however, an active environmental movement did emerge but fell into relative obscurity after 1992. In the post-Soviet context constant changes in state environmental institutions, their often conflicting responsibilities, and the shifting content of environmental legislation have produced a highly unstable and often perplexing setting in which environmentally concerned citizens, advocacy groups, and decision makers must operate.

Acknowledging that most programs encompass a wide range of activities and strategies, Leslie Powell compares strategies in terms of their goals (building civil society versus cleaning up the environment) and their recipients (grassroots versus elite). In chapter 5 she distinguishes strategies that originated indigenously from those that were imported and those that were project based from those that had interactive support.

Powell finds that the success of these assistance programs cannot be measured in terms of improvements in the environment or in terms of greater consciousness among national or local decision makers for environmental issues. Instead, the success of these programs lies in assisting in the establishment and development of environmental advocacy organizations in Russia and, to some degree, in helping to establish new democratic channels between civil society and the political elite for participation and the articulation of interests. Nearly all environmental aid from the West has gone to this third sector in Russia rather than to the state or commercial sectors. Western engagement has empowered social actors, created communication networks both horizontally and vertically, raised the level of public awareness of both environmental and democratic issues, and helped to make civil society groups more professional, organized, and strategic in their planning and activism. She finds that greater positive influence correlates strongly with the degree to which strategies are interactive or responsive to local concerns and to which they encourage coalition building, partly as a result of the demonstration effect of working alongside Western groups. Her findings add to our understanding of how ideas and practices diffuse inside states.

Powell finds that environmental aid has had conspicuously little effect to date on the environment itself or on the implementation of environmental policy. Powell identifies three major reasons for this failure. The first is the weakness of the state, which has exerted little control over industrial and commercial interests and has a difficult time policing itself. Second, channels for articulating societal interests are still weak: The state enjoys a high level of autonomy with respect to the mass public and is not accountable, while democratic processes are either absent or dysfunctional. Third, the link between environmental issues and economic-industrial issues is unbreakable: The sheer magnitude of the two types of problems and their connections to each other make addressing only one and not the other an ineffectual way to resolve environmental issues.

ENVIRONMENT IN KAZAKHSTAN

In the Gorbachev era environmental activism in Kazakhstan centered on protest movements against the testing of nuclear weapons in Semipalatinsk and elsewhere. After the breakup of the Soviet Union, the political climate relaxed considerably, and Kazakhstan witnessed a proliferation of independent organizations across various issue areas. At the same time, however, the environmental situation worsened as the government began to develop the vast energy reserves in the Caspian Sea basin. The environmental NGO sector was fairly well developed in Kazakhstan at the time of independence, and it continued to grow for the first few years afterward. However, even as the environmental situation deteriorated, large-scale environmental movements disappeared from the political arena.

In chapter 6 Pauline Jones Luong and Erika Weinthal focus on the energy sector. They analyze three primary strategies that environmentally oriented international NGOs in Kazakhstan pursued: the provision of small grants and technical support to local NGOs, assistance in information collection and dissemination, and training in decision-making techniques and grant-writing skills to empower local actors and communities to address their own problems.

While local NGOs have proliferated in recent years, the authors find that the NGOs have played a decreasing role in environmental policy making since independence. They argue that this is a result of both domestic and international constraints. At the domestic level local NGOs face institutional obstacles in a political system that has become more restrictive since 1994, and they lack access to organizational resources because of Kazakhstan's continued economic decline. These constraints derive directly from the Soviet legacy as well as from the political developments in Kazakhstan since independence: Limited democratization involves restrictions on press freedom and political mobilization.

At the international level the frequently conflicting interests and strategies of multiple actors—including international NGOs, international donor organizations, foreign oil companies, and foreign governments—have hindered rather than enhanced the role of local NGOs in promoting environmental protection in the energy sector. Efforts have left local NGOs atomized and depoliticized. While outside groups (many with funds from USAID) support local environmental organizations in the hope of promoting a vigorous civil society, they sometimes usurp the local organizations' role, for example, by sending in foreign consultants to draft legislation and advocate specific regulatory regimes. The economic interests of Western oil companies have also directly competed with local NGOs' efforts at democratic activism.

Paradoxically, the authors conclude, international efforts to foster democracy appear to have undermined, rather than contributed, to a robust environmental movement in Kazakhstan. Although local environmental NGOs have grown in numbers because of the financial support of international NGOs, the environmental movement is overwhelmingly reliant on international assistance for its survival, a dynamic that is reinforced by domestic political constraints on activism. In light of the domestic and international constraints, local environmental movements have had little incentive to increase their membership locally. Instead, the goals and strategies of environmental activism have converged with those of donors, toward education on less salient issues such as biodiversity and outreach to the international community while ignoring the most pressing local environmental issues, such as the need for clean drinking water.

CIVIL SOCIETY IN UZBEKISTAN AND KYRGYZSTAN

International organizations have spent millions of dollars to promote democratization in Central Asia. USAID alone spends more than $11 million annually in Uzbekistan and Kyrgyzstan, two countries that represent contrasting levels of democratization in Central Asia. Uzbekistan is a highly authoritarian state, while Kyrgyzstan has taken more steps toward democratic reform. However, the two countries share similar Soviet institutional legacies, have similarly high levels of corruption, are both marked by a disjunction between formal and informal political and economic institutions, have low levels of economic development accompanied by an uneven distribution of wealth, and are both characterized by a weakened public sector infrastructure.

Much of the money earmarked for fostering democracy in the region finances strategies and programs that are designed to strengthen civil society. In chapter 7 Fiona Adamson considers the efforts of international organizations, government aid programs, international NGOs, and local NGOs. Adamson evaluates several strategies, specifying the methods and programs within each strategy and the actors pursuing each strategy.

Adamson details a considerable shortfall between the vision of democracy and the actual results of democracy assistance programs in Central Asia. Western groups and their programs have not succeeded in penetrating deeply into society, and many have interacted with local conditions in ways that unintentionally aggravate a number of problems, such as corruption, income inequality, and aid dependence, all of which are obstacles to democratic consolidation. She finds, however, that the Western efforts have not been without achievements, the most notable of which have been the incorporation of local elites into transnational civil society networks, a growth in official and societal acceptance of NGOs as legitimate social actors, and a few small-scale community development successes.

Adamson's work illustrates the potential for "structural decoupling," whereby the organizational forms and stated aims of international actors diverge from the realities in practice as they struggle to reconcile the conflicts in the environments in which they operate.[30] Much of the ineffectiveness of democracy assistance can be attributed to the challenges that Western organizations encounter as they try to work in contexts that are radically different from those with which they are familiar. Most assistance organizations, for example, have their headquarters in advanced industrial democracies; their overall organizational structure, mission, macrolevel strategies, and programs reflect this context. Local branches, by contrast, must interact with local conditions and must adapt to these conditions in order to survive. Adamson finds a great deal of internal incoherence within international NGOs as a result of such mismatches.

In highly restrictive political and economic conditions like those found in Uzbekistan and Kyrgyzstan, democracy assistance strategies must be especially sensitive to local context. International NGOs need to be responsive and are helped to be so if they employ staff members who are familiar with the context. International actors must be more willing to work with a variety of local groups, such as local community structures and even "government NGOs" and religious organizations. If Western groups work exclusively with the so-called independent NGO sector (largely created by Western assistance), they will continue to reach only a small sector of society. International actors must pay as much attention to the effect that informal processes and institutions such as corruption and patronage networks have on their strategies and programs as they do to formal institutions.

RECONSTRUCTING CIVIL SOCIETY IN BOSNIA

Bosnia-Herzegovina has become a de facto international protectorate since the Dayton Peace Agreement of 1995. International organizations such as NATO make crucial decisions, including establishing electoral laws and determining who will sit on the constitutional court. As in prewar Kosovo, the international NGOs operate under severe constraints. The power to manage violence lies well outside the NGOs' realm; it rests with the twenty thousand multinational U.N. troops of the SFOR (Stabilization Force) and with the Office of the High Representative in Bosnia-Herzegovina. Given the extremely high level of international engagement, the lessons of Bosnia-Herzegovina regarding the effectiveness of international NGOs in helping to rebuild civil society in postwar conditions should be particularly strong.

In chapter 8, V. P. Gagnon examines five NGOs that use four types of strategies to help support civil society. He finds that the most effective strategies involve the physical reconstruction of communities. A key ingredient of success is that international NGOs encourage local actors and local NGOs to determine both priorities and projects: Those that use local expertise and develop strategies in accord with the specific local political context have a greater effect. Success is also more likely where international NGOs engage in an interactive two-way process rather than importing ideas and practices.

The Bosnia-Herzegovina case highlights a number of important lessons for international NGOs that aim to reduce ethnic conflict or to rebuild civil society. Merely generalizing from experience elsewhere, while overlooking the specificities and complexities of Bosnia-Herzegovina, has limited the effectiveness of NGOs. For example, international NGOs' own dependence for funding on institutions such as USAID has so constrained some NGOs that they have invested in strategies in Bosnia, such as party building, that actually exacerbate problems because the existing political power structure is far too dominant. International NGOs are best able to strategize when their funding comes from donors that allow the NGOs familiar with the setting to determine priorities and projects based on what they find there and to operate with a long-range goals in mind. This freedom to maneuver helps resolve what is often a mismatch of the interests of donors and those of the society in which the international NGO is operating.

Gagnon concludes that NGOs and donors need to resolve the disconnects between the needs of society and the interests driving projects and priorities. His work suggests that the efficiency of the democracy network is inhibited when the various nodes in the network are not equally weighted. When outside voices are seen as more authoritative, the distortion is significant. Instead, Gagnon argues that international NGOs in Bosnia should work mainly on helping communities rebuild themselves and their civil society, rather than on importing notions of political party and civil society development derived from Western experiences. Attempts to build democracy in such contexts must come initially from the society in question; it is a mistake to assume that the local environment offers nothing on which to build and that all must be imported.

LIMITS OF THE STUDY AND CONCLUSIONS

The range of cases in this volume is considerable but is not a comprehensive guide to Western democracy assistance strategies in East-Central Europe and Eurasia. No project of this size could reasonably examine the work of the hundreds of international and indigenous NGOs engaged in political transition across the regions. Even in the larger study we could not cover every sector or every country, and we have further limited our focus here to concentrate on a few main areas in which U.S. and European NGOs worked and a representative sample from across the regions. The lessons from these cases should, however, be of interest to practitioners in the field as well as to scholars engaged in the study of transnational influences on internal developments and world politics.

Although this project examined political and social change across the postcommunist states, the findings are by nature a snapshot. Transnational democracy networks and efforts at democracy assistance are extremely vulnerable to jolts, both from the states themselves and from the international system. Shocks come in a variety of economic and political forms, including currency devaluation and war. For example, events in Kosovo in the spring of 1999 had devastating effects on democratization in the Federal Republic of Yugoslavia and negatively affected the West's relations with Russia. Russia's second war in Chechnya, starting in 1999, brought with it a general climate of fear spread by federal authorities under President Vladimir Putin and signaled a retreat from human rights in Russia.

Despite such shocks, this project's focus on strategy allowed participants to ask questions that were independent of the day's events and that pointed out changes that need to be made in Western efforts to help develop and sustain political and social institutions in postcommunist societies. Regardless of the institutionalization of certain practices and ideas, this book suggests that the democratization process is fragile and influenced greatly by issues and forces beyond the control of any one part of the network.

James Scott has observed that "a mechanical application of generic rules that ignores . . . particularities is an invitation to practical failure, social disillusionment, or most likely both."[31] Our investigators encountered this repeatedly in their fieldwork. Investigators often found the same strategies in use across a wide spectrum of states in different stages of international integration and internal transition; the implicit assumption was that one strategy fits many. In the final chapter Mendelson details the implications of these findings for the policy and scholarly communities and recommends changes in strategies to enhance the influence of international NGOs and transnational networks and thereby also the possibility of supporting sustainable institutions in postcommunist societies.

The outcomes of international NGO strategies depended in large part upon the kind of interaction that the NGO had within the local context. A comparison of the case studies shows that international NGOs have played a large role in helping to build institutions commonly associated with democracies but have done little to help these new institutions function well. Because some of these institutions are functioning at a minimal level, if at all, the international NGO strategies have not yet contributed to their sustainability.

The case studies find, for example, that local NGOs and media outlets have become common all across East-Central Europe and Eurasia. In the Czech Republic and in Slovakia international assistance helped to launch self-sustaining media organizations and has supported the creation of local independent television stations. International assistance has been central to the formation of networks of women's organizations in Poland and Hungary. Similarly, in Russia international NGOs have had an impressive effect in helping to sustain women's groups. Such returns for relatively small investments are noteworthy, particularly when we compare these developments to how undeveloped the advocacy groups and other aspects of civil society were in these countries just a few years earlier.[32]

However, international NGOs have had little influence on the effectiveness of the institutions that they helped to create. In nearly every case the investigators found that the new institutions had weak links to their own societies. For example, local environmental NGOs have proliferated in Kazakhstan as a result of financial support from international NGOs, but their political influence has declined. Whereas an environmental movement was central to political reform and independence in the late Soviet period, today it shies away from addressing pressing environmental issues, such as uranium tailings in drinking water. In Poland, Hungary, and Russia women's groups have multiplied even as they have been unable to attract significant domestic support, growing closer to their transnational partners than to the constituents whom they are meant to represent or to the governments that they hope to influence. Each chapter, and especially the concluding chapter, suggests ways in which foreign donors and NGOs might alter their strategies and practices to address the operational nature of new institutions and thereby enhance their effectiveness and sustainability.[33]

Our investigators identified practices and ideas that had little or no local institutional history and traced them to the work of the international NGOs. In certain cases this tracing was relatively simple, because locals had begun to use new and imported terminology on issues ranging from focus groups to feminism and from biodiversity to election monitoring. Investigators could identify changes in behavior that correlated with Western efforts, but they could not say definitively that Western efforts caused the changes. In other cases they found unintended consequences of new speech and behavior. Giving aid to new political parties lacking deep ties to society, as in Bosnia-Herzegovina, risks exacerbating divisions within society rather than creating channels for the democratic articulation of citizens' interests.[34] For example, encouraging political parties to engage in door-to-door canvassing can provoke a backlash in a context where political visits to private homes may lack a peaceful connotation. Many local groups proliferated in Poland, Hungary, Russia, Kazakhstan, Uzbekistan, and Kyrgyzstan around issues that Western donors found important but that lacked wider local resonance. International NGOs providing assistance to women's groups frequently encountered clashes between Western and local perceptions of the most pressing issues for women. Rather than fostering ties with the broader groups that these local NGOs were to represent, these strategies often ended up isolating the NGOs from their communities.

In countries with little or no history of democratic tradition, postcommunist transitions appear to be influenced by how groups reconcile ideas and practices common in the international community with their long-held domestic beliefs and customs. In cases where Western ideas and practices in some way complement the organizational culture of a specific local group, activists are receptive to them. If ideas and practices help solve specific problems (such as increasing a candidate's electoral chances), local activists are particularly likely to adopt them. In contrast, NGOs tend to reject, based on a "logic of appropriateness," ideas and practices that appear to compete with local customs or beliefs.[35]

The case studies reveal frequent clashes of ideas and practices with local customs and beliefs. For example, in several new states in Eurasia local NGOs were, for much of the 1990s, reluctant to coordinate advocacy campaigns with political parties or trade unions because of the negative historical legacies from the Soviet period, when these states used parties and unions to suppress civil society. In Poland, Hungary, and Kazakhstan the interests of donors—whether in forming a network of feminists or in addressing biodiversity—competed with the everyday problems of feeding families and getting clean drinking water. The case studies in this project underscore the finding that a variety of forces—organizational, historical, economic, environmental, and political—limit international NGOs' efforts, although these efforts may be central to many small projects and capable of influencing change on a local stage. The influence of international NGOs appears to be particularly inhibited if they fail to pay attention to these forces.

The diffusion of ideas and practices beyond the people and organizations with which international NGOs work is an important unexamined dynamic in assistance. New practices in media and civic advocacy groups in many countries have, for example, spread across the political spectrum to nationalists and communists. Some NGOs are now considered legitimate in parts of Central Asia. The general public, not just self-proclaimed feminists in Eastern Europe and Russia, is beginning to recognize crisis centers that deal with the consequences of domestic abuse and rape. Such diffusion of ideas and practices underscores the process by which larger populations begin to alter their conceptions of issues fundamental to democracy, such as advocacy on behalf of citizens and protection of civil liberties and human rights.

This summary cannot, of course, do justice to the complexities of each case in this book. We hope that this chapter will help orient the reader to the theoretical concerns at hand as well as the case studies that follow.

NOTES

1. No one yet has done a comprehensive study. For thoughtful analyses of aspects of the issue, see Thomas Carothers, *Aiding Democracy Abroad: The Learning Curve* (Washington, D.C.: Carnegie Endowment for International Peace, 1999); Nancy Lubin, "U.S. Assistance to the NIS," in Karen Dawisha, ed., *The International Dimension of Postcommunist Transitions in Russia and the New States of Eurasia*, pp. 350–78 (Armonk, N.Y.: Sharpe, 1997); Thomas Carothers, *Assessing Democracy Assistance: The Case of Romania* (Washington, D.C.: Carnegie Endowment for International Peace, 1996); Mark S. Johnson, "An Evaluation of Strengthening Russian Democracy Through Civic Education" (an assessment prepared for the National Endowment for Democracy, Washington, D.C., September 1998); Sarah Henderson, "Importing Civil Society: Foreign Aid and the Women's Movement in Russia," *Demokratizatsiya* 8, no. 1 (Winter 2000): 65–82; Matthew Lantz, "The Democratic Presumption: An Assessment of Democratization in Russia, 1994–1998," Strengthening Democratic Institutions Project, Harvard University, September 1998.

2. The Institute of War and Peace Studies and the Harriman Institute of Columbia University obtained funding from the Carnegie Corporation of New York for this project, which was overseen by Jack Snyder and other faculty. Sarah E. Mendelson was the director of research for the project, and John K. Glenn, who shared in the planning and direction of the research, was a postdoctoral fellow with the project.

3. USAID frequently asks the NGOs that it funds to supply it with success stories, which agency officials then use in testimony before Congress. See, for example, "Russia's Economic and Political Transformation: Some Results of USAID Support to Date," *USAID Report*, Spring 1995. See also Strobe Talbott, "Spreading Democracy," *Foreign Affairs* 75, no. 6 (November–December 1996): 47–63.

4. Figures for democracy assistance are notoriously difficult to calculate. Carothers calculates the average funding for democracy assistance in this period as less than 10 percent of total aid to Eastern Europe and the Soviet Union (*Aiding Democracy Abroad*, 61). See table 1.1 for details of assistance from the United States and European Union to Eastern Europe and Eurasia.

5. Fareed Zakaria, "The Rise of Illiberal Democracy," *Foreign Affairs* 76, no. 6 (November–December 1997): 22–43.

6. On problems associated with economic assistance to the regions, see Janine Wedel, *Collision and Collusion: The Strange Case of Western Aid to Eastern Europe, 1989–1998* (New York: St. Martin's, 1998).

7. See Robert Putnam, *Bowling Alone: The Collapse and the Revival of American Community* (New York: Simon and Schuster, 2000); and Peter F. Drucker, *Managing in a Time of Great Change* (New York: Dutton, 1995). See also Putnam, *Making Democracy Work: Civic Traditions in Modern Italy* (Princeton: Princeton University Press, 1993).

8. Claus Offe, "Cultural Aspects of Consolidation: A Note on the Peculiarities of Postcommunist Transformations," *East European Constitutional Review* (Fall 1997): 67.

9. Paul Stubbs, "NGOs and the Myth of Civil Society," *ArkZin*, January 1996, http://www.globalpolicy.org/ngos/role/globdem/credib/2000/1121.htm (November 12, 2001). See also David Samuels, "At Play in the Fields of Oppression," *Harper's*, May 1995.

10. See Václav Havel, *Open Letters: Selected Writings, 1965–1990*, ed. Paul Wilson (New York: Vintage, 1991); Adam Michnik, *Letters from Prison* (Berkeley: University of California Press, 1985); and David Ost, *Solidarity and the Politics of Antipolitics: Opposition and Reform in Poland Since 1968* (Philadelphia: Temple University Press, 1990).

11. See Jean L. Cohen and Andrew Arato, *Civil Society and Political Theory* (Cambridge, Mass.: MIT Press, 1992).

12. See Lester M. Salamon and Helmut K. Anheier, "Social Origins of Civil Society: Explaining the Nonprofit Sector Cross-nationally," working paper no. 22, the Johns Hopkins Comparative Nonprofit Sector Project, Baltimore, Md., 1996.

13. Thomas Carothers, "Democracy Assistance: The Question of Strategy," *Demokratizatsiya* 4, no. 3 (1997): 114.

14. *Transnational* in this context refers to "regular interactions across national boundaries when at least one actor is a non-state agent or does not operate on behalf of a national government or an intergovernmental organization" (Thomas Risse-Kappen, ed., *Bringing Transnational Relations Back In: Nonstate Actors, Domestic Structures, and International Institutions* [Cambridge: Cambridge University Press, 1995], p. 3).

15. For a review of the literature see Martha Finnemore and Kathryn Sikkink, "International Norm Dynamics and Political Change," *International Organization* 52, no. 4 (Autumn 1998): 887–918. On human rights see Kathryn Sikkink, "Human Rights, Principled Issue-Networks, and Sovereignty in Latin America," *International Organization* 47, no. 3 (Summer 1993): 411–42; Audie Klotz, "Norms Reconstituting Interests: Global Racial Equality and U.S. Sanctions Against South Africa," *International Organization* 49, no. 3 (Summer 1995): 451–78; and Thomas Risse, Stephen C. Ropp, and Kathryn Sikkink, eds., *The Power of Human Rights: International Norms and Domestic Change* (Cambridge: Cambridge University Press, 1999). On the security focus see Peter J. Katzenstein, ed., *The Culture of National Security: Norms and Identity in World Politics* (New York: Columbia University Press, 1996); Richard Price, "Reversing the Gun Sights: Transnational Civil Society Targets Land Mines," *International Organization* 52, no. 3 (Summer 1998): 613–44; and Nina Tannenwald, "The Nuclear Taboo: The United States and the Normative Basis of Nuclear Nonuse," *International Organization* 53, no. 3 (Summer 1999): 433–68. On the environment see Paul Wapner, "Politics Beyond the State: Environmental Activism and World Civic Politics," *World Politics* 47, no. 3 (April 1995): 311–40.

16. Margaret E. Keck and Kathryn Sikkink, *Activists Beyond Borders: Advocacy Networks in International Politics* (Ithaca: Cornell University Press, 1998), p. 1.

17. Ibid., p. 8.

18. The Universal Declaration for Human Rights can be found on the U.N.'s Web site, http://www.un.org (November 12, 2001). Other documents can be found at http://www.osce.org (November 12, 2001) and http://www.state.gov/www/global/human _rights/ (November 12, 2001).

19. American NGOs include the National Democratic Institute and the International Republican Institute; the Eurasia Foundation; the Initiative for Social Action and Renewal in Eurasia; the American Center for International Labor Solidarity; World Learning; the International Foundation for Election Systems; and Internews. Private foundations such as George Soros's Open Society Institute, the Ford Foundation, and the John D. and Catherine T. MacArthur Foundation have additionally spent millions of dollars in the region. For a more complete list see M. Holt Ruffin, Alyssa Deutschler, Catriona Logan, and Richard Upjohn, *The Post-Soviet Handbook: A Guide to Grassroots Organizations and Internet Resources*, rev. ed. (Seattle, Wash.: Center for Civil Society International/University of Washington Press, 1999).

20. This volume is part of an emerging literature suggesting the pathologies as well as the power of transnational networks. See Jeffrey T. Checkel, "The Constructivist Turn in International Relations Theory," *World Politics* 50, no. 2 (January 1998): 324–48; Ann Marie Clark, Elisabeth J. Friedman, and Kathryn Hochstetler, "The Sovereignty Limits of Global Civil Society: A Comparison of NGO Participation in U.N. World Conferences on the Environment, Human Rights, and Women," *World Politics* 51, no. 1 (October 1998): 1–35; Michael N. Barnett and Martha Finnemore, "The Politics, Power, and Pathologies of International Organizations," *International Organization* 53, no. 4 (Autumn 1999): 699–732.

21. Jeffrey W. Legro has effectively highlighted the dynamic of international versus domestic norms in "Which Norms Matter? Revisiting the 'Failure' of Internationalism," *International Organization* 51, no. 1 (Winter 1997): 31–63.

22. The group of invited experts included Jeanne Bourgault, formerly of USAID in Moscow; Thomas Carothers, vice president for studies at the Carnegie Endowment for International Peace and former legal adviser at the U.S. Department of State; Larry Diamond, senior fellow at the Hoover Institution; Larry Garber from USAID; Michael McFaul, associate professor of political science at Stanford University; and Kathryn Sikkink, professor of political science at the University of Minnesota.

23. Sarah E. Mendelson and John K. Glenn, "Democracy Assistance and NGO Strategies in Postcommunist States," working paper series no. 8, Carnegie Endowment for International Peace, Washington, D.C., February 2000. Cases that informed the project's findings but are not included here include developments in political parties and elections in Russia (Sarah Mendelson); technology assistance to women's groups (Tina Nelson); Ukraine (James Clem); the Czech Republic and Slovakia (John K. Glenn); developments in independent media in Russia (Anne Nivat) and Ukraine (Marta Dyczok); the promotion of civic education in Romania (Sandra Pralong); and attempts by Western NGOs to reduce ethnic conflict in Estonia (Vello Pettai) and in the states of Central Europe that are home to the Hungarian and Roma diaspora

(Sherrill Stroschein). For an overview of the findings see Sarah E. Mendelson, "Unfinished Business: Democracy Assistance and Political Transition in Eastern Europe and Eurasia," *Problems of Postcommunism* 48, no. 3 (May–June 2001): 19–27.

24. See, for example, Charles Ragin, *The Comparative Method: Moving Beyond Qualitative and Quantitative Strategies* (Berkeley: University of California Press, 1987), and Max Weber, "Objective Possibility and Adequate Causation in Historical Explanation," in *The Methodology of the Social Sciences*, pp. 164–88 (New York: Free Press, 1949).

25. See, for example, "USAID/Russia Activity Description as of March 31, 2000," and "Russia's Economic and Political Transformation: Some Results of USAID Support to Date," *USAID Report*, Spring 1995. These documents are available on request from USAID, Washington, D.C.

26. For statements see then-secretary of state Madeline Albright's address to the Carnegie Endowment for International Peace, September 16, 1999; and then-deputy secretary of state Strobe Talbott's address to Harvard University, October 1, 1999.

27. Bill Clinton, "Remembering Yeltsin," *Time*, January 1, 2000; Strobe Talbott's testimony before the Senate Appropriations Committee, Subcommittee on Foreign Operations, April 4, 2000, available at http://usinfo.state.gov/topical/pol/arms/stories/00040407.htm (November 12, 2001); and Clinton's address to the Russian Duma on June 5, 2000, all cite the presence of sixty-five thousand NGOs in Russia. None of these speeches mentions that NGOs have been subjected to a campaign of harassment by Russia's federal authorities. See Sarah E. Mendelson, "The Putin Path: Human Rights in Retreat," *Problems of Postcommunism* 47, no. 5 (September–October 2000): 3–12.

28. A partial explanation for the reluctance of local NGOs to welcome external evaluation may be found in the organizational constraints under which they operate. When NGOs themselves evaluate their work, they tend to keep the focus of inquiry quite narrow. In contrast to companies engaged in economic assistance in the regions, NGOs tend to have little financial flexibility and small staffs. They are often overextended in their work: Many have field offices in several countries and incomplete control of these outposts. Beyond basic attempts to demonstrate that they have met their short-term (usually six-month) goals—such as how many activists they trained—many NGOs have not viewed it as in their organizational interest to spend precious resources (time, staff, budgets) on anything beyond the evaluation of specific programs. Additionally, when strategies are determined from outside the countries in which they operate, NGOs may not focus on evaluations of these strategies or how they vary according to local conditions. Finally, like any other organization, many NGOs and their donors are reluctant to acknowledge a need for change in either strategies or programs.

29. PHARE originally was an acronym for the European Union's program called Poland and Hungary Action for the Reconstruction of the Economy. The program subsequently became the EU's main instrument for financial and technical cooperation in thirteen countries in Central and Eastern Europe and still is known by its original acronym.

30. John Meyer, *Organizational Integration in Lesotho Primary Education: Loose Coupling as Problem and Solution* (Meseru, Lesotho: Primary Education Project, 1995).

31. James C. Scott, *Seeing Like a State: How Certain Schemes to Improve the Human Condition Have Failed* (New Haven: Yale University Press, 1998), p. 318. See also Albert Hirschmann, "The Search for Paradigms as a Hindrance for Understanding," *World Politics* 22, no. 3 (April 1970): 323–43.

32. The United States allocated approximately $10 billion (FY1992–FY1998) for all bilateral assistance to Eurasia; only $850 million went for democracy assistance to the even larger area of Eurasia and East-Central Europe combined.

33. See also Mendelson, "Unfinished Business."

34. In Burundi assistance to unformed political parties had the unintended consequence of increasing ethnic divisions, thereby paving the way for the mass killings that followed elections in 1993. See Michael S. Lund, Barnett R. Rubin, and Fabienne Hara, "Learning from Burundi's Failed Democratic Transition, 1993–1996: Did International Initiatives Match the Problem?" in Barnett R. Rubin, ed., *Cases and Strategies for Preventive Action*, pp. 47–91 (New York: Century Foundation Press, 1998).

35. James G. March and Johan P. Olsen, *Rediscovering Institutions: The Organizational Basis of Politics* (New York: Free Press, 1989).

Chapter 2

INTERNATIONAL ACTORS AND WOMEN'S NGOS IN POLAND AND HUNGARY

Patrice C. McMahon

In an effort to promote democracy in East-Central Europe, numerous international actors focused their energies on helping women in the region respond to the challenges posed by the transition to democracy and the market. Nongovernmental organizations (NGOs) saw democracy assistance to women's advocacy groups as a way to counter trends that were threatening the status of women and to promote the development of independent women's movements throughout the region. This assistance has undeniably shaped the institutions, ideas, and actors in this sector, but it would be incorrect to suggest that international actors have been the sole driving force in the development of women's advocacy groups. In fact, international involvement has had a paradoxical effect on the development of women's NGOs in postcommunist countries. While international involvement has sped up the process of building a nascent women's lobby and promoted the development of a feminist consciousness, it has simultaneously resulted in the marginalization of women's NGOs that neither depend on nor seek to maintain the support of local actors or national governments.

I gratefully acknowledge the support of the Open Society Institute of New York and the Carnegie Corporation of New York.

Here I explore the relationship between nongovernmental actors and the development of women's advocacy groups in Poland and Hungary. The Columbia University project chose these two countries because democratization has proceeded at a comparable rate and women have experienced similar challenges since the collapse of communism. Despite initial similarities in the development of women's advocacy groups, however, the diverse and fairly developed landscape of women's NGOs in Poland looks dramatically different from the still fledgling and unorganized activities in Hungary today. In both countries I ask similar questions. What have Western NGOs done to promote women's issues? How successful have they been? What are some of the limitations or unintended consequences of this involvement?

The strategies that I assess here are predominately those used by U.S. foundations and Western NGOs such as the network of Soros foundations, the Ford Foundation, the German Marshall Fund, the Global Fund for Women, the Network for East-West Women, and Women's World Banking. Although state funding partially sponsors some Western NGOs (for example, USAID provides funding for the Network for East-West Women, and the Canadian, Norwegian, and Swedish governments provide small grants for women's projects), they develop and implement their goals and strategies without a great deal of government interference. Furthermore, the connections between Western NGOs and local NGOs are quite loose, and local NGOs generally have a great deal of autonomy. Most Western NGOs involved in the development of this sector have been private organizations.

Most prominent among private grant-making organizations is the Soros network of foundations; almost every women's organization or scholar whom I interviewed for this project was in some way touched by its extensive reach in the region. In Poland the Soros Foundation is the largest sponsor of the Stefan Batory Foundation in Warsaw, which has provided assistance to numerous women's organizations and gender-related projects, such as the Center for the Advancement for Women, the Women's Rights Center, and La Strada, the Foundation Against Trafficking in Women. In Hungary the Soros network assists in the development of women's NGOs through the Open Society Institute in Budapest, which has provided money to numerous organizations and projects (including NaNE—Women Working with Women Against Violence; MONA, the Hungarian Women's Foundation; and Roma Women in Public Life). It also supports the Central European University's Program on Gender and Culture and its Small Grants Program, which provides money to women's NGOs and initiatives throughout East-Central Europe and the former Soviet Union.[1] The Open Society Institute in New York initiated its Women's Program in 1997 in an attempt to encourage gender-inclusive projects within Soros-funded national foundations as well as other foundations involved in international issues.

I also examine the strategies of the Ford Foundation, which established the National Women's Information Center in Warsaw and promised funding from 1997 to 2002 to the Stefan Batory Foundation to support women's NGOs in Poland; PHARE (Poland and Hungary: Action for the Restructuring of the Economy), which has provided money to MONA; Women's World Banking, which sought to create Women's World Banks in Warsaw and Lodz; the Global Fund for Women, which has assisted NaNE in Hungary; and the Network for East-West Women, which maintains contacts with most of the women's NGOs in Poland and Hungary.

The information here reflects changes in this sector in the postcommunist period, with a particular emphasis on the late 1990s. Since 1992 I have conducted research on the position of women in postcommunist countries and have maintained close contacts with women's organizations in the region, including Russia.[2] In the fall and winter of 1997–1998 I conducted interviews in the United States with individuals from leading U.S. foundations and Western NGOs, as well as academics involved in women's issues in these countries. In March and April 1998 I interviewed practitioners, funders, policy makers, and academics in Poland and Hungary who have been closely involved in the development of women's NGOs in these countries.[3]

I argue that international actors have undeniably made a difference in the development of women's NGOs in postcommunist countries. However, their efforts would be more successful if assistance were sustained, at least for a couple of years; if assistance targeted organizations and projects that seek to attract the average woman; if Western NGOs persuaded national governments that it is in their best interest to respond to the needs of their female population; and, most important, if Western NGOs encouraged indigenous women's organizations to become involved in the dirty business of politics. While women's NGO activity has blossomed throughout the region, the unwillingness of these groups to get involved in national politics has meant that representatives of women's issues have had little access to decision makers.

My argument proceeds in five parts, beginning with a historical overview of women and transition that focuses specifically on Hungary and Poland. The next two sections first identify and explain the strategies of Western NGOs, then examine their influence on this sector. In the fourth section I discuss the evaluation techniques of Western and local NGOs. I conclude with some lessons learned and recommendations for future involvement.

POLITICAL AND HISTORICAL CONTEXT:
WOMEN AND TRANSITION

Even before the collapse of communism, scholarly and journalistic accounts of the position of women in Poland and Hungary revealed that socialism had hardly fulfilled its promise of gender equality. As in other countries, women received less pay than their male counterparts and were barely represented in positions of power.[4] The Communist Party had intervened in almost every aspect of life; in Poland and Hungary the party directed the formation of mass organizations on behalf of the country's female population.[5] Ambitious communist rhetoric and the presence of large and well-organized women's organizations, however, did not mean that the Communist Party had successfully penetrated traditional culture in either country. The status of women in these countries was precariously dependent upon a state that pledged to support equal rights so long as it, and not women themselves, defined the criteria for equality and parameters of feminism.

Changes in the early 1990s exacerbated the disparities in the treatment of men and women, and, despite important differences among postcommunist societies, women throughout the region suffered disproportionately from political uncertainty and economic restructuring.[6] Moreover, the anticommunist paradigm engendered a patriarchal backlash as these societies struggled to reestablish their traditional cultures. Without socialist principles to guide state policies, the official commitment to gender equality ended. Both countries had some history of women's groups before communism, but neither society had a particularly strong tradition of any independent movement on behalf of women's rights.[7] In both Poland and Hungary the reduction of the state in political and social affairs, and the absence of a culture to promote women's issues, had serious implications for the status of women.

The first postcommunist elections witnessed the end of socialism's affirmative-action policies and the elimination of the quota system that provided for a minimum of female candidates. As a result, the number of female politicians decreased in both countries, as it did throughout the region. In postcommunist Poland women have held, at the most, 13 percent of the seats in parliament, while throughout the 1980s their participation had exceeded 20 percent.[8] In postcommunist Hungary women have comprised 7 to 11 percent of the country's representatives in parliament, in contrast to a figure of more than 20 percent before 1989. In local politics a similar but less dramatic drop was evident. The number of women in the national parliament and local politics had been artificially high because of the Communist Party's quota system. But the failure of these new democracies to attract more women into politics meant that the female population became even more marginalized from public life than it had been during the communist period.

Despite the belief that economic reforms were gender neutral, the move away from socialism and toward capitalism was particularly onerous to women throughout the region. Economic reform meant that women were usually the first to be fired and the last hired. While this was not so in all postcommunist countries, in Poland and Hungary women suffered from higher rates of unemployment than men; most affected were middle-aged women with poor qualifications who were laid off as "redundant labor."[9] Women were also less likely to be retrained and thus experienced a much lower rate of reemployment. Alongside these problems was the reduction (and in some cases elimination) of welfare provisions. Although the closing or the privatization of state enterprises promised new opportunities for all citizens, the economy channeled women's labor into low-status, low-paid positions.

Other issues threatened the position of women in Poland and Hungary. In Poland particularly but in Hungary as well, reproductive rights issues have taken center stage since communism's collapse, along with trafficking in women, prostitution, and violence against women. United Nations reports from 1995 and 1996 confirm that while political and economic changes adversely affected both men and women, the gender gap in politics, along with economic dislocation, put serious pressure on the status of women in these societies.[10]

To varying degrees the Polish and Hungarian governments have acknowledged that the change from communism to democracy and a market economy has been particularly difficult for the female population. Their reactions suggest that since 1989 some governments have been willing to recognize the challenges that women face but that they have not necessarily been interested in responding in any sustained fashion. In Poland in the early 1990s the Parliamentary Group of Women and the Plenipotentiary for Family and Women's Affairs coordinated the activities of numerous NGOs to ensure that women's issues were represented in parliament. Both institutions, but particularly the Plenipotentiary, played a crucial role in reaching out to NGOs and helping them to educate government representatives and the population about economic, political, and social issues affecting women. According to representatives from the Women's Rights Center and the Center for the Advancement of Women, the Plenipotentiary was, in the early 1990s, key to the growth of the women's movement in Poland. Its former director held regular meetings with representatives of women's NGOs and would consult the government on programs and policies from a gendered perspective.

In October 1997, however, Poland's newly installed conservative government introduced significant changes to the machinery responsible for equality practices. It transformed the Plenipotentiary for Family and Women's Affairs into the Plenipotentiary for Family Affairs, with "Women's Affairs" noticeably absent from the title. The office's mandate does not include women's issues or gender equality, and the head of this office is not considered to have a progressive or even positive opinion of gender issues. These changes, as well as the sharp increase in conservative rhetoric by government officials, the Solidarity-supported Radio Maria, and other influential players, have generated an atmosphere of hostility but also resignation among practitioners. Without some government support or machinery to represent women's issues, NGOs become isolated from domestic politics.

Hungary has seen significantly less variation in the government's attitude toward gender issues. While many Hungarian activists whom I interviewed complained that the government is not at all committed to gender equality, some were willing to acknowledge that changes have taken place. In 1992 the government created the Ombudswoman Program Office in Budapest to facilitate contacts between women's NGOs and to reshape and improve the media's coverage of women's issues. In 1996 the Ministry of Labor established the Office on the Status of Women, which has the primary functions of promoting gender issues in the media, coordinating meetings with women's NGOs, and providing research on women's employment issues. The government created the office in response to domestic impulses and, more important, to international pressure; the Hungarian government believed it was a necessary first step toward membership in the European Union. Robert Kiss, the assistant director of the Office on the Status of Women, concedes that Hungary's intense interest in becoming a full member of the European Union inspired its newfound interest in women's issues. The main reason for establishing his office was to reassure members of the European Union that Hungary was sensitive to gender-related unemployment and reemployment issues.[11]

Although many practitioners in Hungary did not feel that the government was genuinely interested in women's issues, they were positive about the creation of this office and its activities. Regular meetings with NGOs and the office's use of the media to promote awareness of discrimination made the office's director, Katalin Levai, a well-respected government official. This office and its origins are testimony to the power that international actors can wield by convincing government officials not only of the benefits of recognizing women's issues but of the negative repercussions that might ensue if the government does not become more sensitive to women's issues. While postcommunist governments have taken some steps to assist women in responding to the effects of transition, the most important actors seeking to improve the position of women are local NGOs, many of which are assisted financially and in-kind by Western foundations and international NGOs.

STRATEGIES OF WESTERN NGOS

Claims that "male-only democracies" were developing in East-Central Europe attracted the attention of Western scholars and practitioners who had begun to look beyond certain institutional configurations to define democracies. The development of civil society, inspired by the writings of Eastern European dissidents, became the catchphrase for Western NGOs as well as governmental actors who were providing democratization assistance to the region.[12] Although academics studying democracy have traditionally ignored gender issues, Western NGOs working in Eastern and Central Europe have not, and they have been involved with women's groups in Poland and Hungary for more than a decade.[13] Women's groups, which had formed voluntarily in an effort to influence state policies on behalf of women's rights, clearly fit into the notion of civil society development.

When asked why women's advocacy groups or women's NGOs were included in their democracy assistance programs for the region, program officers at the Ford Foundation, the German Marshall Fund, and the Eurasia Foundation responded in similar ways, acknowledging the challenges and special needs of this portion of society. Foundation representatives believed that there was a direct link between democratization and women's advocacy groups. By the early 1990s women's advocacy groups in the region had demonstrated that political and economic changes were affecting the female population adversely. Consequently, foundation representatives assumed that if these states were truly to respond to and represent the needs of all their citizens, they needed to support women's groups. Developing this sector meant establishing organizations, providing infrastructural support, initiating training seminars and workshops to educate and empower individuals, and funding specific projects.

The strategies that Western NGOs use reflect what they want to achieve. None pursued one strategy exclusively; in fact, they were likely to fund or be involved in projects that pursued different and even contradictory strategies. Table 2.1 shows the strategies that the foundations used to promote gender equality.

The target of assistance determines the strategy that the foundation will use. International actors can target organizations by providing start-up costs or supporting infrastructural development or can target individuals through education, seminars, or workshops. A third type of strategy involves funding specific projects, either those that stand alone, such as the Women's Beijing Conference Group, or those projects undertaken by an existing organization. Involvement in specific projects tends to be reactive, but other considerations include the dimensions of the strategy, such as the length of the commitment (long term or short term) and the terms of funding (process oriented or product oriented).

In table 2.1 "terms of involvement" describes the method of transfer that the Western NGO is likely to adopt. A proactive strategy is characterized by well-developed goals on the part of the Western NGO. Western NGOs that use proactive strategies tend to have a clear idea of both the outcome that they want and how to achieve this goal.[14] I also use the phrase "terms of involvement" in this chapter to reflect a general style of interacting with local NGOs—Western NGOs are likely to provide conditions and/or explicit instructions for local groups. For example, training seminars and workshops by Women's World Banking were proactive, elite centered, and used imported ideas. In the early

TABLE 2.1 Typology of Gender Assistance Strategies in Poland and Hungary

Target of Assistance
Organizations (infrastructural development)
Individuals or groups (human capital development)
Specific projects (human capital or infrastructural development)

Terms of Involvement	
Proactive	Reactive
Elite-centered	Mass-focused
Imported ideas	Domestic generated ideas
Process-oriented (seminars)	Product-oriented (research)
Short-term	Long-term
Small no. of large grants	Large no. of small grants

1990s this group initiated talks with Polish organizations in an attempt to create Women's World Banks in Lodz and Warsaw, with the ultimate goal of developing branches in other locations throughout Poland. This organization went to Poland with specific goals that it wanted to achieve, based on its experience in Asia and the developing countries.

A reactive strategy is one in which the Western NGO responds to local requests and is less committed to a particular goal or strategy. The Network for East-West Women is a good example of an organization that used reactive, mass-focused strategies with domestically inspired ideas. By facilitating communication between women's NGOs in the region and responding to requests for technical assistance or information, the network has been able to react to ongoing changes and needs.

INFRASTRUCTURAL ASSISTANCE

Because of the inability or unwillingness of the Polish and Hungarian governments to fund women's groups, the primary strategy of Western NGOs has been to provide money and in-kind assistance (such as computers, fax machines, and the like) to develop infrastructures that will create or sustain women's organizations. Since neither Poland nor Hungary had any independent women's organizations in 1989 when communism collapsed, the need to establish offices where women's groups could meet and conduct business was huge. The Soros network of foundations provided particularly extensive infrastructural assistance. Although not all the NGOs that I investigated received Soros money, most benefited in one way or another from Soros involvement in this sector.

While most of the grant-giving international actors (such as the German Marshall Fund, the Soros foundations, and the Global Fund for Women) are inclined to support existing or planned local organizations, the Ford Foundation follows a different approach. Its strategy in Poland is more proactive, top-down, and uses imported ideas. Ford bases its programs or projects on its assumptions about how it can achieve its desired goal. Moreover, unlike many Western foundations involved in the region, Ford still makes its funding decisions in New York. Its local consultant in Warsaw, Grazyna Kopinska, has extensive contacts with women's groups and provides recommendations for funding, but individuals in the United States make the final decision. Ford's proactive approach toward women's NGOs in Poland reflects the Ford Foundation's basic funding strategy of making large long-term investments in a few projects.

For example, Ford based its decision to establish the National Women's Information Center in Warsaw on Ford's experiences in Russia. Because the Ford-funded Center for Gender Studies in Moscow successfully became the hub of activism in Russia, Ford officials believed that founding a similar organization in Poland would have the same effect there. Although the center is located in Warsaw, it is not intended to benefit only elites. It was established in the hope that it would become a national center, helping women's groups and initiatives throughout the country to overcome their isolation by providing them with information about gender-related activities as well as seminars and conferences. According to several practitioners in Poland who were involved in the talks with the Ford Foundation before the center was established, Ford's "vision" had far more influence on the ideas surrounding the development of the center and how it would act than did domestically generated ideas or desires.

The Ford approach to institution building and infrastructural development is distinctly different from the predominant approach of most actors involved in women's NGO development, which is more reactive or interactive (responding to requests from local NGOs). For example, the German Marshall Fund was the first Western supporter of the Women's Rights Center in Warsaw. Urzula Nowokowska, current director of the center, had the idea for it, and local actors made all decisions in its development. According to Nowokowska, the relationship between the German Marshall Fund and the center was very much "bottom up"; the fund had little influence over its activities, although the fund's representative at the time certainly contributed ideas about how the center should develop.

In terms of institution building, the Soros foundations have provided most of the assistance to organizations in Hungary and Poland. They help to establish new organizations that come to them with requests, but they also invest in existing organizations, such as MONA and NaNE in Budapest. Many other U.S. foundations have also provided infrastructural assistance to women's NGOs in both countries, with substantially more money and interest going to Poland. The Global Fund for Women, which has also supported NaNE in Budapest, is one of the few organizations that is committed to providing a large number of small grants to women's organizations (or organizations led by women) for general unrestricted support.

According to several practitioners in the region, since the mid-1990s it has become difficult to find Western NGOs interested in institution building and willing to provide financial or in-kind support to cover overhead costs. Many U.S. and Western European foundations and international actors are moving out of East-Central Europe or farther east to the former Soviet Union because of the belief that they have accomplished their goals and democratic practices have taken hold. Declining interest in the region on the part of the foundations has convinced many NGO representatives that their proposals must be extremely strategic and should emphasize the development of human capital (such as by seminars or workshops). Another belief among practitioners in both Poland and Hungary is that they must reach out to women or groups outside the capital city. According to Western NGO representatives, the most viable proposals come from women's NGOs and focus on specific events.

HUMAN CAPITAL DEVELOPMENT

Empowering individuals or developing skills that are more marketable in the new economy has also figured prominently in the strategies of Western NGOs, particularly for the Network for East-West Women (NEWW), the League of Women Voters, and Women's World Banking. Since the late 1980s the development of human capital has been a common strategy of U.S. foundations for all sectors of civil society. This strategy mostly evolved during the 1990s. Seminars, workshops, and fellowships remain the most obvious manifestations, but in most cases the content as well as personnel involved in these educational endeavors has changed. Not surprisingly, many international actors initially targeted a small group of elites, or individuals, most often from Warsaw and Budapest, believed to be potential leaders in women's advocacy. The international foundations held one- or two-day training seminars in Warsaw or Budapest with Western trainers on finance, accounting, management, or political participation. The foundations also often offered travel and long-term fellowships in the United States or Western Europe. For example, in addition to providing seed money to the Women's Center in Warsaw, the German Marshall Fund provided travel money for the center's director and other key players to attend international or regional conferences.

Women's World Banking (WWB) conducted seminars for elites in Warsaw and in Lodz, a city dominated by female workers, in an effort to create women's banks in both cities. The organization's approach was top-down, proactive, and relied on ideas tested elsewhere in the developing world. According to Polish practitioners who had a great deal of contact with WWB representatives, the organization knew a lot about Poland and the ongoing changes. However, it based its seminars and strategies for responding to these changes on models that originated in countries that are significantly different from Poland. Representatives were unwilling or unable to change WWB's structure or methods to respond to the unique needs of Polish women. Perhaps as a result, and despite WWB's early interest in Poland, it established no Women's World Banks there.

The Network for East-West Women is unique in its approach to human capital development in this region. Its extensive activities are reactive, grassroots oriented, and rely on both domestic and imported ideas to guide the organization's involvement in the region. The network is associated with numerous short-term activities inspired by experiences in the West. For example, the East-East Legal Coalition examines and monitors the legal effect of postcommunist transitions. However, NEWW's most important function is the voice that it gives to women's NGOs and individual women by linking more than two thousand women's advocates in more than forty countries and by providing free Web pages for women's organizations in East-Central Europe and the former Soviet Union. Since 1990 it has been the main facilitator of the spread of information about women's organizations in the region, gender-related activities (including research on women), and fellowships in the United States and Western Europe. It has given a voice to small isolated groups throughout the region and assisted more mature groups to become leaders in the emerging women's movements. NEWW's extensive electronic network provides free computer links, and often computers and training, to women's groups throughout the region. The network (and its Web site) is the first place to go in researching women's advocacy groups in Poland and Hungary.

PROJECTS

According to many practitioners in the region, Western NGOs appear to be more eager to become involved in projects that have short-term identifiable objectives than in providing long-term support for infrastructural development or overhead costs. Involvement in specific projects, for better or worse, involves a beginning and an end, not to mention definitive amounts of financial assistance and commitment. According to Maria Knothe, director of the Center for the Advancement for Women in Poland, numerous sources, including several foreign embassies and USAID, helped underwrite its *Directory of Women's Organizations and Initiatives in Poland,* but these organizations were not willing to provide general support to the center's program for unemployed women.

The Gender Studies Small Grants Program, developed in 1996 by the Central European University's Program on Gender and Culture in Budapest and funded by the Soros Foundation, provides a large number of small grants to groups to pursue projects related to gender. Since 1996 the Program on Gender and Culture has provided up to $2,000 to institutes, centers, programs, and university departments for initiatives related to gender. The program seeks especially to give money to organizations that are located in small cities and towns and that would benefit significantly from such a small amount of money.[15]

The projects underwritten by the League of Women Voters—Building Political Participation in Poland (1992) and Project Demokracia (Hungary), which began in 1994—are rare examples of a Western NGO's addressing women's declining participation in local and national politics. In contrast to the Small Grants Program, the league provides a small number of longer-term grants to democracy-oriented NGOs throughout Poland and Hungary. These projects involve in-country training seminars as well as fellowships in the United States. The strategy thus focuses more on process and is of several years' duration. Using the grassroots framework and strategies that it developed in the United States, the league relies on local politicians and NGO practitioners to create country-specific methods for educating women's groups about how they could mobilize and influence political processes. In Poland, for example, the league invited twenty women to the United States to learn new skills (including prioritizing issues, forming coalitions, and influencing decision makers about issues) in local league offices. When the participants returned to Poland, they organized a conference for more than two hundred individuals in Krakow to educate Polish women about effective political participation and to encourage them to be more politically active. Project Demokracia in Hungary relied on a similar strategy and included a grants program for civic groups and on-site visits. Unlike other Western NGOs, which often support a single project, the league's approach has recognized the need for a longer period of commitment, outreach in smaller cities, and periodic contact.

INFLUENCE AND LIMITATIONS

In response to the collapse of the communist state and the desire of individuals to participate in public life but outside the realm of state control, the whole region has witnessed a blossoming of NGO activity. Women realized early that political and economic reforms were no guarantee that state policies would represent their interests. Recent political and economic changes in Poland and Hungary, as well as women's encounter with communism, affected their views. Thus it is perhaps not surprising that this sector initially developed in similar ways in these two countries. However, by 1998 the similarities had disappeared, and NGO activity in Poland differed substantially from women's advocacy in Hungary.

Although women's NGOs could be categorized in numerous ways, five general types of groups exist in these two countries: liberal or feminist organizations such as NaNE in Hungary; conservative or religious groups such as the Polish Union of Catholic Women; women's sections in political parties or trade unions such as the National Women's Section of Solidarity; professional women's associations such as the Association of Active Women; and research institutes and women's studies centers such as the Gender Center at the Central European University in Hungary. I targeted the most well-known and active organizations working on behalf of women's rights in both countries.[16] Individuals in the United States, Poland, and Hungary kept mentioning the same organizations and "must-see" individuals. Perhaps it should not be surprising that the women's NGOs identified as most important turned out to be liberal/feminist and those supported by Western NGOs. I discuss this issue later.

At first glance, it may appear that of the three strategies used by Western NGOs to assist women's groups in Poland and Hungary, infrastructural assistance has had the greatest influence on the development of women's NGOs. However, a broad consideration of events in the 1990s, particularly the rise and fall of so many local NGOs, suggests that human capital development and specific projects seem to have had a more enduring effect on the development of this sector.

INFRASTRUCTURAL ASSISTANCE

The Polish and Hungarian governments provide little assistance to NGOs and even less to women's NGOs. In 1989, when the first free elections took place, no independent women's organizations existed in either Poland or Hungary. By 1998, however, more than ninety Polish organizations, foundations, or research institutions had declared themselves to be focused on or associated with the women's movement.[17] In Hungary even an approximate number was difficult to establish. Various sources estimated that twenty to two hundred organizations are involved with women's issues and gender-related activities.[18] The proliferation of organizations suggests that international actors have played a role in this sector.

An examination of the landscape of women's advocacy groups in these two countries show that Western NGOs clearly have been crucial to institution building. Western NGOs have in some way supported the most active Polish and Hungarian women's NGOs. In Poland this strategy has had a tremendous influence on the number and diversity of women's organizations established after 1989. In contrast to Hungary, each of the various women's advocacy groups in Poland has developed a specific area of expertise. For example, the Center for the Advancement of Women offers training and assistance to unemployed women. Several reproductive rights–oriented organizations emerged in the early 1990s, although only the Federation for Women and Family Planning continued to exist in any real sense by the late 1990s. It remains an important force in defending women's reproductive rights and providing information and services to women and children. In terms of political activism, Women Also, with a strong U.S. connection, focuses on women's political participation in local government. The *Directory of Women's Organizations* shows that a majority of organizations, particularly those that are fairly active, were supported in part or wholly by international assistance.

Hungary has attracted fewer international donors and international actors to women's advocacy than has Poland. Other than the Soros network, no major foundations are providing a substantial amount of money to women's NGOs. Although some individuals whom I interviewed estimated that Hungary had one hundred to two hundred women's organizations, I could never obtain a list that identified more than twenty women's NGOs, and that list included organizations such as Women for Clear Water, the Women's Chapter of Autonomous Trade Unions, and the Women's Club in Soporon (the only organization outside Budapest), none of which was very active. Even those organizations that both Hungarians and Americans identified as "the most influential" women's NGOs, such as MONA and NaNE, are not nearly as developed as those in Poland. All the organizations that I investigated, however, benefited from Western assistance.

This has not meant, however, that this strategy has always been effective. The limited amount of money devoted to infrastructural assistance has affected the strategy's ability to foster the development of women's advocacy groups in both Poland and Hungary. Moreover, while both countries have numerous women's NGOs, few have a significant following or a staff and office to conduct business. The inability of women's NGOs to be self-sustaining is related to lack of funding but also to the tendency of Western NGOs to set the agenda in these countries by establishing or funding organizations that may appeal to U.S. or Western European constituencies but not necessarily the home country's population. Western NGOs claim that their approach to the region has become more context specific, as they adopt strategies that are more appropriate to specific historical and political circumstances. However, many organizations have fallen by the wayside. The inability of many women's NGOs to attract significant followers suggests that Western NGOs have done a poor job of ensuring that institutions become embedded in domestic society. Western NGOs have certainly helped establish women's organizations in Poland and Hungary, but the lack of sustained interest—both among Western NGOs and domestic constituents—has meant that the women's advocacy groups that do exist have yet to become established or influential actors in domestic society.

In both countries every NGO that I encountered struggled with the dilemma of how to secure funding for the next year. This prevents women's groups from doing what is necessary to attract domestic followers and develop a long-term agenda. According to Antonio Barros of NaNE, the Global Fund was an important contributor to her organization because it was one of the few organizations that was willing to provide money for general institutional support and that responded quickly to her request. Its flexibility and quick turnaround provided this Budapest-based organization with much needed resources at a crucial time in its development. Yet the constant, even feverish, search for money to keep their organizations afloat has meant that most practitioners have little time to carry out their proposed activities.

Simultaneously, the inability of Western NGOs to monitor the activities or outreach of these local organizations has created a situation in which some local NGOs that are particularly good at fund-raising have impressive offices but do little. The problem appears to be that once funders give money to an organization, they are likely to continue providing funds even if the organization lacks domestic support. Twice in Poland and once in Hungary I encountered organizations that occupied impressive modern offices equipped with the best technology but appeared to be devoid of both staff and agenda. Asked about their membership or current activities, the sole representatives of these organizations conceded that their organizations had few active members and were doing little more than applying for more grants.

The inactivity of these NGOs and their lack of domestic constituents are not necessarily the result or fault of the local NGO but may be caused by two other factors. It may be that once a funder supports a local NGO, it continues to do so because it does not want to "lose its investment" or acknowledge that it has made a poor decision. Some NGOs that received seed money or in-kind support may no longer have enough money to support a paid staff. According to Wanda Nowicka, director of the Federation of Women's Planning, Western NGOs were often critical of the work ethic in Poland, demanding to know why women associated with the federation were not working longer or even on the holidays. In fact, Polish women could not afford to volunteer their services; they needed to be paid for any time spent in the office. Conditions in Poland meant that day-to-day life was so demanding that volunteers or even paid employees could not spend their evenings or weekends working in the office.

According to NGO practitioners and academics in the region, another reason for the poor performance of women's NGOs is related to Western NGOs' strategies, which often ignored urgent issues, such as political participation and economic dislocation, and focused instead on issues popular in the United States and Western Europe. Several local practitioners mentioned the attention being paid to the trafficking in women (who tend to come mainly from former Soviet states) and the rights of minority women and suggested that this focus served the interests of the international NGOs rather than the interests or needs of Polish or Hungarian women. Women's NGOs in desperate need of support often organized their activities around the interests evinced by Western NGOs and thus neglected local needs.

HUMAN CAPITAL DEVELOPMENT

International involvement has affected the number of women's groups that have been established and has played a role in the types of organizations that have emerged, the ideas that have shaped them, and the strategies that they have used. The strategy of developing human capital appears to have had a lasting and penetrating influence on the development of this sector. It appears to have been successful in assisting in the development of capable professionals, many of whom now are the leaders of women's groups. According to Maria Knothe, director of the Center for the Advancement of Women in Warsaw, Western NGOs have thus helped to shape the thinking and behavior of those involved in this sector. Thanks to international involvement, Polish women and women's groups have developed critical skills for adapting to the new environment, such as fund-raising, strategic planning, and advocacy. These skills are important to the development of women's NGOs. Moreover, they are universal skills. Western involvement has helped women and women's NGOs understand what it means to be professional. For example, the NGOs establish protocols for hiring, firing, and promotion, and meetings begin and end at specific times. Consequently, while this strategy is often difficult to link to a specific outcome, it is an important facet of how Western NGOs have influenced the way that people behave and the level of professionalization that has developed among practitioners involved in women's advocacy.

Women who participated in fellowships in the United States or Western Europe returned to Poland and Hungary to open women's shelters, develop legal assistance centers, and run for parliament.[19] Contacts with Western NGOs have influenced the strategies that local organizations use. For example, British-born Antonio Barros, founder of NaNE, shapes its approach to the development of its organization. Trainers from Britain and the United States travel to Budapest periodically to train local staff members on strategic planning, outreach, and day-to-day management of an NGO. Nowokowska says that many strategies that she has used at the Women's Right's Center come from what she learned while on a fellowship in the United States. These include establishing a women's hot line, lobbying parliament, and writing to senators about women's issues. Further evidence of the influence of the strategy of human capital development lies in how these women talk—in terms of the importance of strategic planning, networking strategies, and making the media more gender sensitive, a vocabulary that would not have been theirs in the early 1990s.

This strategy also entailed certain drawbacks. Practitioners in both countries complained that most of the early investments in human capital development were not well thought out and therefore not particularly useful. Most often, Western NGOs sponsored one-day seminars or workshops in the country's capital. The individuals running the seminars were often ignorant of the local culture and history, as well as local language. In many cases they spent little time ensuring that Western phases and concepts were translated properly; thus people who attended these early seminars benefited little from this strategy. For example, woman who participated in seminars in the early 1990s recalled her experiences with Women's World Banking. Although her English skills at the time were quite good, she had no idea what the term *strategic planning* meant or how to translate it to Polish conditions. However, eight years later she looked at her notes from these seminars with greater comprehension; she says that only in the late 1990s would these seminars have been relevant in Poland.

Another problem associated with the strategy of human capital development is the high attrition rate among NGO practitioners. Although individuals may receive training in third-sector development or financial management for the purpose of women's advocacy, the Western NGO has no way to ensure that this person will continue to be involved in this sector. Many women who participated in women's activities in the early 1990s have left for more lucrative positions. A final problem is Western bias. Interviewees often cited European foundations and organizations as being more sensitive than Americans to local cultures in using human capital development. However, individuals in Hungary felt that even PHARE programs made little effort to incorporate the experiences and modes of interaction in postcommunist countries. As a consequence of these problems, Western-led workshops no longer are held in Warsaw or Budapest; they have been replaced with more successful seminars conducted in smaller cities by local practitioners during a period of several months.

PROJECTS

In both countries but particularly in Poland, specific project support has helped to create a flurry of activity associated with gender. I was genuinely surprised by the number as well as the sophistication of the meetings and workshops being held throughout the country. The National Women's Information Center (OSKa) in Warsaw publishes quarterly newsletters that identify gender-related activities and projects. While women's advocacy groups in Hungary may also be involved in considerable activity, it was far more apparent in Poland. In fact, the initial similarities in Poland and Hungary have disappeared, and the landscape of NGO activity has evolved quite differently in these two countries. Polish women's advocacy NGOs appeared to be better organized and far more than active than those in Hungary.

A second difference was the large number of gender-related projects taking place outside Poland's capital. Mary Haney, a consultant for USAID, notes that many women's groups outside Warsaw are not active and are not likely to survive because of lack of funding.[20] However, women's advocacy groups are active in Krakow, Poznan, Wroclaw, and other cities and even in small towns such as

Legnica and Torun. In contrast, not one person I interviewed for this study in Hungary or the United States was able to name a women's advocacy group or even a project associated with gender that is located outside Budapest.

A third difference, which may account for the others, is the general level of knowledge about other women's groups and gender-related activities within and outside Warsaw. The Center for the Advancement of Women's *Directory of Women's Organizations*, as well as the National Women's Information Center's quarterly bulletin of gender activities throughout Poland, are signs of the evolution and maturity of women's advocacy groups in Poland. In Hungary in the 1990s, by contrast, no formal or informal communication existed even among groups in Budapest, let alone outside it. Even among NGOs that appeared to have a great deal in common, many practitioners acknowledged that they know little about the activities of other groups.

While providing assistance to specific projects or programs appears to be a way to support women's activities without investing too much money or time in this sector, this strategy has nonetheless had an important influence on this sector. This assistance has been particularly important to small, isolated organizations that need a small amount of money or partnership to conduct a conference or workshop. According to several practitioners in both Poland and Hungary, the Small Grants Program based at the Central European University in Budapest has provided critical assistance to groups in small towns and villages that could never have received money from another source. Grants to emerging organizations that support a small project mean significant gains for a small amount of money. It appears, however, that the Soros Foundation and other foundations involved in these countries are increasingly using this strategy instead of strategies that are more expensive or require a longer time commitment. In a climate of declining interest and funding for East-Central Europe, the funding of specific projects may be the only way for women's NGOs to continue receiving international assistance.

LIMITATIONS

In assessing the influence of Western NGOs on the development of women's advocacy organizations in Poland and Hungary, we must consider three factors. First, international actors have spent considerably less on women's NGOs and gender issues than on ethnic issues or political parties. Even estimating the amount of money given to women's advocacy groups or gender-related activities is not possible because the foundation officials whom I interviewed did not isolate funding for gender-related activities or women's NGOs. Most often, they incorporated funding for women's issues in civil society development or human rights. Moreover, while many foundations were active in Poland, few supported Hungary or Hungarian women's groups.

Second, assistance to women's advocacy has generally been reactive, providing limited support as needed rather than as part of a comprehensive plan or sustained interest in this sector. The amount of democracy assistance to women's NGOs varies from country to country, and the assistance itself is often so meager and scattered that no individual donor or strategy could influence the development of women's advocacy in these countries.

Third, assessing the influence of international actors on the development of women's advocacy groups, and comparing developments in Poland and Hungary, is complex because of the difficulty of isolating international factors from other variables. Government support for this sector, the strength of indigenous NGOs, culture and traditions, and the different challenges facing women in these countries all have their influences. One Hungarian scholar remarked that women's advocacy will always be different in Hungary than in Poland because women's reproductive rights will never be challenged in Hungary by the Catholic Church in the same way that they have been in Poland.[21]

A further problem with isolating the influence of international involvement is related to the issue of selection bias. The list of organizations and "must-see" individuals that I compiled tended to be somehow associated with or sponsored by Western and generally U.S. organizations. According to Robert Kiss, the assistant director of the Office on the Status of Women, Western actors are most likely to work with and give money to liberal or feminist organizations, even if professional associations or women's sections have a better infrastructure or more members. Instead of trying to understand the role of particular civil groups in postcommunist societies, Western foundations put their money into newly created organizations that tend to model themselves on Western organizations. They also appear to focus on issues deemed relevant by their home country, rather than on issues that are considered to be relevant or necessary to Central European societies. Despite these observations, however, when I asked Kiss which organizations were "the most important" and "influential" in Hungary, he listed only liberal or feminist organizations.[22]

Ultimately, it is difficult to say whether liberal/feminist NGOs showed the most promise and were funded by Western NGOs for that reason or whether these groups became the most active and important women's advocacy groups because of the materials and skills provided by Western NGOs. I will simply note that the correlation between Western NGO involvement in predominately liberal/feminist organizations and their prominence in Poland and Hungary is strong.

UNINTENDED CONSEQUENCES

International involvement in the development of women's advocacy groups has not always been able to control its influence. In both countries unintended consequences from international involvement were evident. The most disturbing unintended outcome—infighting among women's NGOs—was evident in both Poland and Hungary. International interest in the development of women's NGOs has led to a substantial amount of competition among women's groups. While infighting might have occurred anyway, even in the absence of international involvement, many practitioners claim that the activities of Western funders (but not of Western NGOs) exacerbate tensions and lack of communication among women's groups.

In Poland women's advocacy groups have been able to work together, but a significant rift still exists among groups that were overlooked when a U.S. foundation decided to create a new women's organization in Poland. Several women expressed disappointment and resentment that this organization was created and "imposed" on them. In Hungary a similar situation has emerged; groups do not always know how much money another group received, and they tended to exaggerate the amount of foreign assistance given to other groups. For example, three practitioners from different organizations in Hungary mentioned "a large grant" that one women's NGO in Budapest had received from a U.S. foundation. In fact, that organization had no connection with the U.S. foundation. The fight for international funds (as well as other divisions) has left women's groups in Hungary fragmented.

Equally important, international involvement has meant that women's NGOs are dependent upon Western actors for resources to maintain their infrastructure, further their skills, or complete their proposed projects. Assistance from international actors has allowed these groups to focus on issues once considered taboo in Polish and Hungarian society, such as violence against women, and to engage in Western-style activities, such as opening shelters, lobbying the parliament, and conducting research on the changing status of women. The absence of domestic financial or moral support, along with their dependence on international actors, has meant that women's NGOs remain isolated from the general public and marginalized from the local decision-making process.

Grazyna Kopinska, the Ford Foundation's local consultant in Warsaw, explained that many Polish organizations adopted feminist ideas from the United States and tried to replicate the American style of activism even where these conflicted with Polish history and tradition. As a consequence, the term *feminism* or the idea of women's advocacy groups conjures up, for much of the Polish public, images of extremists or lesbians. According to Kopinska and others, no women's organization currently represents the average Polish woman. Because adopted Western ideas and strategies conflict with Polish culture, ideas related to women's advocacy have had a difficult time taking hold in Polish society.

As suggested by Kopinska in Poland and by Kiss in Hungary, the inability of women's NGOs to become genuine representatives of the female population has generated increasing criticism in both countries. Many practitioners and academics in Poland and Hungary are eager to replace U.S. feminism with Central European or Hungarian feminism. Western involvement has contributed to the isolation of women's NGOs and their marginalization in local and national politics. In light of growing anti-Western sentiment, the rise of Central European feminism, and declining international support for the region, women's NGOs will in the long run have to rely on and respond to domestic rather than international constituents. Asked where the movement would be if international actors had not been involved in women's groups in Poland, Barbara Liminowska, director of the Women's Information Center, responded that women's groups would be more involved in domestic issues. Instead of depending on external actors, they would rely on and have to work with political parties, the government, and other social groups.

HOW NGOS EVALUATE THEMSELVES

International actors clearly have played a critical role in the development of women's advocacy groups in Poland and Hungary and in the ideas that have shaped the thinking of the women's movements in these countries. But have local NGOs been successful in their endeavors? And has Western assistance made a difference to women in these countries?

In general, indigenous NGOs did not appear to, nor did they claim to, have a well-developed evaluation process for their activities or the strategies that they have used to advocate on behalf of women. If their organizations continue to exist, this will be a crucial sign of success. Local NGOs were quick to provide statistics (e.g., of women assisted per week), hand me glossy pamphlets detailing their programs and projects, or point to legislation on which they were consulted. But when I asked whether women's NGO's have made a difference in improving the position of women or whether they could provide evidence that their organization has made a difference to the female population, representatives consistently made only modest claims. Most responded that they believed their organization had helped women on an individual basis but resisted speculating about its influence on the society.

Several practitioners cited changes in national consciousness regarding women's issues, including an increase in the awareness of discrimination and in the media's coverage of women's issues. MONA representative Zsuzsa Lestal said that when MONA launched a project in 1998, local television and radio stations asked her why she did not notify them, whereas the media previously had shown no interest in gender issues. Almost half the NGO representatives whom I interviewed said that their organization have achieved some of their stated objectives, although none had evidence to support these claims.

Representatives from Western NGOs, including the Ford Foundation, the Soros network, and the German Marshall Fund, were more sophisticated in their evaluations of NGO activity but relied on simplistic quantitative methods, often providing the same information given to them by their local organizations. In addition to reports from the local NGOs, U.S.-based NGOs sometimes relied on internal evaluations of their partners in Poland and on information gathered by outside evaluators. U.S. NGOs generally evaluate their involvement by quantifying women's advocacy, in such terms as the number of women who participated in a seminar or who received a fellowship to the United States. Western NGOs seem unwilling or unable to take this evaluation process a step further and establish a link between their involvement and improvements in women's unemployment, political participation, or status in society. Although it may be too soon to evaluate the ultimate effectiveness of these strategies, some tentative, broad conclusions about the strategies and Western involvement are possible.

LESSONS LEARNED

One of my objectives here was to link several issues—the state of women's NGOs in Poland and Hungary; international involvement in the development of women's advocacy groups; and strategies used by Western NGOs to develop women's NGOs—to determine the importance of Western NGO involvement in the development of women's advocacy groups in Poland and Hungary. In many respects the situation for women in Poland and Hungary continues to deteriorate: Unemployment continues to rise, particularly for older, less educated women in smaller cities; women's political participation remains low; and other forms of discrimination against women are evident.[23] In short, international assistance has not reversed negative trends. Despite this situation, a consensus emerged from my conversations and interviews with activists and NGO representatives in the field and with academics in Poland and Hungary and the United States: Western NGOs have been crucial to the development of women's advocacy groups in Poland and Hungary. They have helped establish organizations and empower individuals, and their involvement has brought respect and seriousness to the plight of women. Most evidence cited for the effect of NGO activity on the position of women was the change in consciousness among elites and within society in both countries. Challenges remain, but at least people are now willing to acknowledge the existence of discrimination and the unique obstacles that women face. Politicians can no longer wholly ignore women's NGOs. In Poland it would be reasonable to argue that the activities of Western and local NGOs have helped to generate a budding, albeit limited, women's movement. In Hungary, however, lack of coordination of disparate women's NGOs means that a critical mass of its citizens has yet to be convinced that a woman's voice is either necessary or important to the process of democratization.

On the basis of the evidence in this chapter, I conclude that women's advocacy organizations need both large, long-term institutional grants and small grants that primarily target individuals. Many in Poland criticize the Ford Foundation for the way that it handled the establishment of the National Women's Information Center, arguing that Ford's strategy had been forced on the local activists. But few disagree with its goal or the need for a national organization with extensive outreach capability. Such a national organization must be developed at the appropriate time, when women's activities have attained a critical mass and NGOs are willing to work together. Poland has reached this point, but it is less clear that Hungary has. Poland's experiences and the higher volume of Western involvement suggest that more Western involvement—particularly assistance in human capital development outside Budapest—could expedite the building of a similar critical mass in Hungary.

Second, the efforts of Western NGOs would be more successful if they funded or formed partnerships with organizations and projects that focused on average citizens. The strategies of Western NGOs must be context specific: Western NGOs cannot impose local NGOs and the ideas around which indigenous groups form—these must be initiated locally, using domestically generated ideas and methods. Women's NGOs in both Poland and Hungary continue in 2001 to be isolated from the general public, which often treats them with disdain for their wholesale adoption of Western ideas and strategies. Western NGOs should target organizations that are sensitive to local cultural context, needs, and interests.

Third, neither Western nor local NGOs can ignore domestic politics. Western NGOs should try to create an incentive structure that would lead government brokers to feel that women's issues are important. The European Union's attitude toward women's issues is an excellent example of the difference that international actors can make. Even if government representatives are not genuinely interested in gender issues, international pressure and incentives can make a significant difference in terms of the government's acceptance of and support for women's advocacy groups. Western NGOs should continue to train local NGOs in how to write proposals and raise money but should also encourage local NGOs to get involved with local and national politics. More than anything else, women's NGOs need local partners, whether they are government organizations or other NGOs. If women's NGOs are to make their voices heard, they must also gain access to government leaders.

Western NGOs should pay closer attention to sequencing various types of assistance. They should first respond to local activities with infrastructural assistance and human capital development. Once a critical mass has developed, Western NGOs should provide larger, long-term assistance to NGOs that are politically grounded and domestically supported.

NOTES

1. Information on the Small Grants Program is available from the Program on Gender and Culture, 1051 Budapest, Nador u.9, Hungary, or from Program on Gender and Culture at http://www.gender@ceu.hu (June 7, 1999).

2. See Patrice McMahon, "Building Civil Societies in East-Central Europe: The Effect of American Nongovernmental Organizations on Women's Groups," *Democratization* 8, no. 2 (Summer 2001): 45–68; Patrice McMahon, "The Effect of Economic and Political Reforms on Soviet/Russian Women," in Nahid Aslanbeigui, Steve Pressman, and Gale Summerfield, eds., *Women in the Age of Economic Transformation: Gender Impacts of Reform in Postsocialist and Developing Countries*, (London: Routledge, 1994).

3. In Poland I conducted many of the interviews in Polish, whereas I conducted all interviews in Budapest in English.

4. Numerous studies have examined the status of women in communist countries. See, for example, Sharon L. Wolchik and Alfred G. Meyer, eds., *Women, State, and Party in Eastern Europe* (Durham: Duke University Press, 1985).

5. In Poland this mass organization was called the League of Polish Women; in Hungary the women's organization was the Democratic Association of Hungarian Women.

6. Unfortunately, the studies of the effects of political and economic reform on women in postcommunist countries are often more journalistic than scholarly; only in the last few years have credible statistics emerged that demonstrate the effects of change on women. A good book on postcommunist women and movements is Nannette Funk and Magda Mueller, eds., *Gender Politics and Postcommunism* (New York: Routledge, 1993).

7. See Renata Siemienska, "Polish Women and Polish Politics Since World War II," *Journal of Women's History* 3 (Spring 1991): 108–25, and Andrea Peto, "Hungarian Women in Politics," in Joan W. Scott, Cora Kaplan, and Debra Keates, eds., *Transitions, Environments, Translations*, pp. 153–62 (New York: Routledge, 1997).

8. "The Status of Women in Poland" (unpublished manuscript prepared as a country report for Fourth World Conference on Women, Beijing, September 4–15, 1995).

9. Ministry of Labor Equality Department, "Status of Women in Hungary," unpublished report, 1997.

10. Darko Silovic, "Human Development Report, Regional Study on Human Development and Human Rights in Central and Eastern Europe," November 15, 1999, Human Development Report, Background Report, *United Nations Development Program*, http://www.undp.org/hdro/silovic.pdf (July 30, 2001).

11. Robert Kiss, assistant director, Office on the Status of Women, Ministry of Labor, interview by author, Budapest, March 1998.

12. Ferenc Miszlivetz, "Participation and Transition: Can the Civil Society Project Survive in Hungary?" *Journal of Communist Studies and Transition Politics* 13, no. 1 (March 1997): 31.

13. For a discussion of gender and democratization see Georgina Waylen, "Women and Democratization," *World Politics* 46, no. 3 (April 1994): 327–54.

14. Kevin F.F. Quigley, "For Democracy's Sake: How Funders Fail—and Succeed," *World Policy Journal* 13 (Spring 1996): 109–18.

15. Christina Crowley, program coordinator, Gender Studies Small Grants Program, Central European University, interview by author, Budapest, March 1998.

16. I based my selection of NGOs on research I did in the United States as well as in Poland and Hungary. Before visiting the region, I asked foundation officers, practitioners, and academics which organizations were the most active and were doing the most on behalf of women's interests. In Poland and Hungary I did the same thing, attempting to develop a short list of organizations and people.

17. See the *Informator o Organizacjach I Inicjatywach Kobiecych w Polsce* (Directory of Women's Organizations and Initiatives in Poland) (Warsaw: Fundacja Centrum Promocji Kobiet, 1997).

18. The Program on Gender and Culture at the Central European University has a database on women's organizations but provided a list of only twenty-two women's NGOs or organizations associated with gender issues. Several practitioners in Budapest suggested that in fact Hungary has about two hundred such organizations. No other organization had even a list of names.

19. Orna Tamches, manager of Emerging Democracies Program for the League of Women Voters Education Fund, Washington, D.C., telephone interview by author, June 1998.

20. Mary Haney, consultant for USAID, telephone interview by author, February 1998.

21. Andrea Peto, interview by author, Budapest, March 1998.

22. Kiss interview.

23. Silovic, "Human Development Report."

Chapter 3

EVALUATING WESTERN ASSISTANCE
TO RUSSIAN WOMEN'S ORGANIZATIONS

James Richter

A key objective of democracy assistance for Russia is the promotion of civil society. No effort to promote civil society in Russia can be successful, however, without explicitly considering the contribution of women. Most studies estimate that by the late 1990s two thousand to four thousand women's organizations were active in Russia (women's organizations are defined as organizations with mostly women members, working in the interests of women).[1] These organizations include educational groups, consciousness-raising groups, crisis centers, human rights groups, environmental groups, cultural clubs, lesbian support groups, charitable organizations, professional associations, employment retraining centers, and political advocacy groups. Women are also the most active members of many other Russian NGOs: One study found that in 1995 more than 80 percent of the members of St. Petersburg's charitable organizations were women.[2]

In this chapter I examine Western assistance to women's organizations, paying particular attention to organizations that identify themselves as feminist. The mission of these organizations is not simply to improve women's lives in a

---

I would like to thank Valerie Sperling, Sarah Henderson, and Julie Hemment for their comments on earlier drafts.

practical sense but also to remove the legal, social, and cultural impediments to women's equal access to government and market resources. I also include in this category crisis centers and hot lines directed against domestic abuse and sexual assault. Although feminist activists may or may not run the individual crisis centers, feminist ideals were the basis for the movement in Russia. I concentrate on this subset of women's organizations for two reasons. First, unlike many other women's organizations in Russia, these groups consider themselves to be part of a transnational social movement. Most founders of contemporary Russian feminism drew their inspiration largely from contact with Western feminists and feminist literature.[3] A conceptual framework for a more "authentically Russian" variant of feminism is only now being articulated. Second, feminist organizations receive a disproportionate share of Western assistance among women's organizations, and they are more dependent than other women's organizations on such assistance for their survival.

My central argument is that although Western assistance has strengthened the third sector, it has not helped, and in some ways has hurt, civil society as a whole. *Civil society* and the *third sector* are often used interchangeably, but there is a crucial distinction between the two terms. *Civil society* refers to an overlapping network of autonomous voluntary associations—formal and informal, political and nonpolitical—that creates a space for public action between the individual and the state. In a strong civil society such associations are woven into the fabric of daily life and help structure citizens' relations with each other and with the state. These associations not only aggregate societal demands and articulate them to government officials but also—and, more important, in some scholars' view—instill the habits of cooperation, solidarity, public spiritedness, and respect for legitimate authority necessary for a stable democratic polity.[4]

The *third sector*, on the other hand, refers more narrowly to the formal, functionally differentiated, and frequently professional nonprofit organizations that interact with state and market actors. Strong third-sector organizations have the skills and stability to provide a service consistently and efficiently over time, to get their message out to the public, to articulate their demands to government officials, and to monitor government actions to ensure accountability. But because many such organizations are run along the same lines as state and market actors, they are less equipped to socialize individuals to become good citizens.

Western assistance cannot create the informal structures that make up civil society; at best, it can reach a fraction of the formal organizations that constitute the third sector. Within Russia's women's movement Western assistance has helped institutionalize and strengthen key organizations to ensure the movement's survival in a hostile economic, social, and legal environment. It has helped women's organizations to communicate and maintain extended contact with each other. The result has been the emergence of a small but growing cadre of nonprofit professionals within the women's movement that can manage their organizations and negotiate with government officials more effectively. However, the real success of civil promotion should be measured not in terms of organizational capacity but in terms of changed institutions and human beings. Such changes happen gradually as a result of the sustained, informal interaction among activists and between activists and the larger society. They often occur not as the expected result of particular projects but as a result of positive externalities, that is, the "benefits that accrue to persons or sectors outside the scope of the immediate organization or program."[5]

Unfortunately, by focusing activists' attention on organizational questions, Western assistance to women's organizations has frequently acted to diminish such positive externalities. In some cases it has widened the gap between the activists and the rest of society. Institutionalizing and professionalizing civic associations frequently transforms them into hierarchical, centralized, and corporate entities that value their own survival more than their social mission. Their dependence on Western assistance often forces them to be more responsive to outside donors than to their constituencies, removes incentives to mobilize new members, and fosters interorganizational competition that discourages open communication. These effects of assistance on third-sector organizations contribute little to the habits of trust, tolerance, and solidarity necessary to civil society. Lacking a firm base in society, the third sector in Russia remains highly vulnerable to political fluctuations, not only in Russia but also in Western countries.

Western donors could partially offset this trend by changing some of their emphases. First, donors should pay closer attention to how decisions are made within organizations to encourage wider participation and transparency. Second, donors should take steps to avoid centralization within the movement as a whole, by spreading out more small grants among a variety of organizations and by increasing their efforts to connect women's organizations with the Internet. Third, and most important, donors should award grants that actively encourage organizations to reach out to their communities with practical services that have immediate, tangible effects on people's lives. Western assistance to crisis centers for abused women, for example, has proved particularly effective in this regard.

These conclusions are based on research trips to Moscow, Nizhni Novgorod, St. Petersburg, and Yekaterinburg during the summers of 1998 and 1999. I interviewed more than forty women's activists and observed a number of conferences, demonstrations, and public lectures. In Moscow I chose my subjects from the list of signatories to a charter for cooperation among women's organizations sponsored by the Movement of Russian Women in April 1997, a group that included both independent and state-sponsored groups, feminist, and some charitable organizations.[6] In Nizhni Novgorod, St. Petersburg, and Yekaterinburg I interviewed women activists whom I identified from local contacts and from a directory of women's organizations published in May 1998.[7] I also interviewed local program officers for several Western granting agencies, as well as representatives from other sectors of Russia's civil society, particularly environmental organizations. Three earlier trips to study women's organizations and trade unions in the town of Ivanovo, as well as subsequent research into the effect of transnational factors on the Russian third sector, also inform my argument; most of the organizations in Ivanovo did not receive financial assistance from Western donors at that time.[8] I also drew upon on the extensive secondary literature on women's activism in Russia.[9]

Since I completed my field research, the pattern of Western assistance to Russian women's organizations has changed in several respects. Most important, in 1998 the Soros Foundation's Open Society Institute opened an office of the Network Women's Program in Russia. The program's budget of more than $500,000 in 1999 and 2000 quickly made it the single largest donor to women's organizations in Russia.[10] The World Bank, the Gender Equality Fund, and the Canada International Development Agency have also begun programs in Russia devoted to women's issues. In addition, both the U.S. Agency for International Development (USAID) and the Ford Foundation have made important changes in their approach to issues of gender. USAID has announced a new effort against the trafficking in women for prostitution in Russia and in the former Soviet Union.[11] The Ford Foundation has cut back on its grants to civil society organizations in the Russian feminist movement and concentrated its support on gender studies in higher education, microfinancing of women's small business enterprises, and the campaign against domestic violence.[12]

This chapter begins by outlining the historical and contemporary challenges facing civic activists in Russia, with particular attention to the role that women and women's organizations have played in Russia's civic life. The next section describes the strategies that Western assistance organizations have used to help Russian women's organizations overcome these challenges. Then I analyze the positive and negative effects of these strategies on the movement. I conclude with some lessons this analysis might hold for future strategies.

HISTORICAL AND POLITICAL CONTEXT

The rapid growth of NGOs in Russia is a rare sign of hope in an otherwise bleak economic and political landscape. A report issued in 1997 by Charities Aid Foundation/Russia notes that more than fifty thousand NGOs had registered with the Ministry of Justice since the collapse of the Soviet Union.[13] Even so, Russia's third sector remains in a precarious situation. The vast majority of the new NGOs have few members and fewer resources; most do not outlive the enthusiasm of their founders. They tend to be little known in their communities, and those that are known often meet with indifference or suspicion. The most effective organizations, as a rule, survive only with the help of state funding or international assistance.

CIVIL SOCIETY IN RUSSIA

Russia has never had a strong civil society. The tsarist autocracy carefully monitored all forms of civic activism, and the Soviet regime banned independent public activism altogether. The social organizations that did exist in the USSR depended upon the regime for funding and personnel and often acted as a means of social control rather than of individual empowerment. Reacting to these efforts by the party-state to dominate all public life, most Russians sought to avoid the public sphere and retreated as much as possible into the sanctuary of their homes, their families, and a small network of trusted friends. The resulting absence of public, horizontal ties among the population left no basis for a coherent civil society when the party collapsed; instead, Russian society consisted of a multitude of small private worlds cultivated in mutual isolation and distrust.

The public activism characteristic of the perestroika period reflected this fragmentation. Though many informal organizations (*neformaly*) emerged when Mikhail Gorbachev relaxed party control, most were small and weak, with few ties to society or to the government. Rather than articulating the interests of particular constituencies, as one might expect in a civil society, these "movement organizations," as Steven Fish has dubbed them, pursued more comprehensive goals of raising public consciousness and transforming society as a whole.[14]

CIVIC ACTIVISM AFTER 1991

The movement organizations did not fare well in the first decade of the post-Soviet era.[15] The economic upheaval of the transition caused most Russians to worry about more immediate, tangible goals than raising public consciousness. A combination of rampant inflation, declining production, and a retreating state created a demand for more practical social welfare organizations, but the response was disappointing. A sense of civic powerlessness dominated society: Many people expected the state to supply their education, employment, housing, health care, and even recreation, as it had under the Soviet regime, and the continued concentration of political and economic power gave them little reason to believe that public action would change anything. Most Russians again retreated into private worlds, relying on their gardens, their networks, and barter to insulate themselves from economic turmoil.[16]

Not all Russians retreated, however; a significant number of activists, mostly women, emerged to fill the gaps left by the retreating state. Unfortunately, few of these organizations had the technical competence to make much of an impact. The new activists had little or no experience in managing independent organizations. Most saw their role as a temporary one of providing services that the state would provide in more stable times and so did not consider how their activities might fit within a broader, more permanent mission. They were working in a chaotic, even hostile, environment. No law regulating NGOs existed until 1995; Russia has no tradition of private giving, and the existing tax code offers few incentives to begin such a tradition.[17]

The greatest challenge facing Russian NGOs, however, is to overcome the legacy of cynicism and suspicion that many Russians feel toward all public organizations. The task is not an easy one. Many early NGOs fueled such distrust by exhibiting little or no commitment to social change. Even committed social service organizations frequently reproduced the Soviet pattern of small private worlds, where the director and a few other activists—often personal friends or former coworkers—allocated organizational resources according to personal loyalty rather than more disinterested criteria. Such practices reinforced the perception that NGOs exist primarily to enrich the organizers, discouraging others from participating in NGO activities.

The Soviet legacy of small private worlds also made it difficult for the new NGOs to work together: They had no common sense of mission, they had few means of contacting each other, and they distrusted people outside their own circle. Anastasia Posadskaya, an organizer of the First Independent Women's Forum, reported with dismay that many of the representatives at the forum had little interest in closer coordination: "We have our group. You have your center. You have your support group. We have already found each other. Why should we organize this? For whom?"[18]

WOMEN IN RUSSIAN CIVIL SOCIETY

Women had played an active role in Russia's small civil society before the 1917 revolution, but the Soviet regime condemned the independent women's movement as bourgeois, as it did other groups. The women's groups that did emerge under the Soviets were created mostly to mobilize women's support for the new regime. Indeed, in the public realm, at least, the status of Soviet women compared favorably in many ways to that of their sisters in the capitalist countries. But whereas the regime's ideology proclaimed the equality of men and women in the public sphere, it never addressed the additional expectations placed on women in their roles as housekeeper and mother, leaving women with the full burden of domestic responsibilities in addition to their work outside the home. Such unspoken assumptions about women's domestic roles limited their opportunities in the workplace as well. Women were concentrated in less prestigious and less remunerative jobs, such as textiles, retailing, health, and accounting, where, it was thought, their "natural" aptitudes as mothers and housewives could be put to good use. Even in these occupations, women would not receive the promotions that they deserved because most supervisors thought the women would be distracted by maternal duties. On average, Soviet women earned only 70 percent of Soviet men's earnings.[19]

WOMEN'S ORGANIZATIONS TODAY

POLITICAL ORGANIZATIONS

When the Soviet regime collapsed in 1991, there were two state-sponsored women's organizations (though they had been administered jointly since 1987). First, the Soviet Women's Committee was designed to bolster the Soviet Union's international image as a champion of peace and women's rights. Second, a network of women's councils, or *zhensovety*, was created to mobilize women within Russia and to act as as a social welfare organization.[20] For the most part the *zhensovety* defined their role as helping women to fulfill their duties to the state as wives and mothers. They arranged public lectures, fairs, and other events to encourage the party's family values and provided material and moral support to single mothers, mothers of large families, and other "problem families."[21]

When the Soviet Union collapsed in 1991, this "official" women's movement reconstituted itself as the Union of Russian Women.[22] For the most part the organization maintained its earlier emphases on political mobilization and social welfare and, as before, retained its policy focus on the social problems facing women in their maternal role. In pursuing this agenda under post-Soviet conditions, however, the organization has taken positions more compatible with Western feminism, such as helping women to get elected to positions of power and defending women against discrimination. In 1993, the Union of Russian Women led a coalition of women's organizations to form a political bloc, Women of Russia, that received 8 percent of the vote and the right to be represented in the Duma. Unfortunately, the bloc proved ineffective within the Duma and failed to gain 5 percent in the 1995 elections, the minimum necessary for representation. Soon after that Yekaterina Lakhova, President Boris Yeltsin's adviser on women's questions, left the bloc to found her own organization, the Movement of Russian Women, which was more closely aligned with Yeltsin.[23]

FEMINIST ORGANIZATIONS

During perestroika, while official women's organizations still pursued the ideal of Soviet womanhood, a number of activists came together to form the first independent women's movement since the Revolution. Inspired largely by contact with feminists and feminist literature from the West, these new activists formed small associations to raise social consciousness about gender inequality.

Some new activists were able to use existing structures funded by the state as a base for their activities. For example, they created the Moscow Center for Gender Studies (MCGS), within the Institute of the Socioeconomic Study of Population of the Academy of Sciences. But the activists also created a number of *neformaly* outside state structures. In March 1991 more than two hundred women from throughout Russia met in Dubna, outside Moscow, to form the First Independent Women's Forum. A Second Independent Women's Forum in November 1992 drew more than five hundred women.

Like members of other movement organizations created during perestroika, Russia's feminists did not fare well in the transition. In addition to problems with funding, space, and time, the feminists had difficulty finding a constituency in Russian society. The reasons for this difficulty are complicated, but two stand out. First, Russian women often identified the struggle for equal rights with Soviet-style emancipation and so accepted the Soviets' narrow definition of equality. Many Russian women in the post-Soviet era say they feel no discrimination; they also feel that such "equality" has not done them any good. Second, feminism's aim to politicize relations between men and women threatens the sanctity of the household, that sanctuary of privacy that Russians had protected fiercely under Soviet rule.[24]

While Russian feminists found few allies at home, they had little trouble forging ties with women in the United States and Western Europe. Indeed, without help from the West the Russian feminist movement might not have survived.[25] The Moscow Center for Gender Studies, for example, suffered the crippling economic difficulties that afflict all Russian academic institutions until it registered as a nongovernmental organization in 1994 and received an institutional grant from the MacArthur Foundation.[26] Even organizations that have not received much direct international assistance, such as the Feminist Alternative in Moscow and the Society of Independent Activists in Tver', have benefited from the resources and networks created with Western help.

CHARITABLE ORGANIZATIONS

Women have been particularly active in the social welfare groups that emerged after the Soviet Union's collapse.[27] Julia Zelikova, a researcher in St. Petersburg, offers three reasons for the disproportionate activism of women.[28] First, women bore more of the costs of reform than men did. Women were the last hired and first fired from state enterprises, and the state budget offered them little help, such as unemployment benefits. Many women created organizations to find collective remedies for their difficulties, including organizations to help widows or mothers of disabled children, professional organizations for women in defense industries, and organizations to retrain the recently unemployed. Second, many new charitable organizations were linked with the Russian Orthodox

Church, where traditional conceptions of "self-sacrificing" Russian woman-hood promoted sympathy for others. Finally, because the reforms had pushed women out of politics and the marketplace, many ambitious, energetic women found no other way to have an active public life. Indeed, many social welfare activists had earlier worked in social organizations sponsored by the old regime, particularly with the trade unions or local chapters of the *zhensovety*, and looked to autonomous social welfare organizations to continue their work (and preserve their social status) under the new conditions. Relying on connections in the regional bureaucracies, these former activists have often been more suc-cessful than other groups in getting local government support for their activities.

COMMITTEE OF SOLDIERS' MOTHERS

One of the best-known and most active networks of independent women's orga-nizations in Russia today is the Committee of Soldiers' Mothers. This organiza-tion began in 1989 to protect Soviet, and later Russian, conscripts against human rights abuses. The committee's activities have included public protests against the brutality of senior recruits against younger ones (*dedovshchina*) and against the conscription of students. In their most celebrated activity the moth-ers sponsored a peace march to Chechnya in 1995 and facilitated the exchange of prisoners in that war. They have staged fewer public demonstrations in recent years but continue their efforts to support and advise young men (and their mothers) about how to avoid conscription, defend themselves against charges of desertion, and receive adequate medical care if they are ill.

WESTERN ASSISTANCE STRATEGIES

Western donors to Russian women's organizations selectively help self-identified feminist organizations more than they do other women's organizations. This is true of transnational feminist organizations such as the Global Fund for Women and the Frauenanstiftung of Germany, as well as of donors such as the Ford and MacArthur foundations, that identify women's rights as a priority within larger contexts of human rights and civil society. Because Russian femi-nists have based their movement on Western ideas, Western donors understood and recognized their mission and priorities. Russian feminists also were more likely than other women's groups to look to the West for assistance. Olga Lipovskaya notes that "feminist organizations are more experienced than non-feminist groups in cross-cultural relations with Western counterparts, have a better knowledge of foreign languages and were the first to set up projects that cooperated with Western organizations and which benefited from funding."[29] Whatever their larger missions, all donors to women's organizations identify building a strong third sector as an important objective in its own right. The strategies that donors use to achieve this goal vary along three dimensions (see table 3.1) that correspond with the different tasks that they seek to accomplish: building NGO infrastructure, public advocacy or community outreach.[30] Needless to say, the boundaries between these tasks are not precise: Assistance to improve relations with the media, for example, may be described either as public advocacy or community outreach.

Grants also differ with respect to their beneficiaries: individuals or organizations. The hope behind grants targeting individuals is the empowerment of women by providing them with the skills and knowledge necessary to pursue their interests more effectively. Examples include training grants to improve organizational capacity, travel grants and exchanges to strengthen networks, and research grants to improve public advocacy. Broadly speaking, grants to organizations are designed to institutionalize the women's NGO sector and preserve a space in which individuals can pursue their interests. The two are often indistinct. For example, representatives of groups providing Internet access to the regions tended to refer to the targets of their efforts as organizations, whereas organizations designed to train activists to use the Internet described their targets as individuals.

A third dimension of variation among assistance strategies concerns their conceptual frameworks and their terms of involvement. Donors pursue proactive strategies when they participate actively in identifying the goals and methods of a particular project, and they use reactive strategies when they respond to local requests and are less committed to a particular goal or strategy. Strategies may be informed by ideas that originated in the West or by ideas generated by domestic actors. Grants may be multidimensional, if they allow organizations to

TABLE 3.1 Typology of Western Assistance Strategies in Russia

Tasks of Assistance

Infrastructure: organizational capacity and networking / public advocacy / community outreach

Target of Assistance

Individual activists, scholars, journalists, NGOs

Terms of Involvement

Proactive	vs.	Reactive
Imported Ideas	vs.	Domestically generated ideas
Multidimensional (program based)	vs.	Unidimensional (project based)
Process oriented	vs.	Product oriented

perform a range of services within a particular program, or unidimensional, if they are targeted to accomplish a specific task or project. Finally, grants may facilitate a process, such as training, education, or communication, or fund the creation of a particular product, such as a database or a research paper.

Apart from the differences in their strategies, Western granting organizations also have certain practices in common. For example, agencies often give responsibility for grant money to one person, usually the local NGO director, because of the lack of a reliable banking infrastructure, the complicated and disadvantageous tax codes, and the undeveloped governance of the organizations themselves. Second, granting agencies also tend to give repeat grants to organizations, partly because of a commitment to build long-term partnerships with local organizations, partly because these organizations prove to be good at what they do, and partly out of inertia. By 1998 most assistance agencies had shifted their attention outside Moscow and St. Petersburg to build up women's organizations in the regions. Even Moscow organizations were likely to win grants only if their project entailed some outreach to organizations in the provinces.[31]

NGO INFRASTRUCTURE

In discussing assistance efforts to overcome inexperience, organizational weakness, and mutual isolation within the independent women's movement, donor organizations use four types of strategies: large multidimensional grants to a few select organizations to act as "resource centers" or umbrella organizations; small multidimensional or unidimensional "seed" grants spread out among many organizations; somewhat larger unidimensional grants to organizations for specific products and/or processes; and individual grants for training, travel, and exchange.

RESOURCE CENTERS AND UMBRELLA ORGANIZATIONS

The strategy with perhaps the greatest effect on the independent women's movement in Russia entails multidimensional long-term grants to pay for the salaries, office space, and other operational costs of a few select organizations that in turn are expected to provide a range of services to other organizations in the sector, including training, legal and financial consultations, facilitating and arranging seminars and conferences, and distributing information regarding the activities of other women's organizations in Russia and around the world. Such grants have established three core organizations in Russia's independent women's movement: A Ford Foundation grant helped create the Information Center of the Independent Women's Center (ICIWF); the Consortium of Russian Women's Non-Governmental Organizations grew out of a grant from Winrock International, a large international NGO based in the United States; and the St. Petersburg Center for Gender Issues was established with help from the German feminist group, Frauenanstiftung. The Moscow Center for Gender Studies (MCGS), supported since 1994 by a grant from the MacArthur Foundation, performs some of these services as well. Because multidimensional grants established each of these organizations (except the MCGS), they must be considered proactive rather than reactive, though in each case they emerged only as a result of a negotiation with Russian partners.

The Consortium of Russian Women's Non-Governmental Organizations was established as part of the United States—Newly Independent States Women's Consortium sponsored by Winrock International's Women's Leadership Program with funding from USAID's Civic Initiatives Portfolio. The Consortium of Russian Women acts as an umbrella organization to link women's organizations throughout the Russian federation. Under its first director, an American named Martina Vandenberg, the consortium emphasized building coalitions among women's organizations as its chief mission. Under its current director, Yelena Yershova, it has made public advocacy a greater priority, reflecting in part her own strengths and experience. In 1998 the consortium's list of activities included training in leadership, advocacy, fund-raising, governance, and strategic planning; organizing seminars and meetings; distributing a newsletter; helping women's organizations to establish Internet access; and distributing seed grants to smaller women's organizations. More recently, the consortium has added to its priorities the struggles against domestic violence and trafficking in women for prostitution, as well as the support of women's small business enterprises.[32]

Through 1998 the Ford Foundation was the greatest benefactor of women's organizations among the private foundations. Most of the foundation's grants to the women's sector have been long-term, process-oriented, and multidimensional grants.[33] In the early 1990s the foundation's largest beneficiary among women's organizations was the ICIWF, which publishes and distributes a newsletter for women's organizations, helps coordinate lectures and seminars, and offers training programs. Ford grants also funded programs to promote women's studies at the university level as well as efforts to promote crisis centers against violence against women. After an internal review in 1998 the Ford Foundation shifted its strategy toward women's empowerment in Russia. Rather than providing support to feminist resource centers like the ICIWF, Ford has instead tried to introduce a "gender lens" into its programs that would consider more broadly how projects might affect the status of women in society. Ford still funds projects in gender education and the campaign to fight violence against women, however, and has added microfinancing of women's small business enterprises to its list of priorities.[34]

Because Ford Foundation grants usually emerge from extensive negotiations with prospective grantees, characterizing them as either reactive or proactive is often difficult. The local program officers—native English speakers with long experience in Russia—have a great deal of influence in the setting of local priorities and awarding of grants, and they have tried to listen to local activists. Still, negotiations are complicated. For example, the ICIWF was created in the early 1990s when Anastasia Posadskaya, then director of the MCGS, recommended that the organizations of the Independent Women's Forum approach the Ford Foundation to fund an umbrella organization that would coordinate their work more closely. The organizations came up with a draft proposal that would unite about thirty different projects in a nonhierarchical organization. After yearlong negotiations a somewhat different vision shaped the grant: a more institutionalized, centralized organization that would act as an information and resource center.[35]

Another large donor to the Russian women's sector has been the John D. and Catherine T. MacArthur Foundation. For the most part the MacArthur Foundation awards grants to individuals for nonpartisan research. But it also awards a small number of larger multidimensional grants to select organizations for institutional development, such as the grant that the foundation awarded to the MCGS in 1994. Unlike the other large institutional grants, the grant to the MCGS did not create a new organization but instead allowed an existing organization to continue the activities that it had always considered to be the core of its mission.[36] MCGS members advised government officials during the perestroika period and played a crucial role in organizing the first and second Independent Women's Forums. Though research remains the organization's first priority, MCGS members have been involved in many different projects funded by Western granting agencies, including a USAID-funded "gender expertise" center involved in policy advocacy, training projects for women NGO leaders, and a gender studies summer school funded by the Ford Foundation.

A third donor offering large, long-term, and multidimensional grants to improve networks among women's organizations is the Frauenanstiftung, which is affiliated with the Heinrich Böll Foundation of the German Green Party. The Frauenanstiftung has an explicitly feminist agenda, defining its mission as "the development and support for women's studies and women's education, documentation and consulting centers, and support for communication and networks between women's organizations."[37] It too awards grants after extended negotiations between foundation officials and selected local activists, though the Frauenanstiftung's grants tend to be more reactive and less restrictive than those of the Ford Foundation. Unlike most other donors, furthermore, the Frauenanstiftung sponsors conferences and exchanges designed to keep its beneficiaries in touch with each other; at least one grantee expressed appreciation for the Frauenanstiftung's effort to make its grant recipients feel like partners in a common enterprise.[38] Some Frauenanstiftung grantees in Russia have included the St. Petersburg Center for Gender Issues, which acts as an educational and resource center for women's organizations in the region, and the Archive-Database-Library (ADL) project, which grew out of the ICIWF as a central clearinghouse for information regarding the history and status of the Russian independent women's movement. (The ADL did not receive a second grant and has since split into three separate components.)

Finally, the Network Women's Program of the Soros Foundation's Open Society Institute began operating in Russia in 1998 and within a year became the single largest donor to women's organizations in Russia. This program has its headquarters in the United States and is directed by the former head of the MCGS, Anastasia Posadskaya. The director of the Moscow office is also a long-time women's activist, Yelena Kochkina. In its first three years the Network Women's Program in Russia has offered many small grants for a variety of activities, including infrastructural support, gender education, improving the image of women in the mass media, and policy advocacy, among others. Since 1999 it has also provided financial support to four "partner organizations," including the ICIWF and the MCGS, as well as the Tver' Center for Gender Studies and the Interuniversity Program for Women's Studies in Ivanovo.[39]

SEED OR MINIGRANTS

Seed grants and minigrants are designed to help fledgling organizations become established within the third sector. The grants can be unidimensional or multidimensional, product or process oriented, but they are usually reactive rather than proactive. The Global Fund for Women, for example, provides grants of as much as $15,000 with no conditions to small promising organizations. Winrock International and the Eurasia Foundation also sponsored a small grant program through the Consortium of Russian Women. These were unidimensional grants to purchase office technology, gain access to the Internet, organize a conference, conduct policy-related research, and publish a newsletter. Because both Winrock International and the Eurasia Foundation depend heavily upon funding from USAID, the consortium's project was discontinued when USAID priorities shifted away from seed programs and toward funding large resource centers and other infrastructure projects.[40] In 1999 small grants again became available through the Network Women's Program of the Open Society Institute.[41]

UNIDIMENSIONAL GRANTS

Many unidimensional grants awarded to women's organizations are designed to strengthen networks. USAID, for example, offered a grant to the Women's Information Network to create a directory of Russian women's organizations. The Eurasia Foundation too has invited applications for grants to fund training sessions, conferences, brochures, newsletters, and databases.

One of the most common goals of unidimensional infrastructural grants in recent years has been to connect women's organizations to the Internet. Most notably, the Network of East-West Women, with funding from Eurasia, Ford, MacArthur, and World Learning, has connected more than two thousand women from more than thirty countries, including ten groups in different regions of the Russian federation.[42] The network also maintains a number of electronic mailing lists, enabling women throughout Eastern Europe and beyond to gain information about their counterparts in other countries. Both the Frauenanstiftung and the Global Fund for Women have also supported the Women's Innovation Fund "East-West," a small organization of just two or three members that teaches computer and Internet skills to women activists.

INDIVIDUAL ASSISTANCE

Training programs are designed primarily to teach NGO activists general principles of organizational administration, such as creating a charter, outlining a strategic plan, projecting an image, raising money, and resolving conflicts. Western instructors provided most of the training in the early 1990s, but more recently Russian graduates of "training-of-trainers" courses have done most of this work, funded by Western assistance.

Western agencies also provide travel grants and exchange programs to enable activists to attend conferences or to learn from the practices of other organizations within Russia and abroad. Ford, Eurasia, and other assistance agencies made it possible for representatives from independent women's organizations to take part in the NGO Forum at the 1995 U.N. Fourth World Conference on Women. In recent years the Network Women's Program of the Open Society Institute ran several grant competitions for travel to conferences and exchange programs and in 2001 announced a new "Global Access" competition designed to improve the ability of Russian women activists to understand and gain access to women's transnational advocacy.[43]

PUBLIC ADVOCACY

In order to improve the condition of women while strengthening the accountability of the Russian government, assistance organizations provide grants to help activists improve their ability to articulate their interests to government officials. In general, foreign assistance strategies to improve public advocacy overlapped or resembled strategies to improve infrastructure. The Consortium of Russian Women and the MCGS, for example, have both received grants from Promoting Women in Development to improve public advocacy.[44] MCGS used its grant to support a "gender expertise" program that analyzed upcoming legislation and its effects on women and organized seminars, press conferences, and publications to disseminate the findings.[45] The Network Women's Program has also made "gender public policy" a priority.

A more unusual form of public advocacy funded by unidimensional grants targets law enforcement officials rather than decision makers. One of the more effective programs for preventing domestic abuse or the trafficking in women and children for prostitution, for example, has been to educate local police about the seriousness of the problem and teach methods of enforcement that have proved effective in other countries.[46]

Finally, the MacArthur Foundation provides indirect support to public advocacy with individual grants for nonpartisan research that "will arm policy advocates with arguments" on issues of national significance.[47] Like the Ford Foundation, the MacArthur Foundation defines its priorities in the United States but awards the individual grants after an open competition judged by a panel of both Russian and American scholars.

COMMUNITY OUTREACH

Donors have offered relatively little support to efforts to mobilize popular support for a feminist agenda. Some exceptions include the efforts of the Ford Foundation and Frauenanstiftung to fund gender-based education, as well as research funded by the MacArthur Foundation to improve the image of women and the women's movement in the media. The Network Women's Program of the Open Society Institute also has identified as priorities both gender-based education and work with the mass media.

Most prominent has been the assistance given by the Ford Foundation; the American Bar Association; Women, Law, and Development, International; and other donors to crisis centers and hot lines designed to help victims of domestic abuse in Russia. The movement against domestic violence in Russia owes its existence almost entirely to ideas imported from the West. Marina Pisklakova, a researcher at MCGS, started the first hot line in 1993.[48] She had always been aware that domestic abuse existed but, like most Russians at the time, had regarded it as a private matter afflicting individual women. She began to see domestic violence as a social problem requiring a social response only through a colleague familiar with Western literature on the topic. She began the hot line after a trip to Sweden, where she learned how to do it. By 1999 about thirty new organizations had arisen in Russia to help victims of domestic violence. In 1998 funding for Pisklakova's organization in Moscow, Anna, came mostly from a multidimensional grant provided by the Ford Foundation. The grant also provides money to support the Association of Crisis Centers, which links such organizations throughout the country. More unidimensional grants have come from Women, Law, and Development and others to provide legal advocacy and psychological help for individual victims, as well as to publish pamphlets and leaflets for mass distribution throughout Russia.

One noteworthy program that made outreach to the larger population a priority was a pilot program in the early 1990s funded by the East-West European Network. The program enrolled more than sixty unemployed women in Moscow in a six-month course that offered job retraining and psychological support. The program still existed in 1998 but at that time depended more on the local employment office for financial support.[49]

THE EFFECT OF WESTERN ASSISTANCE

How well has Western assistance helped the Russian independent women's movement overcome the challenges facing Russian NGOs? First, Western support has made it possible for the women's movement to survive at all. Though some independent feminist organizations have carried on without outside assistance, they probably could not have remained sufficiently active and connected to be called a movement had Western funds not sustained a core of organizations.

Also, Western assistance has helped individual grantees overcome the organizational weakness, inexperience, and mutual isolation that plagued the movement in the early 1990s. Most of my interviewees who were activists and had received Western assistance could state clearly and concisely their organization's mission and its role in contemporary Russian society. They were familiar with the personalities and activities of other women's groups throughout the country. They were confident in handling the legal and financial challenges confronting a Russian NGO and skilled at writing grant proposals. More important, organizations funded by the West were somewhat less likely to depend on one person and more likely to survive a change in leadership than organizations without such funding.[50] They were no longer ad hoc organizations.

Yet if Western assistance has helped the independent women's movement become a vigorous participant in Russia's third sector, it has done little to foster the kind of informal connections—the positive externalities—necessary to integrate it more fully into Russian society. Several factors have limited the donors' effectiveness. First, the continued absence of NGO infrastructure in the regions has limited donors' ability to reach beyond a few urban centers. In many cases regional activists are simply not aware of the possibilities for external assistance. Others recognize the possibilities but cannot write successful grant proposals. Indeed, writing proposals for Western donors is a difficult, culture-specific skill. Most funding agencies recognize this problem and offer help in writing grant proposals, but activists who have contacts in the West or in Moscow fare better than those who do not.[51]

One of the greatest limitations facing the independent women's movement and its Western donors, however, remains the profound resistance to feminism in contemporary Russian society. For example, one of the original purposes of the St. Petersburg Center for Gender Issues was to provide open lectures and seminars to attract and educate nonactivists, but attendance was so poor that the organization shifted its emphasis to helping other women's organizations in the surrounding regions.[52] Feminist organizations also face greater challenges than other organizations in working with the media and other institutions of Russian society that could help put their ideas forward. Active environmental groups usually can find sympathetic primary school teachers to distribute material and information to their students; feminist organizations usually cannot.

In some respects Western assistance actually has widened the distance between the Russian women's movement and the rest of society by creating a cadre of professional activists involved in their own networks, with their own norms and practices. At least initially, funding from the West reinforced the feminists' orientation toward the women's movement in the United States and Western Europe rather than toward other women's organizations in Russia. Few assistance agencies provided organizations with the incentives or the opportunity to define their agendas and activities to reflect the needs that Russian women themselves perceive as most urgent.[53] Rather, they usually identified priorities based on the issues, values, and preconceptions of their own local environments, such as the current emphasis on the struggle against domestic violence. One exception to this trend can be seen in the prominent emphasis on women's economic issues found in the Network Women's Program, whose program officers are Russian activists.[54]

Western assistance has further diminished the positive externalities of civic activism by contributing, perhaps inevitably, to the bureaucratization of the movement. Third-sector organizations devote much of their time and energy to routine activities such as preparing reports to donors and Russian tax authorities and writing new grant proposals. This often requires a professional accountant and other staff members, who may or may not share a commitment to the organization's social mission. Such third-sector organizations increasingly resemble corporate entities that pursue their own organizational interest before they pursue their social mission. Though such organizations are often more effective at presenting demands to governmental bodies and coordinating the activities of disparate organizations, they may undermine the informal, open-ended, and horizontal ties that make up an essential part of civil society.[55]

Organizations that depend on grants often lose their initiative. Multidimensional process-oriented grants allow somewhat more flexibility in this respect than do unidimensional grants, but the requirements of even multidimensional grants often mean that core organizations are expected to do too much with too few resources, leaving their efforts scattered and unfocused.[56] This tendency is further exacerbated by changes in the priorities of donor organizations—"the flavor of the month," as one program officer put it[57]—which make it impossible for organizations to maintain a sustained, focused effort in any one area. Some shifts in priority reflect efforts to broaden and deepen the Russian third sector, such as the new emphasis on reaching out to the regions. Others simply reflect new trends in the West.[58] In either case organizations that depend on grants struggle to keep up. For example, the projects that the Consortium of Russian Women's Non-Governmental Organizations has added to its list of activities since 1998—the struggle against domestic violence and trafficking in women for prostitution, as well as support for microfinance—correspond closely to donors' changing priorities, but member organizations probably have had no time to develop any expertise in these issues.

Third, although Western efforts have succeeded in reducing the isolation of Russian women's NGOs, they have not been as effective at promoting the solidarity and trust associated with civil society. Competition for grants among professional social movement organizations can be divisive in the United States as well, but the mutual mistrust and a near absolute dependence upon a relatively small number of Western donors has magnified the problem among Russian NGOs. Activists in different organizations have become less willing to share ideas with each other; one even swore me to secrecy regarding a project she planned to develop for a grant.[59]

Most damaging, perhaps, has been the common practice of giving one person the responsibility for administering a grant. Whereas Russian feminists, like their counterparts in the West, had sought to avoid hierarchical structures in their movement as much as possible, the donors' practice often forced women's organizations to name a director who then had decisive influence over organizational decisions. In a few cases directors abused this trust to appropriate grants for their own use.[60] But even in the vast majority of cases where directors are truly committed to the cause, the concentration of responsibility and the absence of transparent, participatory procedures feed into the Soviet legacy of mistrust. Rather than instilling habits of compromise and mutual responsibility, the practice has bred ill will and even contributed to rifts in several women's organizations.[61]

Finally, donor practices have had the unfortunate consequence of reinforcing the prevailing belief that assistance resources are distributed according to personal connections rather than merit. As noted, organizations that have competent English speakers or contacts with the West are more likely to win grants. According to the veteran activists Natalya Abubirikova and Maria Regentova, knowledge of English has become "a means of power and control" and "a convertible currency."[62] Western donors also tend to award grants to organizations that have successfully fulfilled grant requirements in the past. Given the extreme importance of personal connections in other parts of contemporary Russian society, it is not surprising that people regard the NGO community as a closed society into which one can gain access only by knowing someone. One activist who worked for a short time at the Soros Foundation said all her friends began sending their applications to Soros because they believed that she would approve them.[63] More troubling, another acquaintance said she would not submit an application for a research grant because she did not know anyone at the foundation and did not want to waste her time.

NGO INFRASTRUCTURE

RESOURCE CENTERS AND UMBRELLA ORGANIZATIONS

The core organizations have served a particularly valuable service in keeping the women's movement alive by providing focal points for coordinating and institutionalizing contacts between women's organizations, especially with organizations in the regions. In December 1995, for example, a seminar sponsored by the ICIWF and the Archive-Database-Library project produced the new Association of Independent Women's Organizations, which included thirty organizations from seventeen different regions.[64] The Web site of the Consortium of Russian Women lists ninety-nine members in thirty-seven different regions, and, as noted, the Association of Crisis Centers had about thirty members in June 1998.[65] Most important, these two organizations have been able to bring together organizations from different branches within the Russian women's movement, including self-identified feminist organizations, members of the Movement of Russian Women, and some charitable organizations in the regions.[66] The Association of Crisis Centers has been particularly successful in garnering support from more traditional women's organizations in the regions. For example, contacts with an American activist—a visit by Susan Hartman of Connect US-USSR in Minneapolis—inspired the hot lines in Nizhni Novgorod in 1998, but the women running them had been activists during the Soviet era and relied upon their connections with local authorities for operational support.

Unfortunately, many of these links were superficial, based on utilitarian motives rather than ideological commitment. Moscow organizations seek to include regional organizations within their circle to win prestige and grants; regional organizations often rely on connections with Moscow organizations to help them write grants or provide them with recommendations.[67] Links to Moscow also bring local credibility and opportunities for travel.[68] One hot line in Nizhni Novgorod was associated with a shelter for abandoned children. The director clearly regarded the children as her priority and the hot line as a means to gain more resources for it.[69] She admitted to having read little, if any, of the voluminous literature supplied by Western-oriented organizations, and she remained skeptical of their feminist philosophy. She accepted feminism "half and half," she said, because in Russia, she believed, men were the victims of domestic violence as much as women.

A more serious danger is that funding of resource centers may concentrate access to Western funding within a few powerful organizations. Several activists—nearly all those whom I interviewed in Ivanovo, Nizhni Novgorod, and St. Petersburg—complained that the large core organizations in Moscow tried to protect their privileged access to Western grants and to the informational and organizational resources that they have accumulated as a result of such grants.[70] At least two activists complained that Western assistance had created a new women's *nomenklatura*.[71]

Several activists also expressed a fear that an organization created to serve the women's movement might be confused with the movement itself. In 1995 Abubirikova and Regentova wrote that the ICIWF "began quite actively to substitute itself for the entire IWF [Independent Women's Center], though it never received any such authority."[72] In 1998 several activists raised similar concerns that the director of the Consortium of Russian Women's Non-Governmental Organizations would begin to present herself as representing the women's movement as a whole.[73]

SEED GRANTS

Seed grants seemed to be quite effective at providing critical initial support to women's organizations in Russia. Many people whom I interviewed maintained that small grants from the Eurasia Foundation, the Consortium of Russian Women, or the Global Fund for Women allowed them to buy the office equipment or learn the grant-writing techniques that enabled them to develop further. The greatest limitation on seed grants is that the organizations that receive them often do not know how to use assistance effectively or are so isolated within a region that they have little effect. One activist in Moscow argued that seed grants to regional organizations often result in computer technology that sits unused in empty offices.[74] Even so, small seed grants offer a relatively inexpensive way to offset the centralization and suspicion that arise when too much Western money is concentrated in too few hands. At least one activist appreciated the minigrants precisely because they made Western assistance more accessible to a wider range of organizations and activities than the larger grants to core organizations were.[75]

UNIDIMENSIONAL GRANTS

The strategy least successful in fostering informal connections between organizations, and between organizations and society, are unidimensional grants, especially reactive ones. Such grants often encourage a blinkered efficiency, where grantees had to worry more about accomplishing a set of discrete tasks than about exploring the best approaches to achieve their overall goal. Several activists complained that unidimensional grants, particularly those funded by government-sponsored organizations, provide little or no flexibility to react to changing conditions.[76] Product-oriented grants were particularly restrictive, but donors' dependence on quantifiable indicators to evaluate process-oriented grants meant that here too activists were more concerned about completing a task than with keeping the process going. Finally, the search for such grants frequently caused organizations to take up projects that fit only tangentially with their mission and that they were ill prepared to fulfill effectively.

One form of unidimensional grant praised by almost everyone with whom I spoke was that designed to link regional organizations with the Internet. In addition to the inherent advantages of rapid communication, participation in electronic mailing lists disseminates information without the need for a coordinating body and so may also help offset some problems of centralization within the movement. Yet these projects also suffered from problems found in other unidimensional grants. In some regions the phone lines needed to support Internet access are expensive and unreliable, yet the grants that helped set up Internet connections did not provide for the maintenance of phone lines. The success of such projects also depended on how they were implemented. For example, Sarah Henderson compared a relatively successful Internet project administered by the Network of East-West Women (NEWW) with a less successful one carried out by the Consortium of Russian Women.[77] As the name implies, NEWW is devoted exclusively to establishing a network among women's organizations. Instructors spent at least a week with personnel from each of ten organizations to introduce them to the new technology and then automatically placed them on an e-mail list, providing them with a ready-made audience and source of information. By contrast, the consortium, which had contracted to provide Internet access to thirty-five organizations, had little previous experience with this sort of project and was running several other projects at the same time. The training sessions were relatively rushed, and the clients were not placed on an e-mail list so that they could immediately take part in discussions among activists. As a result, many of the organizations linked by the consortium often used their electronic mail—if they used it at all—for mostly personal reasons.

INDIVIDUAL ASSISTANCE

Western-funded training has had considerable success in creating a cadre of NGO professionals in the women's sector, but such training has tended to impart general principles of management without necessarily applying them to specific conditions in Russia. In the most egregious cases trainers used material created for less developed countries with high levels of illiteracy, which insulted the many women activists in Russia with advanced degrees.[78] The most inappropriate material has largely disappeared with the increasing number of Russian trainers, but much of the training material in 1998 was still informed by Western models that might not be appropriate to Russia. For example, some lessons on fund-raising focus on writing grant proposals rather than finding imaginative techniques for raising money from indigenous sources.

Training that focuses on abstract concepts without explicitly connecting them to the Russian context tends to divide the third sector from the Russian population. Organizations may adopt ideas in a ritualistic manner to demonstrate their professionalism to Western donors, without necessarily thinking of the practical effect in carrying out an organization's mission. One activist, for example, complained that her organization had spent months working on a strategic plan, which resulted in an ambitious agenda that it could never address.[79] Indeed, the very language of third-sector professionals, with such English terms as *capacity building* and *training of trainers*, helps them talk to each other but has no meaning to the rest of the population.

By contrast, travel grants for conferences and exchanges have been effective for establishing personal ties and diffusing ideas among women's activists. Activists spoke particularly enthusiastically about the "gender summer schools," which bring women from all over the country to participate in two-week intensive seminars on gender studies. They also were enthusiastic about long-term exchanges with other organizations that enabled them to interact with other activists for an extended period. They also praised programs that allowed them to learn from the experiences of activists in other countries, whether through an exchange program or through participation in an international conference. The only potential drawback to such grants is that activists may become involved so deeply in the network of women's activists that they have less contact with women outside that network.

PUBLIC ADVOCACY

Women's organizations always enjoyed substantial access to the political process. Before the collapse of the Soviet Union, the MCGS, as part of the Academy of Sciences, had a hand in drafting laws on the status of women and the family as early as 1990, while Yelena Yershova, director of the Consortium of Russian Women, was a member of the "gender expertise" commission of the Supreme Soviet Presidium.[80] In the Yeltsin era each of the three major power centers of the Russian government—the Duma, the Council of Ministers, and the presidency—had a committee or commission devoted to issues concerning women and families. Activists in the political organizations, rather than members of the independent women's movement, opened these points of entry, but activists in the independent movement used them to gain access as well. They received political figures at conferences and seminars, attended hearings, and drafted legislation. Valerie Sperling of Clark University argues that such contacts between the independent movement and the political organizations have had a significant influence on the latter's willingness to speak out more forcefully for women's equality.[81] Indeed, a key policy consultant to the Movement of Russian Women is Svetlana Aivazova, who began her activism in the F-1 Klub, an independent organization of the perestroika period.

In 1998 both Yershova and Olga Voronina, the MCGS director, expressed pride that the independent women's movement successfully had introduced the terms *gender* and *domestic abuse* into the country's political lexicon.[82] It is difficult to assess precisely how much Western assistance has contributed to such success, but clearly it has provided the independent women's movement with the stability and financial wherewithal to hold the conferences, seminars, and press conferences at which old contacts are sustained and new contacts are made, and to do the research that makes its arguments more persuasive.[83]

A chief strategy of both the independent and political women's organizations has been to pressure the government to comply with international conventions such as the Convention on the Liquidation of All Forms of Discrimination Toward Women, which the Soviet government ratified in 1981.[84] Western assistance has enabled the women's movement to use this lever more effectively by establishing contacts and disseminating information between the Russian women's movement and women's organizations around the globe.[85] Activists particularly praised the grants that enabled independent activists to participate in the United Nations's 1995 Fourth World Conference on Women.[86] As early as 1993 a presidential decree included NGOs in a national council created to prepare the Russian delegation for the conference.[87] After the conference both Yeltsin and the Chernomyrdin government issued resolutions and decrees formally accepting the conference's results and creating the Interdepartmental Commission on Issues of Improving the Position of Women to coordinate the government's work on women's issues.[88] Activists also took part in an international conference funded by USAID to help the women's movement monitor how well Russia has conformed to these results.[89]

The strategy of appealing to international norms to increase political leverage may help women's activists gain symbolic victories that will shape outcomes in the future. In the short term, however, this strategy can divert activists from the more fundamental work of mobilizing support from below. For example, whereas activists cite international conventions and U.N. conferences seeking to eliminate discrimination against women, many Russian women simply do not think discrimination is their problem. Also, Abubirikova and Regentova note that "the energies directed to writing innumerable proposals" in connection with the U.N. forum at Beijing might have been better directed to "give a powerful push" to work out more effective strategies to mobilize women at home.[90]

Indeed, despite women activists' undoubted access to the political process at the federal level, they have produced few significant, practical results.[91] Even Yershova, director of the Consortium of Russian Women, acknowledged that public advocacy at the federal level can "at best get results on paper."[92] For example, a bill on domestic violence that the Women of Russia bloc introduced in the first Duma was so watered down in subsequent drafts that in 1998 the women's movement no longer supported it.[93] There are three reasons for such failure. The absence of public support and understanding for advocates of women's rights leaves them with relatively little clout in the legislature. Second, state institutions are themselves so fragmented and starved for resources—particularly those institutions concerned with social issues—that they have not yet allocated resources to implement and enforce the resolutions regarding the status of women that have been passed. Finally, because the population is so little involved in matters of politics, particularly concerning women's rights, there has been little effort to monitor government compliance with these resolutions.

Acknowledging the lack of progress at the federal level, Yershova argued that her consortium can teach regional organizations lessons about public advocacy that they can use more effectively at the regional level.[94] However, my own observations are that the success of regional women's groups depends mostly on the personalities in charge of local government, the personalities in charge of local women's organizations, and the connections between the two. In Yekaterinburg a grassroots organization called the Urals Association of Women has become a significant actor in local politics largely because of the energy and political acumen of its former leader, Galina Karelova, who is now first deputy minister for labor and social development. In Ivanovo the women's organizations have received strong support from regional officials, won seats on the city council, and influenced legislation to support impoverished mothers and their families, largely because the Ivanovo *zhensovet* was exceptionally active during Soviet times, and because one of the most active women's advocates in the city had been a high official in the Ivanovo Communist Party organization. Neither group had received substantial help from outside donors.

COMMUNITY OUTREACH

As I have noted, feminist organizations continue to have difficulties reaching beyond their own network of activists. Several activists complained that women's activists spend too much time talking to each other.[95] Until recently, Western donors have done little to improve this situation. Even now, most assistance agencies focus on strengthening infrastructure and lobbying efforts. Indeed, by encouraging activists to adopt norms and practices that provide them with privileged access to Western funds, the granting agencies may have created an incentive for Russian women's organizations not to look outside their own narrow circle for new members. As one participant of a seminar for environmental organizations in Lipetsk argued, "The expenditures on mobilizing human resources don't pay for themselves."[96]

In recent years, however, donors have altered their strategies somewhat to encourage activists to work more directly with the larger community.[97] They have been most successful where they have supported activities that are consonant with existing norms and practices. For example, Western programs to promote women's studies and gender analysis in Russia's universities have benefited greatly from the experience and networks of the many Russian feminists who began their career in academics. A database of Russian scholars working in women's studies published in 2000 has more than 250 entries from more than thirty regions.[98] To a large extent the growth in gender studies can be attributed to a natural diffusion of ideas within a scholarly community that only recently gained open access to scholarship in other countries. But in the academic world, as in public advocacy, Western assistance has provided scholars with the stability and the money to pursue this line of investigation and to share their ideas at conferences throughout the country.

Skeptics might raise several questions regarding these academic efforts. First, such programs reach only a relatively small part of the intellectual elite, and many of the model syllabi in these programs consist almost entirely of literature from the United States and Western Europe. To what extent can these programs affect a wider segment of Russian society? Second, such programs have attracted opportunists more interested in the funding than the ideas. Many featured scholars at one conference that I attended in Ivanovo in 1997 (funded in part by UNESCO, the United Nations Educational, Scientific, and Cultural Organization) included university officials who formerly taught classes in Marxism-Leninism and whose papers exhibited little knowledge of existing scholarship. Still, the programs have attracted enough students and serious younger scholars to nourish hopes that social awareness about women's issues will grow.

Efforts to overcome public cynicism and bring women into the public sphere also work better when they offer assistance that tangibly improves people's lives in the short term. One moderate success story has been the proliferation of crisis centers dealing with domestic violence. Feminist activists against domestic violence have worked hard to publicize the issue and make people aware of the existence of these facilities. I saw several advertisements on television during my short stays in St. Petersburg and Nizhni Novgorod. In St. Petersburg the local hot line organization staged a demonstration, followed by a press conference. During the demonstration activists asked passersby on Nevsky Prospect, the city's key thoroughfare, to sign a placard with the slogan "There Is No Excuse for Domestic Violence." In the end, however, the campaign against domestic violence has been able to enlist traditional women's activists largely because their activities correspond to the earlier social welfare function of the *zhensovety* and other Soviet-era social organizations: helping families in crisis without necessarily challenging traditional conceptions of gender. Indeed, some regional activists who belong to the Association of Crisis Centers do not even understand, much less adhere to, the feminist ideals espoused by the leadership of that association.[99]

The women's organization that has reached outmost successfully to Russian society has been the Committee of Soldiers' Mothers. Like the crisis centers, the committee offers services that tangibly improve women's lives. Unlike the feminist approach to domestic violence, the committee's does not seek to transform society; indeed, the assumption that mothers should put themselves on the line in the interest of their sons conforms well with traditional views of Russian femininity. Yet two active feminists with sons told me that the committee's work affected them more deeply on a practical level than anything the feminist organizations have done. The committee's offices in Moscow, St. Petersburg, and Nizhni Novgorod have long lines of petitioners waiting for advice, and weekly open meetings are well attended.

The experience of the committee also offers a sobering lesson about the influence of Western assistance on civil society. The committee pursued a much more aggressive strategy of public demonstrations before 1997, when it received relatively little funding from the United States and Western Europe. Since then, the mothers have held fewer public demonstrations and concentrated more of their resources on individual cases and engaging in public advocacy through conventional channels. This shift resulted in large part from a split within the organization's leadership, precipitated in part by an infusion of money that the organization received as a result of being nominated for the Nobel Peace Prize. In addition, the organization's opposition to the second war in Chechnya has been less popular than its opposition during the first war. However, at least one member of the organization maintained that a strategy of public demonstrations became less advisable once the organization began receiving substantial assistance from the West, because such support would leave the group vulnerable to the charge that it was a paid agent of a foreign power.[100]

CONCLUSIONS AND LESSONS

Western assistance to women's organizations has been a mixed blessing for the construction of civil society in Russia. The entire endeavor is built on a contradiction. To serve as a bulwark of democracy, civil society must be embedded within the formal and informal institutions of Russian society. Western assistance can reach only a fraction of the formally registered organizations and runs the risk of drawing these organizations away from their domestic roots and embedding them instead in a network of international NGOs and third-sector professionals. In selecting feminist organizations over other women's organizations, donors have compounded the problem by assisting organizations whose goals from the beginning were more firmly based in this transnational network than in Russian society.

Does it make sense, then, for assistance agencies to continue funding feminist organizations? I argue that it does. First, the mission of the women's international NGOs and the foundations is not limited to building civil society but also promotes women's rights. This is a laudable goal that only the feminist organizations pursue vigorously. Second, their links to the transnational movement have given them independence from the state in a society where state structures (or their ruins) still dominate. Funding feminist organizations creates an alternative space for women's activism that some of the other, more traditional organizations can also use. Finally, the skilled professionals within the modern Russian feminist movement represent a valuable reservoir of human resources that can serve the third sector more broadly and may engage in other forms of public service.

INFRASTRUCTURE

The strategy of creating strong central organizations to help connect and coordinate the work of regional organizations has generally succeeded in sustaining the movement in a difficult environment. The ability of independent feminist organizations to reach out to activists among the formerly "official" organizations is particularly valuable. Even though such connections may reflect utilitarian calculations rather than ideological commitment, these initial contacts provide a necessary first step toward substantive cooperation. Whatever their motivations, former teachers of Marxism-Leninism are now writing articles about women's experience during the transition; former trade union officials have established a hot line against domestic abuse in Nizhni Novgorod; and former members of the *zhensovety* are attending conferences and meetings where they can talk to feminists. These institutional connections between Moscow and the periphery have caused the independent Moscow activists to take a more active interest in organizations that have roots in domestic institutions and ideologies while providing some traditional activists with a new language (which they may accept at least "half and half") and material resources with which to press their activities more independently of the state.

On the other hand, the tendency of such grants to concentrate power both within organizations and within the movement as a whole is worrisome. Rather than promote the norms and habits of mutual trust, tolerance, and compromise, such centralization fosters distrust and resentment even as it reinforces the hierarchical practices of the Soviet period. To avoid the concentration of power within organizations, assistance agencies should encourage greater initiative and wider participation in the decision making of grantees, even at the cost of efficiency. The experience of the pilot project by the East-West European Network for retraining unemployed women demonstrates the advantages of such an approach. Rather than asking one person to decide how the money should be distributed, the donors asked the women themselves to decide who should get what. Although this process caused some unpleasantness and even led a few people to leave the project, I interviewed two activists who had participated in the project and who maintained that such discussions increased participants' stake in the organization's success.[101]

Western assistance agencies could also take steps to avoid creating hierarchy and mistrust within the movement as a whole. Funding umbrella organizations like the Consortium of Russian Women's Non-Governmental Organizations remains essential, but donors should insist upon decision-making procedures that encourage participation and accountability to constituent organizations. They should also complement large grants to resource centers with seed grants to smaller organizations. Finally, supporting women activists' access to the Internet will give them the opportunity to gain information without having to rely on a few organizations in the center. (However, because many organizations still do not have access to the Internet, donors should not neglect more traditional means of communication.)

Western donors should also design their grants in ways that could foster the positive externalities, the intangible and unquantifiable results that contribute to a stronger civil society. First, grants should encourage innovative thinking about how to solve problems rather than blinkered efficiencies in meeting targets. In this respect long-term multidimensional grants are preferable to short-term grants designed to implement specific projects. When unidimensional grants are necessary, donors should allow grantees as much flexibility as possible in choosing their methods and rely on qualitative rather than quantitative methods of evaluation. Finally, Western donors should allow Russian activists a greater role in identifying priorities and evaluating results. When Western donors do push their own issues, they should remain as consistent as possible and resist the temptation to embrace new priorities simply because they are fashionable.

Similarly, the training sessions provided by Western donors have proved effective at creating skilled professionals but may have had the unintended consequence of distancing the NGO community from the rest of society. Donors should encourage recent trends in training that emphasize imaginative problem solving within a specifically Russian context.[102] A model might be the project of Peace Corps volunteers in Nizhni Novgorod who set up an NGO incubator. It provided local NGO leaders with a small stipend to enroll in intensive hands-on training during which they were expected to accomplish a number of practical tasks for their organizations. By the end NGO leaders had found a number of ingenious methods of raising money from local business and government officials.

Finally, infrastructure grants should try to foster informal connections between activists and between the activists and other Russian women. Sponsoring conferences is a valuable way to introduce activists to each other, but longer exchanges and summer schools are more effective at fostering the informal networks that would extend beyond utilitarian calculation. Similarly, unidimensional grants should not evaluate projects by examining how many different regions a particular grantee has visited but by looking more closely at how the grantee followed up on these visits.

PUBLIC ADVOCACY

Western assistance in the area of public advocacy has helped independent women's organizations make persistent and effective use of the points of access opened by formerly "official" activists. Such assistance has helped activists familiarize policy makers with such concepts as gender discrimination and domestic abuse, which may shape public discourse in future policy debates.

Beyond that, public advocacy has not accomplished much. The gains that women's organizations have made are largely symbolic: At best, they persuade the government to endorse abstract slogans such as "the elimination of discrimination," but these are divorced from the practical realities facing Russian women today. Moreover, existing strategies cannot mobilize the public support necessary to make the government accountable; these strategies focus on government institutions that most people reasonably distrust and offer only the prospect of long-term benefits when most Russians live in short-term time frames.

One exception has been the efforts to work with local police to enforce existing laws on domestic abuse and trafficking in women for prostitution. Such a strategy promotes concrete, observable, immediate improvements that may encourage greater public trust, both in local police and in NGOs.

COMMUNITY OUTREACH

Western assistance has failed most significantly in encouraging Russian women's organizations to reach outside the NGO community to the larger Russian society. Western donors have been most successful in this regard when they have funded activities that built upon existing norms and networks within the activist community and the wider society. In addition, the relative success of the crisis centers suggests that even ideas originating outside Russia may find a receptive audience if they offer tangible, observable improvements in women's lives.

In sum, Western assistance was vital to sustaining a small public realm where women activists could participate in public life independent of the state. This remains true even under the Putin regime, as women's organizations remain almost untouched by pressures placed on environmental and human rights activists.[103]

I have argued here that Western donors might enlarge this realm if they devoted somewhat less attention to the formal aspects of the third sector and more to the informal aspects of organizational life that sustain a movement. In particular, they should examine existing practices that unnecessarily restrict access to Western assistance to a relatively small group of activists, focus activists' attention on organizational administration rather than on outreach to the community, and lead to the pursuit of priorities that do not reflect the perceived needs of Russian women. Fortunately, as donors have acquired more experience in Russia, they have altered their practices somewhat. The new emphases on creating links to more service-oriented organizations in the regions and the introduction of problem-solving approaches to NGO training are significant improvements. The strategies adopted since 1998 by the Ford Foundation and the Network Women's Program of the Open Society Institute also offer cause for hope. Both foundations are trying to integrate a gender lens into all their programs, which may alleviate somewhat the isolating effect that Western assistance has had on overtly feminist organizations. The shift in the Ford Foundation's emphasis toward projects like microfinance and the campaign against domestic violence, which offer clients short-term tangible benefits, has a good chance of bringing more women into the public sphere and overcoming the isolation of Russia's feminists. Similarly, by complementing its support of resource centers with small grants delivered to many organizations, the Network Women's Program will allow additional voices to be heard within the Russian feminist movement, perhaps giving rise to a feminist philosophy that depends less on Western theoretical frameworks and reflects more the experience of Russian women. The program's emphasis on the economic and social problems that pervade Russian women's everyday experience also gives room for hope.

NOTES

1. N. I. Abubirikova, T. A. Klimenkova, E. V. Kochkina, and M. A. Regentova, "Zhenskie organizatsii v Rossii segodnya" (Women's Organizations in Russia Today), in N. I. Abubirikova et al., eds., *Spravochnik: Zhenskie Nepravitel'stvennye organizatsii Rossii I SNG* (Directory of Women's Nongovernmental Organizations in Russia and the Commonwealth of Independent States) (Moscow: Izdatel'stvo "Eslan," 1998), p. 17.

2. Julia Zelikova, "Women's Participation in Charity," in Anna Rotkirch and Elina Haavio-Mannila, eds., *Women's Voices in Russia Today* (Hants, U.K: Dartmouth, 1996), p. 248.

3. Valerie Sperling, *Organizing Women in Contemporary Russia: Engendering Transition* (Cambridge: Cambridge University Press, 1999), pp. 222–27.

4. Robert Putnam, *Making Democracy Work: Civic Traditions in Modern Italy* (Princeton: Princeton University Press, 1993), pp. 86–92.

5. Norman Uphoff, "Why NGOs Are Not a Third Sector: A Sectoral Analysis with Some Thoughts on Accountability, Sustainability, and Evaluation," in Michael Edwards and David Hulme, eds., *Beyond the Magic Bullet: NGO Performance and Accountability in the Post–Cold War World* (West Hartford, Conn.: Kumarian Press, 1996), p. 33. Also see Edwards and Hulme's introduction.

6. A copy of the charter and its signatories can be found in the Movement of Russian Women's newspaper, *Zhenshchina Rossii* (Women of Russia), April 1997, p. 4.

7. The directory is Abubirikova et al., *Spravochnik.*

8. See James Richter, "Promoting Civil Society? Democracy Assistance and Russian Women's Organizations," *Problems of Postcommunism* (forthcoming).

9. Sperling, *Organizing Women in Contemporary Russia*; Rotkirch and Haavio-Mannila, *Women's Voices in Russia Today*; Mary Buckley, ed., *Post-Soviet Women: From the Baltic to Central Asia* (Cambridge: Cambridge University Press, 1997); Linda Raccioppi and Katherine O'Sullivan See, *Women's Activism in Contemporary Russia* (Philadelphia: Temple University Press, 1997); Julie Hemment, "Gendered Violence in Crisis: Russian NGOs Help Themselves to Liberal Feminist Discourses," *Anthropology of East Europe Review*, Spring 1999, http://www.depaul.edu/~rrotenbe/aeer /v17n1/Hemment.pdf (October 25, 2001). More recent literature includes Rebecca Kay, *Russian Women and Their Organizations: Gender, Discrimination, and Grassroots Women's Organizations, 1991–1996* (New York: St. Martin's, 2000); Julie Dawn Hemment, "Gender, NGOs, and the Third Sector in Russia: An Ethnography of Postsocialist Civil Society" (Ph.D. diss., Cornell University, 2000).

10. Yelena Kochkina, "Context for the Development and Results of Activities, 1998–2000" (unpublished report of the Network Women's Program of the Open Society Institute, Moscow, 2001), p. 3.

11. USAID/Russia Democracy Gender Program, Annual Program Statement, July 16, 2001, http://www.usaid.gov/procurement_bus_opp/procurement/annual_pstatements /gender.html (July 30, 2001).

12. I am studying the effect of Ford's new strategies on the Russian women's movement as part of my larger ongoing study tentatively entitled, "Power and Principle: Transnational Advocacy Networks and Russian Activism."

13. This number excludes about 100,000 religious groups, political parties, consumer cooperatives, and professional unions that fall under different legislation. See Paul Legendre, *The Nonprofit Sector in Russia* (Kent, U.K.: Charities Aid Foundation, 1997). My thanks to Lisa Petter for drawing this study to my attention.

14. M. Steven Fish, *Democracy from Scratch* (Princeton: Princeton University Press, 1995), pp. 61–65.

15. A good discussion of the crisis in the environmental movement appears in Sergei Fomichev, *Raznotsvetnye zelyonye* (Multicolored Greens) (Moscow–Nizhni Novgorod: Izdatel'stvo TsODP SoES–Izdatel'stvo "Tretii put'," 1997).

16. Svetlana Aivazova, long-time activist, interview by author, Moscow, May 14, 1998.

17. Yuri Dzhibladze, "Russian NGOs Fight for Fair Taxation," *Give & Take* 2, no. 1 (Winter 1999): 4–5.

18. Raccioppi and See, *Women's Activism in Contemporary Russia*, p. 144.

19. An excellent discussion of the economic status of women in the Soviet and post-Soviet eras appears in Sue Bridger, Rebecca Kay, and Kathryn Pinnick, *No More Heroines: Russia, Women and the Market* (London: Routledge, 1996). See also Zoya Khotkina, "Women in the Labor Market: Yesterday, Today, and Tomorrow," in Anastasia Posadskaya, ed., *Women in Russia: A New Era in Russian Feminism*, pp. 85–108 (London: Verso, 1994).

20. See Genia Browning, "The *Zhensovety* Revisited," in Mary Buckley, ed., *Perestroika and Soviet Women* (Cambridge: Cambridge University Press, 1992), p. 99; Mary Buckley, *Women and Ideology in the Soviet Union* (Ann Arbor: University of Michigan Press, 1989).

21. Browning, "*Zhensovety* Revisited," pp. 106–9.

22. Accounts of the Union of Russian Women can be found in Raccioppi and See, *Women's Activism in Contemporary Russia*, 72–106; and Sperling, *Organizing Women in Contemporary Russia*, pp. 32–33, 37–38, and 111.

23. Aivazova interview.

24. The literature discussing the rejection of feminism in Russia and the rest of Eastern Europe is voluminous. Some of the best discussions appear in Nanette Funk and Magda Mueller, eds., *Gender Politics and Postcommunism* (New York: Routledge, 1993); and Beth Holmgren, "Bug Inspectors and Beauty Queens: The Problems of Translating Feminism into Russian," in Ellen E. Berry, ed., *Postcommunism and the Body Politic*, pp. 18–20 (New York: New York University Press, 1995).

25. Tatianna Klimenkova, activist and scholar at MCGS, interview by author, Moscow, May 12, 1998; Marina Liborakina, long-time NGO activist, interview by author, Moscow, May 19, 1998; Galina Venediktova, women's NGO activist with the Network of East-West Women and Women, Law, and Development, interview by author, Moscow, May 19, 1998.

26. More detailed accounts of MCGS appear in Raccioppi and See, *Women's Activism in Contemporary Russia*, pp. 127–49, and Sperling, *Organizing Women in Contemporary Russia*.

27. Abubirikova et al., "Zhenskie organizatsii v Rossii segodnya," p. 17.

28. Zelikova, "Women's Participation in Charity," pp. 251–53.

29. Olga Lipovskaya, "Women's Groups in Russia," in Buckley, *Post-Soviet Women*, p. 191.

30. See also the chapters by Karen Ballantine and Patrice McMahon in this volume.

31. Chris Kedzie, program director, Ford Foundation, personal e-mail, July 27, 1998; and Kochkina, "Context for the Development and Results of Activities," p. 9.

32. Consortium of Women's Non-Governmental Organizations, n.d., http://www.wcons.org.ru/about/about.en.shtml (July 9, 2001).

33. Mary MacAuley, speech to conference of the Association of Crisis Centers, Moscow, May 21, 1998.

34. Moscow Office of the Ford Foundation, 2000, http://www.fordfound.org/global /office/index.cfm?office = Moscow (June 14, 2001); also Chris Kedzie, personal e-mail, June 22, 2001.

35. Natalya Abubirikova and Maria Regentova, unpublished, untitled manuscript, 1996.

36. More detailed accounts of MCGS appear in Raccioppi and See, *Women's Activism in Contemporary Russia*, pp. 127–49; and Sperling, *Organizing Women in Contemporary Russia.*

37. Frauenanstiftung (The Women's Foundation), "FAS — The Women's Foundation," 1996, http://www.owl.ru/eng/zhif/fas-mirr.htm (October 26, 1998).

38. Galina Grishina, women's NGO activist, interview by author, Moscow, May 8, 1998.

39. Kochkina, "Context for the Development and Results of Activities," p. 9.

40. Bernadine Joselyn, program officer, Eurasia Foundation, interview by author, May 27, 1998; Irina Pirugova, public relations representative, Initiative for Social Action and Renewal, interview by author, May 25, 1998.

41. Kochkina, "Context for the Development and Results of Activities," pp. 14–15.

42. Network of East-West Women, "Organizational History and Program," http://www.inch.com/~shebar/neww/neww1.htm (October 22, 2001).

43. Yelena Kochkina, "Conceptions for 2001" (unpublished report of the Network Women's Program of the Open Society Institute, 2001), p. 2.

44. From October 1995 through May 2000 the International Center for Research on Women and the Centre for Development and Population Activities in Washington, D.C., co-managed a grants program called Promoting Women in Development (PROWID), which was funded by USAID's Office of Women in Development. PROWID sought to improve the lives of women in developing countries and in economies in transition. Its Web site address is http://www.icrw.org/prowid.htm (November 8, 2001).

45. Yelena Kochkina, long-time activist, interview by author, Moscow, May 6, 1998.

46. Lyudmila Yermakova, crisis center activist, interview by author, Yekaterinburg, June 15, 1999.

47. Galina Ustinova, program director, MacArthur Foundation, interview by author, May 19, 1998.

48. Marina Pisklakova, founder of first Russian hot line, interview by author, Moscow, May 27, 1998.

49. Lyusa Kabanova, Russian activist for the East-West European Network, interview by author, Moscow, May 17, 1998.

50. Sarah Henderson, "Importing Civil Society: Western Funding and the Women's Movement in Russia," *Demokratizatsiya* 8, no. 1 (Winter 2000): 65–82.

51. Valentina Konstantinova, activist and scholar at MCGS, interview by author, Moscow, May 15, 1998; Irina Yurna, NGO activist, interview by author, Moscow, May 18, 1998; Yevgeniya Verba, director, NGO resource center, interview by author, Nizhni Novgorod, May 29, 1998.

52. Olga Lipovskaya, author, interview by author, St. Petersburg, June 7, 1998.

53. Anonymous women's NGO activists, interviews by author, Moscow, May 1998.

54. Kochkina, "Conceptions for 2001," p. 5.

55. Richter, "Promoting Civil Society?"

56. Yuliya Zhukova, women's NGO activist, interview by author, St. Petersburg, June 7, 1998; Rosa Khatskelevich, director, NGO resource center, interview by author, St. Petersburg, June 1998. For other accounts of how changing priorities have caused organizations to overextend themselves, see Henderson, "Importing Civil Society"; Aleksander Borovikh, "'Zver' po imeni URTs" (The Beast by the Name of URC [Universal Resource Center]), *Den'gi i blagotvoritel'nost'*, no. 17 (October 1997): 16–17.

57. Bernadine Joselyn, program officer, Eurasia Foundation, interview by author, Moscow, May 26, 1998.

58. Anonymous NGO woman NGO activist, interview by author, Moscow; Joselyn interview.

59. Konstantinova interview; anonymous NGO woman interview. Also see Sperling, *Organizing Women in Contemporary Russia*, 234–36, and Kay, *Russian Women and Their Organizations*, 202–6.

60. Anonymous woman activist, interview by author, St. Petersburg, June 1998.

61. Abubirikova and Regentova, untitled ms.; Konstantinova interview; Zhukova interview; I would add, however, that organizational splits because of resources are also common among organizations that receive less money from Western organizations, such as the Committee of Soldiers' Mothers and the Green Party in St. Petersburg.

62. Abubirikova and Regentova, untitled ms., p. 14.

63. Yurna interview.

64. Sperling, *Organizing Women in Contemporary Russia*, chap. 7. Also see *Vestnik Zhenskogo Informatsionno-obrazovatel'nogo proekta* (Newsletter of the Women's Informational-Educational Project), no. 5 (1996): 1–5.

65. Consortium of Women's Non-Governmental Organizations, "Consortium of Women's Non-Governmental Organizations: About," 1999, http://www.wcons.org.ru /about/about.en.shtml (June 29, 2001).

66. Despite reservations about the centralization of the Consortium of Russian Women, for example, almost all the activists whom I interviewed noted that their interactions with the organization had been positive. This observation fits with Thomas Carothers's discussion of the positive implications of the shift toward "going local" in democracy assistance during the late 1990s. See his *Aiding Democracy Abroad: The Learning Curve* (Washington, D.C.: Carnegie Endowment for International Peace, 1999), pp. 227–31.

67. Yelena Yershova, director of the Women's Consortium, interview by author, Moscow, May 18, 1998; Tatianna Troinova, women's NGO activist, interview by author, May 22, 1998.

68. Sperling, *Organizing Women in Contemporary Russia*, chap. 7, presents the skeptics' arguments in detail.

69. Galina Kondratenko, director of a children's home and domestic violence hot line, interview by author, May 28, 1998.

70. Women's NGO activists, interviews by author, Ivanovo, June 1996, Nizhni Novgorod, May 28, 1998, and St. Petersburg, June 1998. Also see Sperling, *Organizing Women in Contemporary Russia*, chap. 7; and Kay, *Russian Women and Their Organizations*, pp. 194–206.

71. Interviews of Women's NGO activists, Moscow, May 1998, and St. Petersburg, June 1998. A similar argument is found in Kay, *Russian Women and Their Organizations*, pp. 196–206.

72. Abubirikova and Regentova, untitled ms., p. 24.

73. Interviews of anonymous women NGO activists, Moscow, May 1998, and St. Petersburg, June 1998.

74. Elvira Novikova, long-time women's NGO activist, interview by author, Moscow, May 6, 1998.

75. Natalya Bychkova, women's NGO activist, interview by author, Moscow, May 19, 1998.

76. Aivazova interview; Grishina interview; Zoya Khotkina, author, interview by author, Moscow, May 26, 1998.

77. Sarah Henderson, "Fostering Women's Activism in the Regions: Ford Foundation and the Women's Movement" (paper prepared for the annual conference of the American Association for the Advancement of Slavic Studies, St. Louis, Mo., November 18–21, 1999), pp. 18–24.

78. Larisa Fedorova, women's NGO activist, interview by author, Moscow, May 5, 1998; Novikova interview; Natalya Berezhnaya, activist and long-time diplomat, interview by author, Moscow, May 14, 1998.

79. Anonymous women's NGO activist interview, St. Petersburg, June 1998.

80. My thanks to Valerie Sperling for this information.

81. Sperling, *Organizing Women in Contemporary Russia*, chap. 4.

82. Olga Voronina, MCGS director, interview by author, Moscow, May 13, 1998; Yershova interview. Several other activists also made this same claim.

83. An excellent discussion of the women's movement's access to political organizations appears in Sperling, *Organizing Women in Contemporary Russia*, chap. 4.

84. Information Center, Independent Women's Center, "Polozhenie zhenshchin i Natsional'nyi mekhanism: Pozitsiya zhenskikh ne pravitel'stvennykh organizatsii" (The Situation of Women in the National Mechanism: The Position of Women's Nongovernmental Organizations) (paper prepared for the conference Paths to Realizing the Peking Platform of Action on the Status of Women, November 1996).

85. Sperling, *Organizing Women in Contemporary Russia*, chap. 7.

86. Fedorova interview, Moscow, May 15, 1998; Klimenkova interview; Liborakina interview.

87. Information Center, "Polozhenie zhenshchin i Natsional'nyi mekhanism."

88. Ibid.

89. Ibid.

90. Abubirikova and Regentova, untitled ms., p. 14. Also see Sperling, *Organizing Women in Contemporary Russia*, chap. 7.

91. It is conceivable that even the women's movement's access to the political process has diminished under the Putin presidency, which has been the experience of other sectors of the Russian NGO community. In two quick visits to Russia since Putin came to power, however, I heard few complaints about his policies toward feminist organizations.

92. Yershova interview.

93. Liborakina interview.

94. Yershova interview.

95. Natalya Abubirikova, author and activist, interview by author, Moscow, May 8, 1998; Nadezhda Azhgikina, journalist and activist, interview by author, Moscow, May 15, 1998.

96. Sergei Fomichev, "Yeshcho raz k voprosu o krizise" (Once More on the Question of Crisis)," *Tretii put'*, no. 29 (1993): 6.

97. This change in donors' strategies was not confined to postcommunist countries. See Carothers, *Aiding Democracy Abroad*, pp. 227–31.

98. Zoya Khotkina, "Gender Research in Russia and the NIS: Who Is Who?" 2000, http://www.owl.ru/win/books/dbras_who_is_who (October 23, 2001).

99. Hemment, "Gendered Violence in Crisis."

100. Anonymous activist, Committee of Soldiers' Mothers, interview by author, Nizhni Novgorod, June 1, 2001. My thanks to Sarah Mendelson and Valerie Sperling, who were also at this interview and asked the right questions.

101. Kabanova interview; Bychkova interview.

102. Thomas Carothers notes that such pedagogical methods have become increasingly common in recent years as a result of the learning curve. See his *Aiding Democracy Abroad*, pp. 231–35.

103. See Sarah E. Mendelson, "The Putin Path: Civil Liberties and Human Rights in Retreat," *Problems of Postcommunism* 47, no. 5 (September–October 2000): 3–12.

Chapter 4

INTERNATIONAL ASSISTANCE AND THE DEVELOPMENT OF INDEPENDENT MASS MEDIA IN THE CZECH AND SLOVAK REPUBLICS

Karen Ballentine

The development of independent mass media was one of the main pillars of international efforts in the 1990s to assist the democratization of the postcommunist states. Indeed, after 1989 a plethora of international, state, and nongovernmental actors became involved in one or another aspect of media development: training journalists, providing technological improvement, reforming the legal-regulatory framework, enhancing the financial and managerial performance of media outlets, and developing professional associations for journalists, broadcasters, and other media professionals. Virtually all these international actors were motivated by the same underlying idea: that independent and pluralistic media are an essential bulwark of a mature and effective democracy, serving both as a watchdog of potential abuses of power by elected officials and as an inclusive arena of informed debate and discussion of issues affecting the body politic. Democracy assistance to the media sector was also prompted by the realization that, as a result of decades of highly intrusive Communist Party censorship and state subsidization, the newly liberated media lacked the skills, resources, and know-how to perform these democracy-supporting functions in a new and challenging transitional environment.[1]

For their contribution to this research I would like to thank Juraj Alner, international news editor, *Narodna Obroda*; Caroline Barker, second secretary, British Embassy, Bratislava; Ingrid

Most international actors viewed the promotion of independent mass media not as an end in itself but as an intermediate goal within a larger effort to support sustainable democracy.[2] International assistance doubtless had a positive influence in shaping the norms and practices of the postcommunist media, enhancing their professionalism and their viability, and helping to integrate them into a larger transnational media community. This assistance also made a crucial difference to the professional careers of individual journalists and, in some cases, to the survival of particular nonstate media outlets. However, the importance of this support at the aggregate sectorwide level depended in large part on wider progress toward democracy. Where the consolidation of democracy was relatively unproblematic, media assistance is best characterized as facilitating the development of the independent media but not decisive to its very existence. In contrast, where democratic transitions remained partial or were threatened by significant authoritarian reversals, international assistance played a more crucial role in ensuring the material and financial basis necessary for independent media to operate.[3]

Whether media assistance has actually contributed to the larger goal of promoting democracy is more questionable. As elsewhere, whether mass media has a democratizing influence depends on the degree of democratic commitment among prevailing power holders and the prevailing political culture. Without a permissive political and normative framework, the other seeds of international media assistance may not yield the desired democratic fruit. Paradoxically, in the short to medium term international media assistance may be the least effective means of achieving the broader goal of supporting democracy where democracy has yet to be consolidated—that is, precisely where it appears most needed—and most effective where it is least needed. In any case these abiding environmental constraints create attribution and measurement problems that make it extraordinarily difficult to provide a definitive evaluation of the wider influence of international media assistance programs, either individually or together.

Baummanova, grants officer, Foundation for Civil Society, Bratislava; Kathy Sterner, Democracy Programs section head, and Zdeno Cho, media project adviser, USAID Bratislava; Lubomir Fifik, head of the Union of Slovak Television Artists: Olga Holeckova, Prague Center for Independent Journalism; Serge Koperdak, consultant, Pro-Media Slovakia; Martin Lengyel, journalist, Radio Twist, Bratislava; Tanja Rajnakova, media project coordinator, Open Society Foundation, Bratislava; Tatiana Repkova, former editor, *Narodna Obroda*, and consultant, Pro-Media; Andrej Skolkay, media specialist, Department of Political Science, Comenius University: Biljana Tatomir, program director, and Algis Lipstas, project manager, Soros Regional Media Program; Katarina Vajdova, director, Bratislava Centre for Independent Journalism; Jaroslav Veis, press spokesman for Speaker of the Czech Senate who is the former editor of *Lidove Noviny* and former director of the Prague Center for Independent Journalism; Sasa Vucinic, managing director, Media Loan Development Fund, Prague; Marcel Zajac, program officer, Foundation for Civic Activity, Bratislava; Rudolf Zeman, then the director of the Czech Syndicate of Journalists; Irena Zemankova, Foundation for Civil Society, Prague.

The particular strategies of assistance that appear to have been most effective in contributing to the interim goal of media independence and professionalism have displayed some or all of the following features: They are sensitive and responsive to the changing needs of the various local media; they develop strong local partnerships and give local partners and beneficiaries wide leeway in project design and implementation; they target infrastructural needs and build human capacity in a complementary fashion; they provide long-term, specialized, and skills-oriented training using local talent rather than short-term general training by outside advisers; and they strategically limit support to a small number of niche projects sustained for a longer period of time.

Much of the analysis that follows is based on fieldwork that I undertook in the Czech Republic and Slovakia in 1997 and 1998 and reflects the state of affairs at that time. By 1997 the Czech Republic had largely completed the consolidation of its democratic transformation, and many international assistance agencies were in the process of winding down their activities. By contrast, Slovakia was experiencing significant difficulty in achieving democratic consolidation, with the government of Vladimir Meciar increasingly hostile to political and media pluralism. For this reason more actors were undertaking a greater number of media assistance projects in Slovakia than in the Czech Republic at this time. The weight of my analysis on Slovakia reflects this reality.

Comparing the Czech and Slovak republics permitted an examination of how the same strategies work in different, more or less hospitable, political environments and how international assistance organizations subsequently adapted to increasingly divergent political conditions. These two countries share a common background as constituent republics of the Czechoslovak Federation. They began the postcommunist transition with similar legal and political environments and with comparable (albeit not identical) media cultures and structures. In both countries international democracy assistance, including projects designed to support the development of independent media, began at roughly the same time and with similar strategies.

The contrast between these two political and media environments permits a consideration of the question of where, on the macrolevel, international media assistance priorities and resources are most effective. As Thomas Carothers has argued, there may be a particular methodological advantage to assessing foreign assistance in "gray-area cases," such as Slovakia between 1994 and 1998, "where the democratic transition is neither moving forward nor backward very quickly or clearly." Such indeterminate cases may

much better illuminate the strengths and weaknesses of democracy assistance than do societies that moved rapidly to a successful democratic consolidation—or those which have lapsed from an initially positive transition back to some form of dictatorship. In gray-area cases, external democracy assistance is neither a dispensable supplement to a strongly self-propelled process nor a futile rocket off an impenetrable wall. Instead, the assistance becomes more deeply drawn into the local processes of the attempted political transition, resulting in a more thorough testing of the strengths and weaknesses of the program.[4]

Alexander Motyl shares this view and points to the policy consequences by proposing that "Western aid may be able to make the greatest difference in the intermediate countries, where the future seems relatively open, realistic progress may be great, and outside intervention could therefore be most effective."[5]

My findings attest to the validity of these propositions where the interim goals of fostering media independence and professionalism are concerned. While the Czech independent media sector is more developed, international assistance has been more critical to the continued development and, in some instances, the viability of independent media outlets in Slovakia. Without international assistance the Czech media environment probably would be much the same as it is today, after more than seven years of broad international assistance. In Slovakia, however, the absence of international media assistance between 1994 and 1998 probably would have left the struggling independent media more vulnerable to the Meciar government's legal and economic machinations. At the very least the size and scope of the independent Slovak media would be considerably more circumscribed than it was, while some independent media outlets that would otherwise have been viable in an open economy and polity would likely have been pushed from the scene.

As with other aspects of transitional democracy, indigenous political dynamics, especially the degree of elite commitment to open markets and democratic norms, ultimately determine the development of independent media. For intermediate cases, however, well-timed and well-placed international assistance can provide some interim life support that may yield positive long-term benefits. Moreover, while the cumulative effect of assistance is relevant to macrolevel considerations of international donors that seek to have maximal influence in promoting media independence and professionalism, this finding alone says little about the actual effectiveness of discrete assistance strategies within each country setting. As I will detail in this chapter, some strategies have been more effective than others.

Because U.S.-based NGOs were the largest providers of media assistance in these countries, this analysis focuses on their activities and strategies as they have evolved since 1990.[6] In particular, the strategies that I evaluate here are those that were used at the time by the International Media Fund and its successor, the Pro-Media Program of the International Research and Exchanges Board (IREX) (both supported by the U.S. Agency for International Development, USAID), the Independent Journalism Foundation's Centers for Independent Journalism, and the network of Soros foundations, including the local Open Society foundations in each country, the Media Loan Development Fund, and the Regional (now Network) Media Program. I bring into the analysis the work of other, largely European-based agencies such as the British Know-How Fund and European Union–sponsored programs under Poland and Hungary: Action for the Restructuring of the Economy (PHARE), as well as the direct assistance activities of government agencies such as USAID and the U.S. Information Service, where it provides useful elaboration and contrast.

I have divided this chapter into five main sections. The first sets the context by briefly describing the Czech and Slovak media as they were constituted when international assistance agencies first arrived. I then discuss the analytical framework of the study, define basic concepts, and introduce a typology of media assistance strategies that categorizes the targets of assistance and the terms of involvement. The three main categories that I examine are human capital development and two types of infrastructural development: media outlets and regulatory framework. After situating specific NGO projects within this typology, I discuss the influence and limitations of different strategies in these three target areas. Then I discuss how local NGO administrators and media beneficiaries evaluated the assistance programs. In conclusion I consider the lessons these cases may offer to future efforts to aid independent media in transitional societies.

HISTORICAL CONTEXT: MEDIA DEVELOPMENTS AFTER THE VELVET REVOLUTION

THE CZECH REPUBLIC

In the Czech Republic, where observers concluded by the mid-1990s that democracy and pluralism were "consolidated," the mass media made rapid progress on a number of dimensions. After 1989 the media quickly provided a broad range of perspectives, tapped diverse sources, and staked out a large degree of editorial independence from political elites. The Czechs' historical experience with democracy, their relatively strong dissident movement, and the abrupt and complete transfer of power to an elite strongly committed to democratic norms were key factors. While in the early years of postcommunism many of the new, privately owned newspapers were openly allied with political parties, by the late 1990s this was rarely the case. Freedom of the press and freedom of expression were enshrined in the Basic Charter of Rights and Freedoms and were generally observed in the courts. Until September 1997 a law remained on the books that proscribed the defamation of the president and the republic; although the law was widely condemned as an infringement of press freedom, there were few convictions, and most of those found guilty under this provision received suspended sentences or presidential pardons.[7]

In the mid-1990s scores of private newspapers and periodicals, at both the national and local levels, reflected a wide range of interests and opinions. By March 1996 more than half the Czech print media were under foreign ownership, but most were run by Czech editors and journalists and had a high level of Czech content.[8] Reflecting a regionwide trend of popular apathy and a global trend toward sensationalism, the most popular newspapers have been tabloids. In addition to the state news agency, a private news service established in 1994 was by 1997 providing regular feeds both domestically and abroad. As with the print media, publishing and distribution companies had considerable foreign investment.

The government formally reconstituted Czech State Radio and Television as public service broadcasters, governed by a democratically accountable state broadcasting council. Competing with Czech Public Radio were more than sixty private radio stations, making for a very crowded marketplace. Many of these outlets were heavily in debt and had a small market share, conditions that made for a fiercely competitive market.

The two state-owned television channels competed with two major private networks, Prima (formerly Premiera) and Nova TV. In 1997 the latter had more than a 70 percent audience share (compared to the two public channels' combined share of 25 percent). Central Europe Media Enterprises (CME), at the time a growing international media giant active in the region, owned 80 percent of Nova TV.

Since 1997 CME's activities have become controversial following reports that it has disregarded the ownership, advertising, and content provisions of Nova TV's license (staples of its programming are reruns of U.S. television shows and and chatty news shows) and because CME has been busy consolidating a veritable mini-empire extending through the Czech Republic and beyond; CME holdings include other private television networks, radio stations, and newspapers.[9]

The development of professional associations for journalists, publishers, and broadcasters proceeded rapidly, and they have become well integrated into European and international professional associations. On several occasions journalists and broadcasters demonstrated some capacity to defend their corporate interests against political intrusion; in particular, in 1996 they succeeded in preventing the adoption of a restrictive press law.

Until 1997 Prime Minister Václav Klaus's uncompromising embrace of laissez-faire democratic capitalism dominated the Czech Republic's political environment. His ideology and policy framework led to minimal state regulation of the media sector. This antiregulation ethos was powerfully reinforced by both the corporate quest for profits and, perhaps unexpectedly, by a dissident political culture that regards even democratic forms of media regulation, including self-regulation, with abiding suspicion.[10] Observers have cited the lax regulatory environment and relatively passive regulatory bodies as principal reasons why CME has been able to violate the terms of its broadcast license with apparent impunity.[11]

While the Czech mass media displayed many of the characteristics of a robust and independent media, the forces of laissez-faire had their own deleterious effect on journalistic professionalism and on the capacity of the media to act as the fourth estate, that is, to be the public's watchdog and to convey accurate information. Some editors protested that owners' preoccupation with revenues has compromised their independence.[12] Another much noted problem was the threat of commercial corruption of individual journalists, some of whom took up selling coverage for cash and presented as "news" what was really commissioned advertising.[13] While this practice was not widespread, it was prevalent enough to provoke professional concern about journalistic ethics and media credibility. Nonetheless, Czech journalists resisted efforts to adopt a voluntary press code. According to Rudolf Zeman, then the director of the Czech Syndicate of Journalists, the vast majority of journalists were highly averse to the formal adoption of professional standards. In principle the syndicate — a professional association — supported a common ethical standard, but it opposed both a West European–style press council and a system of accreditation for syndicate members that would permit effective enforcement of self-regulating standards.[14]

The print media remained governed by an obsolete and inconsistent press law, instituted in 1966 and amended in 1990. New legislation has gone through a number of drafts but has been held up by disputes about the lack of provisions to protect journalists' sources and to require state bodies to disclose public information to the press.

In 1997 the *Economist* claimed that the Czech media rank fourth among the world's freest presses, ahead of both Germany and the United Kingdom. This ranking, however, may more accurately have reflected the Czech media's passion for the free market than the intrinsic attributes of the media in Germany and England. While the Czech media have acquired many features of a robust pluralistic media, and while their independence has been secured, both market dynamics and residual political, legal, and cultural practices present obstacles to the media's capacity to act as a consistent and effective supporter of democratic accountability and an informed citizenry.

SLOVAKIA

Between 1994 and 1998 Slovakia underwent a period of neoauthoritarian retrenchment. In contrast to the 1989–1994 period, when the media made major strides in casting off state control, a high degree of political intrusiveness characterized the media environment during the mid-1990s. Former prime minister Vladimir Meciar's ruling coalition made efforts to establish various forms of de jure censorship, most notably in 1995–1996 with this unsuccessful effort to enact the Law on the Protection of the Republic, which would have criminalized the dissemination of "false information that damages Slovakia." More common were the Meciar government's de facto efforts to manipulate the financial, regulatory, and material prerequisites for the operate of the nonstate media. These included punitive tax increases; selling printing and distribution facilities to Meciar allies, who subsequently denied these resources to selected outlets critical of Meciar; selective denial of broadcast licenses; an unofficial ban that prevented state-owned companies from advertising in the "opposition press"; and periodic shutdowns of the broadcast transmissions of independent radio stations on flimsy financial pretexts.[15] More ominously, individual journalists suffered legal, verbal, and sometimes physical attacks, and in June 1997 someone vandalized the facilities of the newly established independent Slovak News Agency in what many observers concluded was a government-inspired action.

While these political and economic pressures were undoubtedly serious, Western advocates and monitors of press freedom tended to exaggerate the threat posed by Meciar's actions and to discount the significant achievements of the private Slovak media, as well as their evident resilience in the face of government efforts to undermine them. For two successive years, for example, the Committee to Protect Journalists ranked Meciar among the "top ten worst enemies of the free press worldwide"—a distinction usually reserved for the most egregious dictators—even though the most serious charge against him was his unsuccessful attempt to pass the Law on the Protection of the Republic.[16] Even more inaccurately, the European Fund for Freedom of Expression ranked Slovakia as "a country where the media have little freedom," even claiming that state censorship, though more subtle, was "just as effective as in previous times," that "the written press is largely controlled by the state," and that "control over radio and television is practically complete."[17] Freedom House's annual survey of press freedom ranked Slovakia as "partly free" in 1997. While this standing accurately reflected Freedom House's exclusive preoccupation with measuring state policies toward the media, some thoughtful Slovak observers protested that such categorical claims perpetuated a distorted picture that obscured positive developments.

In fact, as in the Czech Republic, Slovakia had a significant degree of media pluralism, with a half-dozen nationwide dailies for a population of five million, as well as numerous regional papers, monthlies, and weeklies that offered a range of political views and diverse sources of information. The quality of news reporting also showed significant improvement since 1990, especially in the area of economic and financial news, where the weekly *Trend* and the daily *Narodna Obroda* were recognized as standard-setters for the region. Slovakia also had twenty-four privately owned regional and local radio stations, six privately owned regional and local television stations, a burgeoning cable industry (by 1997 seventy-three independent cable operators held licenses), and a newly established independent news agency, which rapidly became a regular news provider to many private media outlets. CME-backed Markiza TV, launched in late 1996, was the second major private network, alongside VTV and the two government-controlled channels, STV1 and STV2. The arrival of Markiza, which offered more popular programming and more balanced and diverse news coverage than state television, effectively thwarted Meciar's domination of the Slovak television scene for the two-thirds of the country that received its signal.[18] After 1997 Markiza enjoyed an audience share well ahead of STV1's and STV2's.[19]

Throughout the Meciar era the Slovak media displayed a dogged capacity to defend its constitutionally enshrined rights to operate free of state interference. Although still weakly developed, several professional associations for radio broadcasters, print journalists, and television producers helped to defeat the government's attempts to pass restrictive media legislation. Most notably, in 1997 independent media associations forced the government to abandon its efforts to criminalize the "false spread of information" deemed damaging to Slovakia. The Slovak independent media also assisted one another in securing access to printing and distribution facilities when the government interfered with their regular sources.

In comparison to its Czech equivalent, the Slovak Syndicate of Journalists was relatively more open to the creation of a nationwide, European-style press council, with a self-administered code of ethics and a system of accreditation to promote and enforce professional journalistic standards, although it had yet to be implemented. In part, the motive may have been preemptive, as the government may have been seeking to exploit the weakness of journalistic ethics as a pretext for renewed censorship. Given the profound polarization that beset Slovak politics at the time, it was no surprise that the independent syndicate had a state-supported rival, the Association of Slovak Journalists, essentially a communist-style organization that supported the policies of the ruling coalition while seeking to undermine support for the syndicate. In 1997 relations between these rival associations were generally poor; nevertheless, they did cooperate in efforts to develop a common press code.

Despite its resourcefulness and vigor, the Slovak independent media faced a number of daunting challenges. The most immediate was their economic viability. As in the Czech Republic, the media market was saturated and increasingly competitive. Production costs and indebtedness were rising, and the size of the market was limited. In Slovakia the media had the additional disadvantage of reduced investment resources. They had fewer foreign investors to rely on, while indigenous investors tended to be owners of newly privatized companies, many of whom had close connections to the Meciar government or were otherwise dependent on it for political favors.

Although state radio and television were formally reconstituted in 1992 as public service broadcasters, which meant they were to be subjected to democratic control by nonpartisan radio and television councils established by the Slovak parliament, the Meciar government reasserted an effective monopoly over their programming and personnel decisions. Indeed, one of Meciar's first moves on being elected prime minister in 1994 was to pack the boards of the Radio and Television Councils with party loyalists. As a result, Slovak opposition parties lost all representation on these bodies as well as routine access to state television and radio in general. The program content of STV1 and STV2 became limited largely to biased political broadcasts and soporific shows celebrating the cultural and other achievements of the Slovak nation, a genre that could be described as "nationalist realism." Progovernment state radio and television had a comparative advantage against their privately owned competitors in terms of subsidies and as the only radio and television networks broadcasting nationwide.

The government repeatedly sought to make examples of independence-minded journalists and outlets that boldly criticized Meciar's policies or attacked him personally. A number of lawsuits charged journalists with defaming state officials or slandering the premier. In 1996 the opposition Bratislava daily, SME, was suddenly denied access to its customary printing and distribution network and forced to rely on a printer at the other end of the country, at great expense. In the fall of 1997, among several other incidents of official harassment, the government temporarily denied Radio Twist its broadcasting frequency, allegedly for failure to pay arrears on licensing fees owed to the state telecommunications company.[20] Finally, in a failed bid to cripple the independent media, in 1997 the Meciar government attempted to impose a fourfold increase in the value-added tax on newspapers.

Meciar's hostile behavior, as well as the highly polarized social and political environment that his government has engendered, threatened the well-being of the independent media. Perhaps inescapably, the media tended to replicate the profound and antagonistic society-wide split between those for and against Meciar. Thus many independent papers and some radio stations displayed a partisan bias, routinely giving favorable coverage to opposition views. This rigid polarization was a major impediment to the further consolidation of a nonpartisan professional media.[21] As in wartime, accurate and balanced reporting was the first casualty in what many see as nothing less than a definitive battle about the future political identity of Slovakia.

ASSISTANCE STRATEGIES
OF INTERNATIONAL ACTORS

Regardless of their varying roles and mandates, international, state, and non-governmental assistance agencies shared the same overarching rationale for as-

sisting independent media: that it is an indispensable component of a functioning democracy and that the media in postcommunist countries lacked the req-
uisite skills and capacity to function as professional—nonpartisan, objective,
and balanced—sources of information and as viable commercial enterprises.
These outside agencies also tended to share a repertoire of assistance tools: most
commonly, conducting in-country training sessions and sponsoring placements
abroad; offering technical, legal, professional, and managerial consultancies;
provisioning media outlets with equipment, either through loans or in-kind
grants; and, more rarely, providing direct financial support. At the sector level
the majority of assistance organizations ran similar projects at similar times.

For the purposes of this analysis *strategy* refers to the conceptual and practical modalities that link particular activities to the fulfillment of desired goals. In
the area of media assistance discrete strategies were not always evident, not even
to those involved in assistance activities. This appears to have been particularly
true during the initial stages of assistance (1990–1993), when—as with other
forms of democracy support—designing coherent strategies of assistance took
second place to providing as much visible aid as quickly as possible, both in
order to satisfy donors that their money was being put to work and to enhance
the palpable benefits of democracy to newly enfranchised citizens.[22] This early
neglect of *strategic* assistance may also have been shaped by an assumption that
the transition to democracy in what was then a unified Czechoslovakia would
be comparatively rapid and unproblematic, and that the scattershot provision of
training seminars and equipment drops would be sufficient to sustain an independent media.[23] Finally, as Thomas Carothers has elaborated elsewhere, while
early U.S. assistance efforts had a relatively clear idea of which model of democracy they were using (essentially a replication of U.S. institutions), they
were less sure of practical approaches models or discrete ways of replicating
these institutions in new and diverse environments.[24]

As with other forms of democracy assistance, the agencies modified their assumptions once the complexities of the situation in the Czech Republic and Slovakia became evident. Media assistance efforts can be divided into three general
phases: an initially heavy emphasis on journalist training and equipment drops,
followed by programs aimed at the wider legal and organizational infrastructure
(reflecting a shift from supplying armies of foreign consultants to building indigenous capacity), and, later, a greater emphasis on enhancing the media's economic viability and developing the regional media. Journalist training was still
the mainstay of this activity, particularly in the Czech Republic, but evolved
from general and abstract lessons on the fundamentals of Western journalism to
the development of technical skills and specialized practical knowledge. Gradually, programs and projects became more diversified, as individual agencies recognized the comparative advantage in devoting their energies and resources to
certain niche areas. Even among those with a greater concern for developing

explicit strategies with clear goals and measurable results, however, some people whom I interviewed had difficulty articulating the strategy or strategies that they used. They often tended to fall back on descriptions of generic program goals and activities rather than articulate the criteria or methods by which specific activities were supposed to lead to the attainment of those goals.

This said, differences in strategies of media assistance were apparent, if only implicitly. Any attempt to categorize these different assistance strategies is rendered problematic by the fact that most assistance agencies—whether consciously or not—are likely to pursue many different strategies at the same time, and these strategies at best approximate, rather than exactly reflect, any pure type. For heuristic purposes I have adapted the following schema, which are set forth in table 4.1.

Terms of involvement refers to the dominant modalities by which international actors—implicitly or explicitly—provide assistance to the media sector. A proactive approach is one in which the international NGO (or the funder[s] to which it is beholden) has well-developed goals, priorities, and strategies for assistance. It may therefore also be associated with a higher degree of outside (as opposed to local) initiative, with imported ideas rather than domestic ones, and with generic models of media assistance, rather than locally specific ones.[25] Conversely, a responsive strategy describes assistance efforts that are designed to be highly responsive to the changing needs of the local partners and beneficiaries, as well as to their initiatives, concerns, and ideas. Assistance strategies are seldom purely proactive or responsive; even the most proactive strategies tended, over time, to shed preconceived notions and incorporate a significant level of domestic ideas and initiative in the process of implementation. There seldom has been an exclusively responsive strategy, which would mean leaving all decisions to local partners and beneficiaries.[26] For this reason I have qualified each with the term *interactive* to reflect the existence of varying degrees of international-local synergy while keeping intact the distinction between the overall thrust of each dominant strategy.[27]

The terms of involvement also reflect variation on a number of other dimensions. Assistance efforts may be multidimensional, in that several distinct activities are undertaken in parallel under a more-or-less coherent, longer-term, local program, or unidimensional, with a focus on a single project, usually to be conducted within a comparatively limited time frame. Unidimensional projects are typically implemented by visiting consultants in collaboration with local partners selected for the purpose, with responsibility for management and oversight remaining at the home base of the international assistance agency.

Both program-based and project-based activities may be either process oriented or product oriented. That is, they may involve activities that focus on the long-range incremental development of media skills and infrastructure (process oriented) or on those aimed at delivering a specific product for a specific need,

TABLE 4.1 Typology of Media Assistance Strategies in the Czech
and Slovak Republics

Target of Assistance

Individual journalists, editors, managers, etc. (human capital development)
Media outlets (infrastructural development)
Regulatory and associational framework (infrastructural development)

Terms of Involvement

Proactive/ interactive	Responsive/ interactive
Multidimensional (program-based)	Unidimensional (project-based)
Process oriented	Product oriented
Imported ideas	Domestic generated ideas
Selective	Nondiscriminatory

such as providing consultation on a proposed media law, holding a one-time conference on journalistic ethics, or publishing handbooks and subsidizing professional journals (product oriented).

Finally, assistance strategies may be described as either selective or nondiscriminatory in terms of the identities of the beneficiaries. Selective strategies are those that restrict assistance to beneficiaries that meet specified criteria of eligibility. A common example of this strategy was to limit assistance benefits to the nonstate media. Another was to restrict assistance to a subcategory of the nonstate media that met certain requirements, such as commercial viability. Nondiscriminatory strategies, by contrast, are those that aim to spread the benefits of assistance to the media sector at large, without demanding any "fitness" tests.

Targets of assistance designates the main types of beneficiaries. In general, international actors seek either to promote human capital development by targeting individual media professionals or to develop the infrastructural underpinnings of media independence. Infrastructural support can be divided into two types: supporting the managerial, technical, and commercial capacities of individual media outlets or assisting the development of professional associations and the legal-regulatory framework. International actors may be engaged in a mix of activities that support infrastructural as well as human capital development, supporting media outlets, associational bodies, and the regulatory framework as well as individuals.

Perhaps more than any other single factor, the identity and mandate of assistance organizations (both the international NGOs and their funders) influenced the strategies that were used. For example, PHARE-supported activities in media assistance reflected the European Union's concerns with both promoting democracy and assisting these countries to meet the institutional and regulatory requirements for eventual membership in the European Union. Therefore the activities that they promoted tended to be proactive, were more focused on reforming the legal, normative, and regulatory infrastructure of the media sector, were generally nondiscriminatory toward all state and nonstate media rather than selective, and were often more product oriented, funding specific projects, such as draft legislation on broadcast and press laws and publications on European standards for press councils and journalistic ethics.

In contrast, U.S.-based agencies were largely concerned with selectively promoting the independent (nonstate) media, largely reflecting the distinctly American bias against state-owned or public sector media. Partly for this reason, and partly in response to local needs—especially in Slovakia where investment was more restricted—U.S. assistance efforts were also more likely to focus on the process of developing a viable commercial infrastructure for media outlets. Several NGO efforts, such as the Centers for Independent Journalism (Independent Journalism Foundation), the Knight-Ridder Fellowship Program, Article 19, PressNow, and Freedom Forum reflect their identity as organizations founded by journalists for journalists. On the whole these tended to be focused on promoting media professionalism by providing human capital development through training, fellowships, and consultancies; were more process oriented; and were more receptive to collaboration and domestically generated ideas.

The next section examines in greater detail and with specific examples the media assistance strategies for each target of media assistance by international actors since 1990.

HUMAN CAPITAL DEVELOPMENT

Human capital development was by far the largest single category of assistance efforts. The reasons for this are both principled and practical. The principled reason is that the norms, skills, and practices of working journalists, editors, producers, and managers are critical variables in determining the overall performance of credible, professional, and independent media. The practical rationale is that individual training—in the form of seminars, workshops, consultations, or placements abroad—is a relatively low-cost way to promote new norms, practices, production techniques, and management models to a relatively wide number of beneficiaries and with results that are quick and quantifiable, if not always meaningfully so.

In the initial phase of media assistance, the vast majority of initiatives were aimed at human capital development and, in the case of the more consolidated Czech Republic, continued in this vein. Between 1992 and 1995 a main vehicle of U.S. government assistance was the International Media Fund, a USAID grantee that was created explicitly for this purpose. According to an official of USAID in Bratislava, the International Media Fund initially pursued a generic multidimensional approach (including technology drops) that was designed at USAID headquarters in Washington, D.C., with little initial concern for tailoring aid to specific local conditions.[28] In collaboration with direct U.S. Information Service (USIS) training programs, the International Media Fund conducted a global program of media training on a generally scattershot and nondiscriminatory basis, its aim being to sow the seeds of training assistance as flexibly and broadly as possible. Training was largely aimed at midcareer professionals and consisted mostly of in-country workshops and seminars run by foreign media consultants but also included some short-term internships and long-term university-based placements in the United States for promising local journalists.

Human capital development was also the primary thrust of the Independent Journalism Foundation, founded in 1991 and largely supported by private U.S. funding, to help journalists to upgrade their professional skills. The Independent Journalism Foundation founded a Center for Independent Journalism in Prague in 1991 and another in Bratislava in 1993. These quickly became major local NGO partners for other international agencies as well as a primary institutional base for a series of in-country training seminars and workshops. In addition, the centers took on the functions of press center, media advocate, and informal professional development network. Except during the start-up phase of the flagship center in Prague, the Centers for Independent Journalism were staffed and managed by local media professionals and overseen by an American acting as regional coordinator.

The initial reliance of the Independent Journalism Foundation on foreign trainers shifted to using journalists from the region to conduct local training; foreign consultants came primarily to provide supplementary, specialized technical training. The staffs of the Prague and Bratislava centers sponsored and administered both training programs and projects that were predominately responsive in nature. These programs reflected a synthesis of internationally and domestically generated ideas and a responsiveness to beneficiaries' needs and initiatives. The centers worked closely with media outlets, with nascent professional associations, and with other Western agencies. They ran the Freedom Forum Library resource centers; they were a main partner for the Soros foundations' "Medianet" project, which supplied access to the Internet to a network of local press and radio outlets; and they administered competitions for a number of foreign fellowships for journalism training abroad, including those sponsored by the U.S.-German Marshall Fund, the Guardian Foundation, the Knight-Ridder Foundation, the British Know How Fund, and other donor agencies.

The Soros foundations' network has acted largely as a funder and coordinator rather than as a direct administrator of media assistance programs. Reflecting the distinctive Soros ethos, the local Open Society foundations in Prague and Bratislava and the wider Regional (Network) Media Program were run exclusively by experienced locals and established flexible and close relationships with local partners, including the Centers for Independent Journalism and professional associations for journalists and broadcasters. According to a director of the Regional Media Program, it did not seek to implement any standard global approach to its assistance activities but to remain highly responsive to the needs and developments of the media in the different countries in which it was involved.[29]

Training was just one of several planks in a multidimensional program. As with other international agencies, upgrading regional media has been a major priority. On the whole, the Soros foundations were more directly involved in infrastructural development activities, including both financial support and technical and capital provision to individual media outlets and to the sector at large. Soros staff members consciously coordinated their training efforts to accompany and reinforce the provision of technical equipment. For example, the Medianet program not only supplied computers and Internet access to local media outlets but provided training on how to use them. Likewise, in the process of fulfilling its main objective of providing direct capital loans to select media outlets, the Media Loan Development Fund provided extensive consultation in the development of business plans (marketing, programming, advertising) so that even executives whose outlets failed to qualify for loans gained improved professional skills.[30]

The IREX Pro-Media Program, established in 1995 as a successor to the International Media Fund to implement USAID's media assistance programs, focused its efforts on infrastructural development, working predominately with individual media outlets but also with the sector as a whole. However, because most of its support was public money from USAID (under a cooperative agreement with IREX), there were political constraints on Pro-Media's ability to provide direct grants of financial and technical resources.[31] Instead, Pro-Media pursued its goal of infrastructural sustainability indirectly, in part by providing training seminars and workshops in finance, management, and advertising as well as on-site consultations and short-term U.S. study tours for media managers. These activities sought to expose media professionals to Western advertising and marketing ideas and techniques in a process-oriented effort to enhance the practical business skills of media executives.

Initially, Pro-Media sought to conduct training in collaboration with local partners, such as the Center for Independent Journalism, but by 1997 had discontinued this practice in favor of providing direct training to media outlets.[32] Pro-Media activities were managed by in-country resident advisers, most of whom have been Americans, but Pro-Media increasingly has brought in local journalists in a consulting capacity. Overall, however, its strategy has tended to be proactive—it had a relatively fixed set of goals and methods aimed at a niche need—and was inspired by imported marketing and management ideas.

MEDIA OUTLETS
(INFRASTRUCTURAL DEVELOPMENT)

Infrastructural assistance to individual media outlets consisted of programs designed to strengthen media outlets' overall technical endowment, financial profile, and managerial skills, with the latter focused on developing the particular skills, especially marketing and advertising, needed to become profitable. Although upgrading the media outlets' technology—both equipment and skills— had been under way since the early phase of assistance, activities aimed at commercial viability began later (in 1995 or 1996) and were developed in response to the expressed needs of media outlets whose commercial development was too slow and whose sustainability looked questionable, both to local media and to foreign funders. One impediment to profitability derived from a media culture in which everyone wanted to be a journalist and no one wanted to be a manager, as well as a culture in which "selling news"—or even having the skills to do so—had not been a high priority.[33] By far the larger and more serious impediments to commercial viability, however, lay in the broader economy, including the slow pace of market reforms, the lack of local and foreign investment, and politically inspired attempts to control access to investors.

For these reasons this type of assistance was targeted at "gray-area countries" such as Slovakia and was not undertaken where outside investment or access to investors was relatively unproblematic, as in the Czech Republic. For example, the Media Loan Development Fund did not provide loans to media outlets in Poland, the Czech Republic, Hungary, or Slovenia, because the investment situation in these countries was relatively good, nor did the fund work in countries where the political and legal environment was too crippling, such as Belarus. Pro-Media considered as potential candidates media outlets operating in countries with a nascent pluralism and a permissive legal framework and that needed cash but could get it nowhere else.

Similarly, Pro-Media focused its efforts in countries that were, for either political or economic reasons, still in the early or intermediate phases of transition.[34] Like the Soros Regional Media Program, Pro-Media targeted the independent regional media, mostly local radio and some local television stations; it provided little support to national television or radio, whether state run or privately owned. The reasons for these exclusions varied but included a lack of suitable partners in the case of state-run outlets, the high cost of giving meaningful assistance to national television, and independent national broadcast and print media that had better access to regular investment resources than did local media.

In the early phase the International Media Fund and USIS, among others, provided direct technical assistance through a series of equipment drops to local print and broadcasting outlets. Typically, these involved recording, editing, fax, and computer equipment donated by Western media outlets or purchased directly. By 1996 such direct technical provisioning was less common, although the Soros Regional Media Fund, working closely with the local Soros foundations, continued to arrange for small-scale technical aid grants (less than $50,000 per outlet) on a case-by-case basis. In order to enable local Slovak television stations to upgrade their technology, Pro-Media negotiated a discount for purchasing digital production equipment for a group of stations and subsidized as much as 20 percent of the cost to each outlet. The Soros Foundation's network, meanwhile, provided the innovative Medianet program, which supplied computers and Internet access to local radio outlets in Slovakia. The outlets were permitted to keep the equipment at no cost if they used it in demonstrable ways, such to set up home pages, use the Internet as a supplementary news and information source, and exchange information with other journalists.[35] In a similar effort to forge technical links to new information sources, Pro-Media negotiated an arrangement whereby local Slovak radio stations would increase their use of the Independent Slovak News Agency and it would provide the stations with training on information access.

For both political and economic reasons direct financial subsidies to the Slovak media were rare, although some agencies had undertaken this kind of support in other countries. More common were either direct loans or indirect support through management consultant and training programs. The largely Soros-funded Media Loan Development Fund was the first in the region to undertake a media loan program, acting essentially as a development bank to provide direct loans to eligible media outlets, to assist them in developing their own broadcast or print facilities and sustainable business practices. Precisely because it was in the business of making loans, the Media Loan Development Fund had a highly selective strategy of picking winners, that is, of providing financing only to those outlets that were independent of the state and of political parties, met strict market-based criteria, and had developed a rigorous and viable business plan. In practice this meant helping those independent outlets that demonstrated good financial prospects but that were at risk of going under because they did not have access to regular sources of investment and distribution. The Media Loan Development Fund worked closely with applicants for three to fifteen months to help them restructure their operations and devise competitive business plans.

The Pro-Media program sought to promote commercial viability indirectly, by addressing the demand as well as the supply side; for example, Pro-Media conducted workshops for local businesses to show them the benefits of advertising their products in the local media. Pro-Media also undertook the first sector-wide market research study of Slovak radio, so that both the outlets and potential advertisers would have a firm grasp of audience demographics. Unlike the Media Loan Development Fund, Pro-Media consciously avoided a strategy of picking winners among the independent media, instead seeking to sow the benefits of its assistance as widely as possible. Given the saturated nature of the Slovak media market, it was widely believed that by 2002 only half these outlets would survive. Therefore Pro-Media sought to give all comers as much business acumen as possible to meet the challenges of this competitive environment.

REGULATORY AND ASSOCIATIONAL FRAMEWORK (INFRASTRUCTURAL DEVELOPMENT)

International efforts to help reform the legal and regulatory framework and strengthen the development of indigenous professional organizations form the third major category of assistance. In general, European-based organizations such as PHARE, the British Know How Fund, the International Federation of Journalists, Article 19, and Press Now were well ahead of U.S. actors in providing support for the development of the regulatory structure, although the U.S. organizations increased their attention to this area after 1996. The primary strategy consisted of instituting individual projects that were highly product oriented, such as holding conferences or workshops that sought to acquaint local journalists with the role of Western press associations. More sustained efforts to effect a broader, long-term restructuring of professional associations emerged only in the late 1990s, as NGOs and funders alike became increasingly concerned with ensuring the sustainability of professional journalism.

Assisting the reform of the legal and regulatory framework involved direct advocacy by international press-monitoring groups, such as Article 19 and the Committee to Protect Journalists, which sought to use public censure to pressure governments to alter offending practices. It also involved indirect efforts to strengthen the capacity of local media professionals to participate effectively in the design and implementation of democratic media legislation. To this end international agencies provided legal consultation in the drafting of media and broadcast legislation, offered legal opinions targeting the deficiencies of existing legislation, and sponsored a variety of conferences and publications on relevant international legal instruments.[36] Typically, both European and U.S. actors relied on the expertise of foreign media law experts. Pro-Media, for example, employed the U.S. law firm of Covington and Burling to analyze controversial Slovak media legislation and constitutional statutes, such as the May 1998 amendment to the Slovak election act that severely circumscribed political advertising and campaigning in the independent media.

International efforts to promote the development of professional media associations typically went hand in hand with the promotion of overall regulatory reform. In part, this was because the establishment and enforcement of sector-wide professional standards, while an important end in itself, was also seen as a way to ensure that the media are both more responsible and more capable of

defending their corporate interests while removing a pretext for politically motivated forms of government regulation. Here, assistance efforts were of two main
types: those aimed at the organizational development of accredited professional
associations and those aimed at the creation of a common code of professional
conduct that these associations could implement and enforce. One strategy for
achieving these goals was to sponsor conferences and publications through which
local media professionals and state officials could become better acquainted with
international norms and practices regarding press councils, journalistic standards,
and associational models.[37] Another was to offer direct institution-building support to indigenous media associations, primarily the Czech Syndicate of Journalists and the Slovak Syndicate of Journalists but later also professional trade
unions such as the Association of Regional Broadcasters, the Union of Television Authors, and publishers' associations in each country. In the Czech Republic, for example, PressNow provided money so that the Czech Syndicate of
Journalists could put out a monthly newsletter for its members, while the U.S.-
German Marshall Fund subsidized the publication of *KMIT*, a wide-ranging
monthly magazine aimed at media professionals that discussed recent media developments, press ethics, and new media technologies.

Most international assistance for organizational development took the form
of periodic consultations. For example, PHARE sponsored a comprehensive
survey of journalists in Slovakia by a local media analyst to get a picture of working conditions, career profiles, and professional needs, so that the Slovak Syndicate of Journalists would have a firmer base for its own restructuring plans. After
1996 Pro-Media also created a long-term program to help transform the nascent
Slovak Syndicate of Journalists and the Slovak Association of Regional Broadcasters into full-fledged professional organizations. One of Pro-Media's main
goals was to help make these into national organizations, with fully equipped regional offices that would bring regional professionals from all eight territorial
districts into the larger professional community and would promote the norm of
decentralized self-organization.

INFLUENCE ON CZECH AND SLOVAK MEDIA

International support had a positive influence on the norms and practices of the
postcommunist Czech and Slovak media, enhancing their professionalism and
their long-term viability and helping to integrate them in a larger transnational
media community. This assistance made a crucial difference to the professional
careers of individual journalists and, in the Slovak case, to the continued viability of particular privately owned media outlets.

The relative importance of this support at the aggregate sectorwide level depends in large part on wider progress toward democracy. In both countries, but
especially in the Czech Republic, strong indigenous impulses to reform the

media sector in accordance with Western norms and practices already existed and were reinforced and accelerated by international support. In Slovakia international assistance agencies were compelled to negotiate the dilemmas posed by the profound division that high politics had created between the state and privately owned media. In this case international assistance often went beyond "facilitation" to provide resources that were otherwise scarce or lacking.

Whether media assistance actually contributed to the larger goal of supporting democracy is more questionable. Because so much of what constitutes media independence lies in the wider economic, political, and cultural environment, international donors and NGOs can do only so much in attempting to fulfill their self-described task of promoting not just an independent media but one that plays a supporting role in developing democracy. International actors often treated these two goals as one, assuming that the mere existence of independent media is, ipso facto, proof of its democratic performance. They have been somewhat reluctant to recognize that much of any media's democratic influence depends on the prevailing political culture and the degree to which power holders are committed to democracy. Affecting this larger political and societal framework is largely beyond the control of international assistance agencies.[38] The analysis that follows therefore seeks to assess the effects of media assistance on the interim goal of promoting viable and professional independent media.

HUMAN CAPITAL DEVELOPMENT

International training efforts clearly helped to speed the development of professional and technical skills of working media professionals. Particularly in the Czech Republic, and to a lesser extent in Slovakia, media outlets no longer acted as the mouthpieces of particular political parties as they did in the early years of the transition; by the mid-1990s few evinced strong partisan affiliations with specific political parties. Journalists increasingly displayed reporting skills in line with Western norms of accurate and balanced reporting of different viewpoints. Indeed, some graduates of international training programs became so accomplished that Western media outlets offered them jobs. Their reporting displayed a greater separation of fact from opinion and greater effort to get the facts straight. Some newspapers adopted the U.S. practice of having separate editorial pages. Again, just how much these improvements can be attributed to international training is difficult to determine. One area that appeared to have benefited directly from international training efforts was investigative reporting.

The relative effects of different strategies of training is always a controversial topic. Most funders and some NGO administrators maintained that in-country training efforts were the most effective, because they reached the greatest number of people with the most economical use of resources while enabling better coordination between human capital and infrastructural development. In contrast, journalists who participated in both in-country training and in foreign internships or university placements said that they gained much more professional expertise from the placements abroad—that nothing is more useful than actually being in the newsroom or editing suite of a Western media outlet and getting hands-on experience.

From the point of view of local journalists, the early training programs were the least effective, primarily because they emphasized abstract and academic lessons about the fundamentals of reporting. Given that training was the mainstay of international media assistance, it is not surprising that many media professionals throughout the region complained of "training fatigue" or of "being overtrained." They also evinced some resentment, again especially during the early phases of support, about strategies that relied on—and were seen disproportionately to benefit—quick visits by foreign trainers who lacked adequate local knowledge. This perception had the unintended consequence of making the putative beneficiaries less enthusiastic and receptive to the efforts of Western trainers. With time, most international agencies altered their training profiles to offer more workshops and consultations on specialized practical topics such as television news reporting, radio editing, and media management, and to use more local trainers.

Moreover, especially in the earlier phases, what might have been appropriate kinds of training were sometimes offered at inappropriate times or under inappropriate conditions such as training broadcasters to use new recording technology to which they did not have access; offering training in English when most journalists did not speak it well; offering workshops on television production in areas that had no suitable local stations; or offering lessons on respecting international copyright laws, when other problems, such as coping with the threat of financial collapse, were far more pressing.[39]

The main beneficiaries of media training programs were midcareer professionals, and increasingly those from regions outside the capital cities, where the professional level had been lower to begin with. Although training the next generation of media professionals received less support and attention at the outset, the teaching of journalism at the university level also improved noticeably. The teaching of journalism was once the preserve of academics with little practical experience, but practical instruction by working professionals now receives greater emphasis. As a whole, however, university-level training in this period remained underdeveloped, lacking adequate equipment, textbooks, and instructors. The quality of training improved over time, as assistance agencies shifted their focus from general (and reportedly often dry) seminars on the basics of reporting or radio broadcasting to more specialized technical and managerial topics, such as television news production or radio station marketing. At the same time indigenous training capacities increasingly developed a solid institutional base, although they remained highly dependent upon Western funders for financial support.

Two main environmental factors limited the overall effects of international assistance to human capital development: the prevailing political climate and the dominant indigenous norms that affect media culture. The political limitations were acute in Slovakia, where the society-wide polarization of pro- and anti-Meciar factions created a volatile, partisan climate that often tested journalistic professionalism. Precisely because the Czech Republic enjoys greater democratic stability, the limiting effects of the prevailing media culture were more evident. Slovakia too, however, shared this constraint, and Western professional codes of conduct were slow to take full root in the media culture of Slovakia. In any society normative transformation is a slow and complex process that is the most difficult to effect by deliberate design—especially where those norms are seen as alien to the local tradition. In these cases the corrupting effects of commercial competitiveness and, within the older generation, a lingering dissident discourse that is highly value laden and resistant to regulation impeded the process.

MEDIA OUTLETS
(INFRASTRUCTURAL DEVELOPMENT)

Although the independent media outlets at this time still did not have state-of-the-art technology, they were much better equipped than they had been five or six years earlier, and international technical assistance was a major reason why. Few media outlets, especially local ones, had the resources to secure this technology on their own. The production values of local radio and television programs improved significantly. Likewise, virtually all media gained regular access to the Internet and established their own home pages. On the whole, these programs particularly benefited the regional radio and television media outside Prague and Bratislava and thus helped them to become more competitive with national outlets.

At the same time the provision of technology was not a smooth process in the early phase of assistance. For example, donated Western equipment was often somewhat outdated and incompatible with existing equipment and therefore unusable.[40] Another problem was that some funders put restrictions on which brands of equipment the funders could underwrite. Following a standard USAID requirement, for example, the International Media Fund was obligated to provide equipment that was manufactured in the United States, sometimes at greater expense and often involving additional compatibility problems.

It is still too early to tell how much of an influence international support has had on the commercial viability of media outlets, in part because this type of assistance is still relatively recent and aims for long-term sustainability.[41] This said, as a result of Pro-Media's market research initiative, the majority of local Slovak radio outlets acquired a firm understanding of their audience share and their expansion potential, as well as the data analysis software to update this information regularly. Pro-Media reports that of the thirteen participating local radio stations, one has used this information to restructure its programming and marketing profile, while another has seen its advertising revenues increase.[42] A Media Loan Development Fund loan played a crucial role in helping the independent Slovak national daily *SME* finance the establishment of its own printing facilities, thereby assuring its long-term survival, after the Meciar government blocked its access to its regular printer.[43]

The major limitation of both strategies lies in their exclusive focus on the privately owned media. Given the Meciar government's tight control of the state-run media, as well as its effort to interfere with the commercial viability of the independent media, this exclusion is understandable, even necessary. One unintended consequence, however, was that it tended to reinforce the commercialization of media content. As elsewhere, the priority of selling squeezes out less popular public interest programming, but in a country with a nascent and highly polarized public sphere, this trend could prove detrimental to the wider goal of developing democracy. Another is that the state media sector was deprived of the benefits of financial and managerial training that could prepare it to compete in a pluralistic media marketplace as a democratically accountable public service media in the post-Meciar era.

Ultimately, the viability of individual media outlets depends on a range of factors that international actors cannot influence directly, such as the vagaries of an oversaturated market and arbitrary political intrusions.[44] In the case of Slovakia, for example, some of the most commercially successful operations were precisely those that the Meciar government tried to shut down through punitive taxes, denial of broadcasting licenses, or frivolous libel suits. International actors had little power to protect individual outlets from such intrusions, but international support for commercial viability did manage to negotiate these limitations well, supplying the kind of support that most local media professionals desired most.

REGULATORY AND ASSOCIATIONAL FRAMEWORK (INFRASTRUCTURAL DEVELOPMENT)

Of all categories of assistance, support for regulatory reform and the development of professional organizations appeared to have the fewest perceptible effects. Given the dependence of regulatory reform on domestic political factors as well as the pervasive cultural bias against common journalistic standards, any international effort to effect change in these areas was likely to encounter major difficulties, regardless of the strategy chosen.

Thus, despite the profusion of Western legal and technical consultations, neither Slovak nor Czech journalists had yet succeeded in achieving new coherent press laws but remained governed by a hybrid of communist and postcommunist legislation. On a number of occasions, however, each group managed to prevent undesirable legislation from being enacted, manifesting some potential for collective action on behalf of their corporate professional interests.[45] Meanwhile, both syndicates, as well as functional associations such as the Czech Union of Publishers, the Slovak Union of Television Authors, and the Slovak Association of Regional Broadcasters, managed to increase their access to and influence on relevant parliamentary commissions and working groups while improving their knowledge of media law in general.

The development of professional associations proceeded slowly. By 1997 most had become members of the relevant international professional bodies and had established working ties across borders. The main problem lay in the persistently low level of their internal consolidation. On the whole, the functional associations, such as the Slovak Association of Regional Broadcasters, the Slovak Union of Television Authors, and their Czech equivalents, made faster progress than the journalists' associations. Perhaps this was because they were able to draw upon tighter and smaller social networks and because it is generally easier to get consensus on the technical and legal issues with which these bodies are concerned than with more the contentious issue of ethical reporting standards. In 1997 the Czech and Slovak Syndicates of Journalists claimed formal memberships of four thousand and twenty-three hundred, respectively. In fact, most were members in name only.[46]

In both countries a stubborn bias against participation in organizations of any kind was an abiding legacy of the communist era and one that even the growing activism of the syndicates in defense of professional interests had difficulty transcending. But there were other reasons why these organizations were slow to develop. In the Czech Republic, where the syndicate in the mid-1990s was still identified with the older "generation of '68-ers," young journalists were highly unwilling to join because they viewed the older generation, whether dissident or conformist, as tainted by their communist past.[47] In the Slovak case the prevailing political polarization, manifested by an organizational rivalry between the independent syndicate and the government-created Association of Slovak Journalists, made many journalists reluctant to join.

The same problems bedeviled efforts to promote journalistic ethics and establish a common code of conduct by which members of the profession would hold accreditation. The Czech Syndicate, for example, steadfastly rejected the idea of a press council. Likewise, it was highly averse to the creation of an association-wide professional code and criteria for membership, preferring instead to keep membership open and to leave ethical issues to individual journalists to work through for themselves. In principle, the Slovak syndicate supported both a common journalistic code and a European-style press council; in practice, however, it was slow to act on this commitment. Most working journalists did not see much value in establishing an industry-wide professional code, and even those outlets that did adopt their own journalistic standards kept them in the bottom drawer. The prevailing attitude was summed up by the then director of Nova Television, who in 1996 was quoted as saying, "We don't need ethical standards because we are professionals."[48]

EVALUATING INTERNATIONAL ASSISTANCE STRATEGIES

As with all forms of democracy assistance, developing and implementing reliable methods of evaluation and self-evaluation for media assistance activities has been a constant source of concern, as funders are understandably eager to ensure that their resources are being used effectively. According to several local NGO administrators and media beneficiaries, however, evaluation was often also a source of difficulty. They appreciated the need for financial accountability but often expressed frustration with funders' reporting requirements, which frequently changed from one reporting period to the next as funders' priorities changed. This forced local NGO administrators to engage in the time-consuming task of reevaluating their results according to changed standards.[49]

Another common complaint was that reporting requirements tended to stress quantifiable results: how many journalists had been trained, how many regional media outlets had participated, or how many workshops were held. As a means of measuring the relative success of efforts supporting the economic viability of media outlets, quantitative indicators were considered appropriate. However, where activities were targeted at more intangible goals, such as human capacity development, local NGO administrators and media beneficiaries viewed these quantitative measures as poor proxies at best, existing mostly for donor consumption.

Overall, in evaluating qualitative change, local program administrators tended to be wary of attempts to measure performance strictly according to preconceived Western standards of professional journalism, such as the separation of fact and opinion. Even in the West these standards are not uniformly shared or practiced, and journalistic norms vary from culture to culture without necessarily diminishing the reliability of media reporting or the quality of professional journalism. Typically, local NGO administrators tended to balance ideal measures of media independence with an empirical appraisal of the actual progress that journalists and media outlets had made in adapting to the manifold economic and professional challenges of their newly democratizing societies.

To their credit some Western funders of media assistance programs showed increasing sensitivity to these local concerns and modified their evaluation methods to include qualitative as well as quantitative measures. In 1998, for example, Pro-Media began issuing quarterly reports on the basis of USAID's standard results framework, which supplements quantitative criteria with a more sophisticated appraisal of the cumulative effect of activities on the quality and performance of those media outlets that have received assistance.

In seeking to discover which assistance strategies NGO administrators and aid recipients considered the most effective in promoting independent media, it was necessary to get beyond the obligatory recitation of facts and figures. I asked interviewees a series of open-ended questions, including: "Which of your projects or programs do you feel were most successful, and why?" "Which assistance strategies do you feel were most effective in assisting the development of independent media?" and "What type of training did you find most beneficial to your professional development?" This approach had the advantage of eliciting the respondents' own criteria for success and effectiveness while allowing them to speak at length about the qualitative effect of particular assistance efforts. Reflecting the relatively underdeveloped articulation of overall assistance strategies mentioned earlier, however, respondents generally offered more detailed comments on concrete activities and tasks than on the relationship that these activities had to the broader goals of media assistance that Western donors typically espoused.

CONCLUSION: LESSONS LEARNED

The efforts to assist the mass media in these two transitional countries suggest several practical lessons that may contribute to more effective media assistance elsewhere. All international assistance agencies operate under the donor-driven need to show results quickly. Often this sense of urgency precludes opportunities for proper planning and coordination of assistance activities, let alone a clear understanding of the local political context and media culture to which these activities are addressed. While such constraints are not likely to disappear, the funders can strike a better balance between the desire for quick and visible results and ensuring that assistance is optimally designed. In order to promote a mass media that is both professional and supportive of democratic culture, funders should give special attention to distinguishing opposition media from independent media, integrating media support with other efforts at civil society and democratic development, and ensuring diversity within the mass media. To their credit the more astute NGOs—having confronted realities in these countries—undertook midcourse corrections that incorporated many of these insights to good effect.[50]

STRATEGIC THINKING

NGOs need to engage in more careful, strategic planning before they begin their assistance efforts: Too often, start-up projects scatter resources in all directions, duplicating the work of other agencies and providing generous support at inappropriate times or in inappropriate circumstances. International actors that may have a clear idea of the end goal have given less thought to the process and methods of attaining it. Often they fall back on catchall programs. The tendency for some donors to create new media assistance vehicles ex nihilo (such as USAID's Independent Media Fund), rather than adapting and deploying the skills and knowledge of existing journalism NGOs, wasted time and resources. In both countries that I surveyed, it took nearly six years to establish a coherent division of labor among international media assistance actors.

Donors could avoid these problems by resisting the impulse to do everything themselves. Instead, they might use a clear but flexible division of labor, in which, for example, journalists take the initiative for training journalists through their own national and international NGOs and professional associations; legal and regulatory reforms are left to the appropriate international and local bodies, rather than to consultants flown in on an ad hoc basis; and financial and managerial support is provided by specialized grant and loan funds created for this purpose and staffed with specialized practitioners of media management, production, sales, and marketing.

Of course, any division of labor presumes a high level of communication and coordination among a variety of assistance actors, a condition that is not always met. Over time, nearly all the major media assistance agencies surveyed did manage to establish some informal coordination and sometimes even cooperation. This learning curve could be shortened by expanding central Internet databases (such as those launched by the International Freedom of Expression Exchange, the International Federation of Journalists, and the Soros Network Media Program), which could provide a clearinghouse of concise and comprehensive information for donors, NGO partners, and beneficiaries about who is doing what, how, and where.

The experience of international media assistance in these countries underscores the need to undertake discriminating assessments of recipient needs from the outset. In the early 1990s such assessments typically took second place to the desire of international donors to get as much aid in place as quickly as possible. This logic appears to be a central factor in the early reliance on training courses by outside experts and indiscriminate equipment drops. These cases also highlight the importance of taking into account the prevailing political and economic conditions affecting media development in different countries and designing strategies accordingly. In places where democracy is relatively well established, and where the market generates enough investment resources, media independence is likely to be a less pressing issue than media professionalism. Here, as many international actors have since learned, assistance may be most profitably directed to specialized training in new technologies, the development of regulatory and associational frameworks that can help establish and enforce codes of professional conduct, and the integration of local media into a larger transnational information and professional community. In places where the political and commercial environment is less secure, these activities should be subordinated to efforts to provide individual media outlets with an adequate technical and financial base.

PROMOTION OF PROFESSIONALISM, NOT POLITICS

International actors must be extremely wary of the trade-off involved in mistaking avowals of democracy for evidence of professionalism and of mistaking opposition media outlets for independent professional media. In virtually any endeavor to promote democratic development in transitional countries, a natural strategy is to seek out and support those indigenous individuals and organizations that most visibly ally with democratic ideals. However, opposition to the state and commitment to democracy are not necessarily the same thing. Moreover, even those journalists and media outlets that embrace democratic norms do not necessarily embrace or practice the norms of professional journalism, and they can be just as prone to biased journalistic practices as any state-run media.[51] While such an approach may help to professionalize opposition media, it risks perpetuating a highly partisan press, thereby compromising the achievement of objective fact-based reporting and undermining the credibility of assistance agencies as nonpartisan actors.

When society is profoundly polarized and governments are actively hostile to the very existence of an independent media, such partisanship may be unavoidable, and international actors may have little choice but to work with the opposition media. If so, they should be careful to pick those individuals or outlets that are, above all else, demonstrably committed to professional journalism. At the same time international assistance should be directed at nurturing an institutional and normative infrastructure, for example, by assisting the development of professional associations, which places an inclusive ethos of journalistic professionalism ahead of partisan politics.[52]

INTEGRATION OF MEDIA SUPPORT AND OTHER FORMS OF DEMOCRACY ASSISTANCE

Media support needs to be integrated with other democracy promotion activities, especially those aimed at strengthening civil society organizations and local government reform. Virtually all the major state and international donors (USAID, PHARE, the British Know How Fund, the Soros network of foundations) treated media assistance as part of their democracy assistance programs, and international NGOs, such as Pro-Media and the Independent Journalism Foundation, also justified their media projects in terms of their putative benefit to democratic development.

Ironically, however, few if any projects explicitly linked the media with other areas of democracy assistance.[53] An effective way to reinforce both the positive influence of the independent media and the capacities of civil society might be to create media watchdog groups or media literacy programs that assist indigenous NGOs, local officials, and the general public in understanding the role of the press in democratic conditions and help citizens to become critical consumers and users of the mass media and the information that they disseminate. By providing additional incentives for responsible and accurate journalism, such projects would also help to overcome the profound lack of popular confidence in the credibility of the mass media that pervades virtually all transitional societies. At the time this study was conducted, however, no such projects existed.

PROMOTION OF DIVERSE FORMS OF MEDIA

There is a need to mitigate the corrosive effects of the commercial media in environments where a democratic public sphere is still nascent. While promoting commercial viability is doubtless a necessary condition for a self-sustaining independent media, the goal of market success is often in conflict with the goal of promoting a well-informed citizenry. The quest for revenues often comes to dictate content, such as imported entertainment and sensational news at the expense of public interest items. In virtually all established democracies, the public service media are a vital component of a pluralistic marketplace of ideas.[54] While most European-based agencies did support efforts to transform the state media into public service media, virtually all U.S.-based agencies, the dominant actors in the media sector, ignored this area. One negative consequence of this neglect is that the norms and practices of the public service media were poorly developed, while the state-run media—which remained dominant in any case—had little exposure to professional production and reporting values, continued to operate with poor management and technology, and were ill equipped to assert managerial and editorial autonomy against political intrusion, to which they remained the most vulnerable.

Finding appropriate partners and devising effective assistance to the state sector can, of course, be problematic in conditions where the state-run media are instruments of ruling governments hostile to press freedom. However, the exclusion of this sector from the benefits of assistance risks perpetuating the politicization of the media and undermining the creation of a coherent profes-

sional identity for the media as the fourth estate. The neglect of the public service media also undermines the human capital and infrastructural capacity for
the development of indigenous public interest and cultural programming that
can effectively compete with imported and commercial programs.[55] One way to
extend the benefits of assistance to the state media sector while limiting the risk
of abuse is to support human capacity development. An approach worthy of
wider adoption is the British Know How Fund's active, consistent, and assertive
efforts to include in journalism and management training programs individual
media professionals who worked in the state sector and to support their participation in inclusive professional associations.

NOTES

1. For an overview see Megan Kearns, "U.S. Assistance to the Information Sector in
Eastern Europe," working paper, Project on East European Media and Society, Univer-
sity of Texas, 1994, p. 2, available at http://www.utexas.edu/ftp/depts/eems/megan.html
(November 12, 2001).

2. The Pro-Media Program of the International Research and Exchanges Board
and the International Journalism Foundation (IJF), for example, explicitly ties media
support to democracy building: The broad goal of the former is "increased [and] better
informed citizen participation in public policy decision-making"; the goal of the IJF is
"helping the people of East and Central Europe make informed decisions by supporting a free press." See International Research and Exchanges Board (IREX), *Annual
Report, 1998*, www.irex.org/publications-resources/annual-report/1998/ (November 13,
2001). See also International Journalism Foundation, Mission Statement, http://www
.ijf-cij.org (November 12, 2001).

3. This finding is also corroborated by preliminary evidence from Croatia and Serbia,
where the fledgling independent media were extremely circumscribed by hostile governments throughout the 1990s, especially during the wars, and where international assistance has provided surrogate technical and infrastructural support at critical junctures.
(Staff of Soros Regional Media Program, interviews by author, Budapest, July 1997; and
staff of Media Loan Development Fund, interviews by author, Prague, July 1997).

4. Thomas Carothers, *Assessing Democracy Assistance: The Case of Romania*
(Washington D.C.: Carnegie Endowment for International Peace, 1996), pp. 7–8.

5. Alexander Motyl, "Institutional Legacies and Reform Trajectories," in Adrian
Karatnycky, Alexander Motyl, and Boris Shor, eds., *Nations in Transit, 1997* (New
Brunswick, N.J.: Transaction, 1997), p. 21.

6. U.S. government and nongovernmental agencies provide an estimated 80 percent of the total international funding for independent media assistance in Slovakia
(staff of USAID, interviews by author, Bratislava, June 1997).

7. "Czech Republic," in Karatnycky, Motyl, and Shor, *Nations in Transit, 1997*, p. 122.

8. Ibid.

9. See Jan Culik, "Truth, Freedom, and the Pursuit of Profits," *Transitions* 4, no. 3
(August 1997): pp. 88–92.

10. In both countries an aversion to even self-regulation was most pronounced among the "generation of '68-ers," journalists who resumed their careers after the Velvet Revolution and whose ethos was shaped by their participation in the anticommunist struggle (Rudolf Zeman, director, Czech Syndicate of Journalists, interview by author, Prague, June 1997). On the difficulties that the generation of '68-ers encountered in the transition to democracy, see Andrej Skolkay, "Postcommunist Journalism: Problems and Issues" (paper presented at the annual conference of the Association for the Study of Nationalities, Columbia University, New York, April 1998); and Jiri Pehe, "Reshaping Dissident Ideals for the Postcommunist World," *Civnet Journal*, March–April 1998, http://www.civnet.org/journal/journal_frameset.htm (November 12, 2001).

11. Culik, "Truth, Freedom, and Pursuit of Profits" p. 88; and Kevin Done, "Nova TV: European Company Licensed to Print Money," *Financial Times* (London), September 3, 1997.

12. Jaroslav Veis, press spokesman for Speaker of the Czech Senate and former journalist, interview by author, Prague, June 1997.

13. Veis and Zeman interviews.

14. Ibid. In 1999 the Czech syndicate finally adopted an ethics code and established a supervisory ethics committee. This may have been enabled by the appointment of a new, younger leadership. See "Czech Republic," in Adrian Karatnycky, Alexander Motyl, and Aili Piano, eds., *Nations in Transit, 1999–2000*, (Rutgers, N.J.: Transaction, 2001), p. 226.

15. Ron Synovits, "Slovakia: Using Taxes to Inhibit the Press: An Analysis," *RFE-RL*, November 13, 1997, http://www.rferl.org/nca/features/1997/11/F.RU971106133017.htm (November 12, 2001). See also Committee to Protect Journalists, *Attacks on the Press*, annual reports, 1997, 1998 (New York: Committee to Protect Journalists, 1997, 1998).

16. Committee to Protect Journalists, *Attacks on the Press*, 1997.,

17. European Fund for Freedom of Expression, *Democracy's Progress in Central and Eastern Europe: 1997*, third report (Paris: European Fund for Freedom of Expression, 1997), pp. 94–95.

18. Andrej Skolkay, media specialist, Department of Political Science, Comenius University, interview by author, Bratislava, June 1997.

19. In 1996 the audience share of Markiza was already 48 percent ("Slovakia," in Karatnycky, Motyl, and Shor, *Nations in Transit, 1997*, p. 342).

20. The evidence strongly suggests that this was simply a pretext and that the Meciar-led government was punishing Radio Twist for its critical reporting (Martin Lengyel, Radio Twist, interview by author, New York, November 1997). See also Committee to Protect Journalists, *Attacks on the Press*, 1997.

21. Skolkay interview.

22. Staff of Media Loan Development Fund, interviews by author, Prague, July 1997.

23. Staff of USAID Democracy Programs in Slovakia, interviews by author, Bratislava, June 1997.

24. Thomas Carothers, "Democracy Assistance: The Question of Strategy," *Demokratizatsiya* 4, no. 3 (1997): 111.

25. His definition differs slightly from that developed by Kevin Quigley to distinguish between funders' styles "on the bases of where the impetus for grant-making rests." See Kevin F.F. Quigley, "For Democracy's Sake: How Funders Succeed and Fail," *World Policy Journal* 13 (Spring 1996): 111.

26. Soros-supported assistance efforts come the closest to typifying a purely reactive strategy.

27. Again, this usage diverges from that of Quigley, who uses the term *interactive* to describe situations where "it is difficult to locate the impetus [of grant making] precisely and there is a high degree of collaboration between the grant seeker and the funder" (Quigley, "For Democracy's Sake," p. 111).

28. USAID staff interviews.

29. Staff, Regional Media Program, interviews by author, Budapest, July 1997.

30. Media Loan Development Fund staff interviews.

31. As a government agency, USAID avoids direct financing of media outlets.

32. According to Zdeno Cho, coordinator of media programs for USAID, this collaboration was discontinued for "organizational reasons," although other observers alluded to irreconcilable differences concerning the assistance strategies preferred by USAID and Pro-Media and those preferred by local partners (Zdeno Cho, interview by author, Bratislava, June 1997).

33. According to Sasa Vucinic, managing director of the Media Loan Development Fund, in Eastern European media outlets management either fell by default to the worst journalists on staff or was reluctantly taken up by the most active working journalists, who had little time to devote to managerial tasks (Vucinic, interview by author, Prague, July 1997).

34. Vucinic interview; Serge Koperdak, Pro-Media consultant, interview by author, Bratislava, June 1997. Pro-Media had operations in Albania, Belarus, Bulgaria, Croatia, Hungary, Romania, Serbia, Slovakia, and Ukraine. For descriptions of its activities in these countries, see Pro-Media's semiannual reports.

35. Tatiana Rajnakova, media coordinator, Open Society Institute, interview by author, Bratislava, June 1997; Biljana Tatomir and Algis Lipstas, Regional Media Fund, interviews by author, Budapest, July 1997.

36. Poland and Hungary: Action for the Restructuring of the Economy (PHARE), Article 19, the International Federation of Journalists, and PressNow cosponsored an international conference in Prague in 1996 called "Freedom of Expression and the Media in International Law and Practice."

37. For example, PHARE, the British Know How Fund, the French Institute, the Foundation for Civil Society, and the Hans Seidel Stiftung cosponsored a 1996 international seminar in cooperation with the Slovak Union of Television Authors called "Ethics and the Development of the Communication Sector." The Slovak Syndicate of Journalists, PHARE, and the International Federation of Journalists cosponsored a 1996 conference and publication called "Journalist Ethics and Press Councils."

38. Changing the larger cultural and political climate was the stated objective of a variety of journalism advocacy groups and human rights monitors such as Freedom House, the Committee to Protect Journalists, PressNow, Article 19, and the International Forum

for Freedom of Expression, all of which seek to defend the media by mobilizing international opinion against violations of journalists' rights and media freedoms.

39. Vucinic interview; Martin Lengyel, Radio Twist, interview by author, Bratislava, June 1997; and Katarina Vajdova, director, Center for Independent Journalism, interview by author, Bratislava, June 1997.

40. Olga Holeckova, Center for Independent Journalism, interview by author, Prague, July 1997; Vucinic interview.

41. Pro-Media was established in 1995 and took nearly two years to set up a fully functioning office in Slovakia. The Media Loan Development Fund was also created in 1995. Because of its highly selective and careful vetting and consultation process, the fund had approved only nine loans in all of Eastern Europe by July 1997 (Koperdak and Vucinic interviews).

42. IREX, *Annual Report, 1998*.

43. Vucinic interview.

44. USAID staff interviews.

45. In 1996 lobbying by the Czech syndicate helped to prevent passage of a law that would have obliged journalists to disclose their sources. The repeated blocking of Meciar's attempts to pass the Law on the Protection of the Republic in 1995–1996 may be partly attributed to the lobbying efforts of the Slovak syndicate, although President Mikhal Kovac would likely have vetoed it in any case.

46. Veis, Holeckova, Zeman, Lengyel (Bratislava), and Koperdak interviews.

47. Tellingly, Holeckova cited the rigidity of the Czech Syndicate of Journalism as the main reason that the Czech Center of Independent Journalism conducted so few collaborative projects with it in the mid-1990s (Holeckova interview).

48. Veis interview.

49. Donors and NGO administrators were generally reluctant to provide details about either the methods or the results of their internal evaluations. One consultant to a U.S.-run program attributed this reluctance to frequent changes in personnel, organization, and mission—meaning that it had not yet developed a satisfactory system of evaluation.

50. For example, since launching Pro-Media II in 1999 (which extends assistance to the Balkans and the Caucasus), Pro-Media's program has been committed to "flexible and demand-driven programs . . . designed to meet specific needs on the ground" and "to a 'bottom up' versus 'top down' approach," which is responsive rather than proactive. See IREX, *Annual Report, 1998*.

51. For example, in the early postcommunist years Western observers routinely hailed the Prague daily *Lidove Noviny* as a standardbearer of independent journalism, largely because of its long-established samizdat identity as an anticommunist, dissident publication. In fact, *Lidove Noviny* suffered from low journalistic standards, engaged in some highly dubious reporting, particular in its biased and inflammatory coverage of Czech-Slovak relations before the Velvet Divorce, and ultimately proved unable to establish itself as a credible source of impartial fact-based reporting. It has lost its best journalists and is unprofitable. Ironically, the daily *Pravo*, the successor to the communist organ *Rude Pravo*, has become recognized as one of the best sources of hard

news reporting by any Czech daily (Veis and Holeckova interviews). See also Skolkay, "Postcommunist Journalism."

52. On the importance of promoting an integrated marketplace of ideas in democratizing states, see Jack Snyder and Karen Ballentine, "Nationalism and the Marketplace of Ideas," *International Security* 21, no. 2 (Fall 1996): 1–36.

53. The only activities that sought to promote some intersectoral democracy assistance were the Foundation for Civil Society's programs in Prague and Bratislava for training NGO leaders to write press releases and conduct press briefings, the Center for Independent Journalism (IJF) workshops for government press representatives, and the EU-funded Foundation for Civil Society support for a weekly radio spot featuring NGO activities (Ingrid Baummanova, program officer, Foundation for Civil Society, interview by author, Bratislava, June 1997; Katarina Vajdova, director, Center for Independent Journalism, interview by author, Bratislava, June 1997; and Irene Zemankova, program officer, Foundation for Civil Society, interview by author, Prague, July 1997).

54. John Keane, "Democracy and the Media: Without Foundations," in David Held, ed., *Prospects for Democracy: North, South, East, West*, pp. 235–53 (Stanford, Calif.: Stanford University Press, 1993).

55. Lubomir Fifik, head of the Union of Slovak Television Authors, interview by author, Bratislava, June 1997.

Chapter 5

WESTERN AND RUSSIAN ENVIRONMENTAL NGOS:
A GREENER RUSSIA?

Leslie Powell

Since the mid-1980s foreign governments, multilateral institutions, and foreign and international foundations have committed well over a billion dollars to address environmental issues in the Russian Federation.[1] By and large, foreign and international funders have viewed these efforts as either democracy assistance or technical assistance, quite distinct from the even larger sums involved in economic assistance packages. While a billion dollars for environmental assistance may sound impressive, its effect on environmental protection and natural resource management in Russia has been quite limited, even marginal. However, its effect on the development of citizens' environmental advocacy groups in Russia is notable.

In this chapter I consider the assistance programs of foreign and international foundations (nongovernmental organizations or private donor foundations) that are actively providing environmental aid to Russia. I find that the success of these assistance programs cannot be measured in environmentally progressive change or in heightened concern among national or local decision makers for environmental issues. Indeed, using those criteria to gauge the influence of these programs would lead to only one verdict: that they have been a failure. However, these programs have succeeded in substantially assisting the establishment and development of third-sector organizations in Russia. To some degree they have helped to forge democratic channels between civil society and political society that previously did not exist and that allow Russians to express interest and participate in environmental policy making.

Foreign and international foundations have granted nearly all their environmental aid to the so-called third sector in Russia, as opposed to the state or commercial sectors. This aid has empowered social actors, created communication networks both horizontally and vertically, raised the level of public awareness of both environmental and democratic issues, and helped to make civil society groups more professional, organized, and strategic. This success has come by way of imported Western ideas of communication, coalition building, strategy, and professionalism that have taken hold firmly among many civic advocacy groups in Russia. However, despite these successes, no significant alteration has occurred in the state-society balance of power.[2]

Aid from foreign and international foundations has, as yet, had conspicuously little effect on the environment or on the implementation of environmental policy. The major reasons for this failure are the weakness of the post-Soviet state, and of channels for societal participation, and the connection between environmental and economic or industrial issues.

First, the Russian state not only has little control over industrial and commercial interests but it has a difficult time policing itself: The state bureaucracy has been a major violator of environmental law in Russia. Meager budgetary resources and nearly continuous administrative and organizational flux—the constant instability of elites and institutions—contribute to the state's weak and ineffectual nature vis-à-vis environmental protection and natural resource management. Since his accession on New Year's Eve 1999, President Vladimir Putin has worked successfully to strengthen the state and now presides over the first federal budget surplus; however, the state overall remains bloated and ineffectual in a number of areas.

Second, channels for societal participation are still weak. The state enjoys a high level of autonomy: It lacks accountability, and democratic processes are absent or malfunctioning. In addition, the party system is weak in a representational sense, both generally and with respect to environmental interests. Although the larger parties pay lip service to environmental issues, even the "green" parties (KEDR and the Green Party) are either green in name only or politically powerless.

A third cause of failure is the inextricable link—as well as the undeniable tension—between environmental and economic or industrial issues. The sheer magnitude of both problems and their connection to each other means that resolving environmental issues by addressing only one and not the other is impossible. Industrial pollution, for example, is a problem that cannot be fully addressed without simultaneously tackling the health and reconstitution of the economy as well as the industrial infrastructure of the country. Yet most Western nongovernmental organizations that fund environmental aid programs do not address the economic or industrial sources of environmental problems. Economic assistance is usually considered an issue area separate and distinct from democracy or technical assistance. There are exceptions. For example, the European Union's program of Technical Assistance to the Commonwealth of Independent States attempts to combine environmental and industrial or commercial issues in many of its assistance programs. However, such issue linkage is absent from the strategies of most foreign nongovernmental assistance programs.

The Western nongovernmental funders that do use holistic programs and build coalitions among environmental, economic, social, and state actors have had a more substantive effect on both the development of third-sector groups and the political-environmental process in Russia. Thus those Western foundations whose sole goal is to assist in the development of the third sector, making it in effect the third leg of the democratic stool, have achieved some level of success. If the goals, however, are to improve Russia's environment as well as its environmental policies and practices, assistance programs would be much more effective if the grantors paid attention to building coalitions among the various sectors rather than giving money only to third-sector groups.

The arguments that I make in this chapter draw primarily on interviews that I conducted from June to August 1998 with representatives of most of the key Western groups providing environmental assistance to Russia as well as with those of many important Russian recipient groups. I conducted most in Russia and many in the Russian language; a few took place in the United States. This chapter is also informed by a nearly yearlong trip in 1999 during which I researched environmental politics in Russia. Most of the assistance programs considered here commenced only in 1992–1993, after the breakup of the Soviet Union, and thus had been active for less than ten years, making evaluation a challenging task. Several foundations were involved with Soviet citizens' groups in the perestroika period but had been able to send money into the country and cooperate in a substantive way only after the collapse of the Soviet system. Thus while their involvement may predate the 1990s, their funding programs and unfettered collaboration do not.

The Western organizations that I chose for this study have a high profile in the sphere of environmental assistance to Russia. Russian funding recipients mentioned them repeatedly in conversation, and their names appear frequently in the literature on Western interaction with the environmental movement in Russia. In addition, I selected a relatively diverse set, ranging from those that mainly work on advocacy (such as Greenpeace) to those that function mainly as donors to local groups (such as the Initiative for Social Action and Renewal in Eurasia [ISAR] and the John D. and Catherine T. MacArthur Foundation) to those that engage at the highest political level as well as in worldwide scientific movements (such as the World Wide Fund for Nature and the Green Cross).

In this chapter I first trace the history of environmental politics in the Soviet Union and Russia. I then go on to analyze the primary strategies used by Western NGOs engaged in environmental assistance to Russian third-sector groups, and I provide examples of each. Next I address the effects and limitations of these assistance strategies, as well as several theoretical explanations for the weakness of third-sector environmentalism in the post-Soviet context. I identify the double-headed strategy of interactive cooperation and multisectoral coalition building as having the greatest influence. Then I assess how Western NGOs evaluate their own assistance programs, make some suggestions for enhancing this process, and consider several lessons learned. Finally, I bring readers up to date on relevant political developments since I researched and wrote this chapter.

HISTORICAL AND POLITICAL CONTEXT:
TRANSITIONS AND ENVIRONMENTALISM

The case of environmental politics in Russia under conditions of democratization presents compelling issues. First, the poor state of the environment in Russia, as well as in the entire former communist bloc, has become an international cause célèbre.[3] Environmental issues are, by their very nature, transboundary and even planetary in consequence. Given the size of the territory involved in the case of Russia, which spans a sixth of the earth's landmass, environmental issues are of concern to diplomats, scientists, activists, and the public everywhere.

Second, the environmental movement during perestroika was a powerful vehicle for citizen protest and the promotion of sweeping political change. It offered an entry point for Western foundations seeking to assist the development of the third sector in the Soviet Union. Given the relative strength, reach, and organization of the Soviet environmental movement in the late 1980s, Western NGOs that wanted to work with citizen advocacy groups in the Soviet Union were able to get started quickly with environmental groups, even when those same Western groups had no experience in working on environmental issues.[4]

Third, the subsequent weakness of the environmental movement, as well as of the third sector in general, in the post-Soviet context presents challenges for scholars as well as practitioners. Given the vivacity and evident influence of the Soviet environmental movement in the late 1980s and early 1990s, what accounts for its dramatic decline?

Russians who are environmentally active often claim a long history for environmentalism in their country, dating to tsarist times.[5] Because of the controlling and repressive nature of the Soviet political system, environmentalism in the Soviet Union was for the most part either an outright fiction or a result of efforts by the Communist Party leadership to turn what could have been an autonomous social organization into a state-sponsored and thus highly controlled activity. Ecological groups in the Soviet period were allowed to address *only* nature conservation and uncontroversial scientific issues.[6] Organizations such as the All-Russian Society for the Protection of Nature (VOOP) were top-down constructs that channeled citizens' concerns for the environment away from overtly political issues and toward a sort of benign, uncritical, nature-loving exercise.[7]

The Stalin-era rush to industrialize contained the seeds of the Soviet approach to the environment, namely, that humans could and should be the master of nature. Official Soviet ideology claimed that the socialist command economy—centrally organized and rational—was incapable of disturbing the environment in any significant way; disorganized capitalism disrupted nature with its polluting and destructive environmental externalities. Under Stalin it became the norm for Soviet industrial enterprises to be formally responsible for policing their own environmental impact and conformity with environmental regulations. Thus polluter and police were one, and because the imperatives of industrial growth were far stronger than environmental concerns, the environmental impact departments of industrial enterprises were exceedingly weak or highly corrupt.

Under Mikhail Gorbachev citizens were allowed to engage in autonomous, self-organized activity free of state control. After Soviet authorities finally acknowledged the extent of the 1986 explosion at the Chernobyl nuclear power plant, and when Soviet citizens learned that their government had made a concerted effort to suppress information about what had happened, citizen protests against nuclear power and other state-sponsored, environmentally questionable activities (such as the infamous river diversion project in Siberia) burst vigorously into the open.

In 1988 the state took its first step toward responding. The Central Committee of the Communist Party and the USSR Council of Ministers adopted a resolution called On the Radical Reconstruction [Perestroika] of Environmental Protection Activities in the Country. As a result, the State Committee on Nature Protection (Goskompriroda) was formed. Important in at least a symbolic way, its creation was "a significant change from the traditional Soviet view of environmental problems as discrete technological issues . . . . The structure of *Goskompriroda* reflected a progressive, systemic approach to environmental protection in recognition of the fact that environmental degradation had grown in size and complexity to become a regional, national, and international concern."[8] The Goskompriroda created a public council that sponsored unprecedented open hearings on environmental issues. During the first years of its existence, however, Goskompriroda operated in a virtual vacuum with respect to environmental legislation, policy, and practices.[9] Only several years later, after the complete dissolution of the state, would a more solid legal and regulatory environment be established.[10]

Since 1992 Russia's environmental efforts have been chaotic. Frequent changes in state environmental institutions, unclear relationships among these institutions, their often overlapping responsibilities, and the shifting content of environmental laws have produced a highly unstable and often perplexing setting in which environmentally concerned citizens, advocacy groups, and decision makers must operate.

A telling example of such institutional instability is the history of Goskompriroda itself. Since its inception in 1988 this agency has undergone three major face-lifts. Even before the breakup of the Soviet Union, it had already been transformed from a state committee into the USSR Ministry of Ecology. In 1992 it became the Ministry of Protection of the Environment and Natural Resources of the Russian Federation. This transformation entailed the abolishment of seven USSR ministries and four republican ministries and the partial merging of several state committees.[11] In 1992–1993 the new Russian Federation's environment ministry and the partially merged state committees engaged in a power struggle. The result was a weak new ministry after the various state committees were able to reclaim most of their former responsibilities. After Yeltsin's reelection in the summer of 1996, the ministry was demoted once again to the status of a state committee and renamed Goskomekologia. In May 2000 Putin abolished the state committee altogether and relegated its primary function—that of environmental monitoring—to the Ministry of Natural Resources. Environmentalists considered this move absurd, given that the Ministry of Natural Resources is, at core, in the business of resource usage, not protection. The comments of an observer speaking of an earlier time remained true: "The structure of executive power is in a permanent state of reorganization, enlargement, disenlargement, and even liquidation of some bodies, which have to be restored again later."[12]

In addition, the overall political turmoil of Russia's transition from authoritarian centralism adds to the confusion on the environmental front. As power shifted from the center to the regions under the numerous and varying power-sharing agreements that Moscow signed with the majority of the eighty-nine "subjects of the federation" (including oblasts, *krais*, and republics), the locus of power and responsibility for environmental issues became ever blurrier. Beginning in the early 1990s, individual "subjects" began establishing their own regional ecological departments, while the Russian Federation Ministry of the Environment (later Goskomekologia) simultaneously created its own branch offices in the regions. The relationships between these regional authorities were not always clear and differed from region to region. By and large, Goskomekologia's branch offices performed an evaluative, regulatory, and monitoring (*kontrol'nyi*) role, tracking polluters and payments of fines. Regional ecological departments, on the other hand, tended to take a more active, executive (*ispolnitel'nyi*) role, by disbursing funds for environmental projects and helping to set regional environmental policy. In a few regions only one or the other agency existed, in which case it wore both hats, further obscuring the lines of authority. In Moscow in 1999 the head of the city's environmental protection department and the head of the city's Goskomekologia branch division were one and the same man.

Many observers of and participants in Russian environmental politics agree that power over environmental issues now resides in the regions, not the center. Thus as a Russian sociologist of social movements noted, Goskomekologia's branch offices in many regions were no more influential than NGOs in the sense of having little actual power in the regions and no funding to speak of.[13] But given the varying power of regions vis-à-vis the center, as well as the varying configurations of power and personalities within each region, such statements, while generally true, were not universally so. Goskomekologia's funding was cut so drastically after 1998 that many regional and local branch offices had to lay off a significant percentage of their staffs before dissolving them altogether. Funding for the regional ecology departments, however, is more secure, as regional administrations have direct control of these budgets.

Environmental legislation in post-Soviet Russia has also been in flux. Environmentalists consider the 1991 Soviet Russian republic (RSFSR) law, On Protection of the Natural Environment, to be the most progressive piece of environmental legislation produced by Russian lawmaking bodies to date. Many consider it to be even more progressive than the Environment for Europe convention adopted at the European Ministerial Conference in Aarhus, Denmark, in June 1998 in the extent of its provisions for public participation in environmental decision making. The 1991 Russian law provides for a significant role for both individuals and NGOs to assist with monitoring and enforcement activities and guarantees the rights to free association and access to information, to seek legal redress for environmental degradation, and to make public demands for and participate in environmental impact assessments (EIAs).[14]

Unfortunately, many laws that Russia has passed since 1991 have been less forward looking in both ecological and participatory terms.[15] A 1995 EIA law does not provide for public participation in state EIAs and sets up procedures and restrictions so complex that citizens' groups usually cannot comply.[16] One long-time observer has called the 1996 Russian Federation law on public environmental review "terrible, but better than nothing"; it requires state organs to provide environmental materials associated with industrial projects to the public for review but only "at the eleventh hour and fifty-ninth minute."[17] In addition, "a veil of secrecy surrounds the activities of the ministries and agencies as they issue numerous regulations that often contradict laws and violate citizens' rights"; even the most progressive laws are poorly enforced.[18]

STRATEGIES OF WESTERN NGOS

The programs of most foreign and international NGOs typically encompass a wide range of activities and strategies, many of which have evolved over time and have been greatly influenced by the indigenous Russian groups with which they work. Thus categorizing each foundation is nearly impossible. Nonetheless, we may compare the various strategies in play in several ways. Table 5.1 illustrates one way. The foundations listed represent general types, not a hard-and-fast match, and are meant as examples only.

The NGOs under consideration devote the overwhelming majority of their assistance to third-sector actors, that is, nonstate, noncommercial actors. The divide between grassroots and elite recipients is therefore in some ways a spurious one. *Elite* in this context does not necessarily refer to state actors; instead, it may refer to nongovernmental actors who are not focused on the masses. Whereas the British donor Charities Aid Foundation provides assistance to community-based initiatives, the MacArthur Foundation is committed to supporting intellectual and academic efforts, especially when the projects proposed are policy relevant. I call the latter focus *elite*.

Where assistance is provided to state actors (a small percentage of the total), the more traditional conception of *elite* applies. The MacArthur Foundation has on several occasions granted funds to the Russian Federation Ministry of the Environment and to individual state-run nature preserves (*zapovedniki*). The World Wide Fund for Nature (WWF) assists regional and national parliaments with the drafting of environmental legislation and has provided money, equipment, and training to *zapovedniki* around the country. While *zapovednik* personnel may not enjoy a high level of decision-making authority, they are nonetheless State Forest Service employees and are therefore more elite than grassroots.

The divide between support for the third sector generally and support for environmental groups is much clearer (see table 5.1). Western NGOs have mission statements or charters that set forth their overarching goals and thus determine their strategies. Of the groups under consideration here, about half aid environmental groups as a way to support the development of the third sector more generally, and the others support environmental groups because they themselves are environmentally active. Thus, for example, the Pennsylvania-based, nonprofit group Ecologia works exclusively with Russian environmental NGOs

TABLE 5.1 Strategies of Western Environmental NGOs
by Goal Orientation and Type of Recipient

		Goal Orientation	
		Civil Society	**Environment**
Recipient	**Grassroots**	Charities Aid Foundation	Ecologia
	Elite	MacArthur Foundation	World Wide Fund for Nature

TABLE 5.2 Strategies of Western Environmental NGOs
by Idea Source and Type of Involvement

		Idea Source	
		Indigenous	Imported
Type of	Project Financing	A	B
Involvement	Interactive Assistance	C	D

to promote high-quality monitoring of waterways, whereas the Charities Aid Foundation supports environmental groups as part of its effort to support the development of Russian nonprofit groups in general.

Table 5.2 illustrates another way to categorize strategies that the Western NGOs use. Nearly all the NGOs use a combination of these strategies, and examples of each (A, B, C, and D) are discussed below. An interactive strategy entails some level of substantive, programmatic cooperation or collaboration between donor and recipient, whereas project financing is limited to donations of money or equipment without substantive participation by the donor organization in the project itself. Alternatively, the difference may be thought of as that between process-driven and product-driven strategies, respectively, though the line between these concepts often is blurred. Simply put, a process-driven strategy is one in which the funder is engaged at some or all points between the start and end of a project, whereas a product-driven strategy tends to be limited to only the start and end points.

A: PROJECT FINANCING FOR INDIGENOUS IDEAS

Perhaps the clearest example of a strategy of project financing for indigenous ideas was the massive funding program called Seeds of Democracy that was administered by the U.S. nonprofit organization ISAR under a cooperative agreement with the U.S. Agency for International Development (USAID) from 1993 to 1997. Seeds of Democracy awarded approximately five hundred small grants (up to $5,000, for a total of about $1 million) to environmental NGOs throughout Russia. The competition process required indigenous groups to submit project proposals. All proposals that secured grants were indigenous ideas and subject to minimal guidelines from ISAR (no commercial ventures, no purely scientific projects, preference to projects that benefit the community at large or have a policy angle). Over time, groups seeking funding through the Seeds of Democracy project, having become aware of ISAR's preferences, tended to tailor their project proposals to include community-at-large or policy elements. Thus indigenous and imported ideas eventually were mixed. ISAR itself did not become substantively involved in any of the funded projects; it merely acted as a funnel (albeit an interested party) for grant money.

B:PROJECT FINANCING FOR IMPORTED IDEAS

In 1991–1992 Battelle Memorial Institute in Washington, D.C., established the Center for Energy Efficiency (CENEF) in Moscow. Several U.S. government agencies and U.S.-based foundations, including the World Wildlife Fund and the MacArthur Foundation, provided seed money. The basic concepts underlying CENEF—energy conservation by both industrial and household consumers and promoting collaboration on energy issues among regional administrations, industrial energy consumers, the media, and the public—originated primarily with CENEF's U.S.-based founders. By the late 1990s CENEF had become a self-sustaining nonprofit organization. CENEF spent most of its seed money in the first few years of operation and developed a client-based, contractual approach to its subsequent financing. With several subcontracted projects from Battelle (most of which originated with the U.S. Environmental Protection Agency) and many new contracts with the World Bank, the United Nations' Environment Program, and—most important—various Russian regional administrations and municipalities, CENEF has become a highly skilled nonprofit consulting group dedicated to energy and environmental issues.[19] As such, it stands as a positive example of a self-sustaining project that was originally created and financed with grants from Western sources.

C: INTERACTIVE ASSISTANCE FOR INDIGENOUS IDEAS

In the late 1990s the U.S.-based nonprofit group Sacred Earth Network and its Russian partner, Ekotok, responded to indigenous requests for assistance by developing a regional organization for the environmental movement all over Eurasia. Until then, Sacred Earth–Ekotok had been in the business of giving computers and communications equipment to more than four hundred environmental NGOs in the former Soviet Union and running training seminars on electronic communications. In regions such as the North Caucasus, Kamchatka, and southern Siberia, Sacred Earth–Ekotok trains regional environmental NGOs that wish to cooperate and become better coordinated among themselves. The goal is to create coalitions among NGOs, regional authorities, and the public to better address environmental issues that cannot be solved by a single organization.

D:INTERACTIVE ASSISTANCE FOR IMPORTED IDEAS

There are many good examples of interactive assistance for imported ideas. The most obvious is the professional training performed by many NGOs, such as ISAR and a Russian-American nonprofit organization called Golubka that specializes in NGO training. Such training consists of lessons in strategic planning, tactics, and the identification and use of human, informational, and financial resources. One indicator of the wholly imported nature of these ideas is that in a popular handbook for Russian environmental groups, the terms *strategic planning, fund-raising,* and *press releases* are translated (transliterated) as *strategicheskoe planirovanie, fandraizing,* and *press-relizy.*[20] Training of this kind has been so widespread that some Russian activists, previously trainees, now specialize in training others.

Another example of the strategy of interactive assistance for imported ideas is the way in which Green Cross Russia (a chapter of the worldwide environmental advocacy organization Green Cross International [GCI] founded by Mikhail Gorbachev at the 1992 Rio Earth Summit) has achieved a promising level of cooperation with the Russian army and other state organs in Russia. One of GCI's global programs addresses the environmental legacy of wars, especially the cold war. To this end GCI seeks to mitigate the social, environmental, and economic consequences of chemical and nuclear contamination from military buildup. Green Cross Russia, responsible for implementing this program in Russia, has forged an official agreement of cooperation with the army, which subsequently initiated its first public outreach program on environmental issues. Green Cross Russia has also successfully concluded a cooperative agreement with the Ministry of Atomic Energy, which has, as a result, granted much greater public access to information about Russia's nuclear power and weapons industry. Other NGOs and the public have thus all benefited from greater access to environmentally sensitive information.

INFLUENCE AND LIMITATIONS

Citizen advocacy groups committed to environmental issues in Russia played an uneven role in the transition to democracy during the 1990s. Before the mid-1980s such groups did not exist in the Soviet Union. Gorbachev's liberalization policies allowed the first mass-mobilized, antistate protest movements to emerge. Because of the confluence of the interests of environmentalists, nationalists, prodemocracy activists, and others, Soviet citizens in the mid- to late 1980s came together, formed autonomous organizations, and helped bring about transformative political and economic changes. Given environmentalists' scientific bent, state authorities often viewed environmental groups as the least overtly "political" and therefore the safest, of all protest groups. Nationalists, human rights proponents, and others often joined environmental protest movements partially out of shared interests but also partially as a cover for more overtly political activities.[21]

Since the breakup of the Soviet Union, however, environmental advocacy groups in Russia have dramatically weakened and are far less populist. Although thousands of environmental NGOs may now be active in Russia, most are local, small, often short lived, and frequently oriented around only a single issue.[22] The environmental movement in Russia has tended to be fragmented, weak, and strapped for cash.

Since Putin's ascendance, environmental NGOs in Russia have come under increasing pressure from the federal authorities. Many groups have reported being harassed by the Prosecutor General's Office and by police and security forces, taking their cue from Russia's KGB-reared leader. In the summer of 1999, for instance, Putin made public statements charging, without evidence, that Russian environmental NGOs were engaged in espionage.[23]

However ominous these developments are for the third sector and democracy overall in Russia, the rise and rapid fall in influence of environmental NGOs well predates most of the harassment of environmentalists by the federal authorities.[24] While this harassment has no doubt contributed to the weakness of the environmental movement, the stark contrast between the vigor of the movement in the late Soviet period and its decline in the post-Soviet period is primarily attributable to numerous, mutually reinforcing factors, all of which bear on the ability of Western NGOs to assist in the development of the movement. These factors include a weak state, the economic crisis, "movement surrogacy," and the loss of many of the movement's early leaders.

First, the state's weakness has tended to stunt most third-sector groups in Russia. If the third sector is to develop into a robust network of institutions mediating between state and society, it needs solidly institutionalized procedures for governance and advocacy. Citizens' groups also need a coherent target audience within the state to cooperate with or confront. If third-sector groups are to be able to articulate their interests through established channels and acquire real influence over legislative and policy decisions, the state must be effective and institutionalize procedures for governance. The weakness of the state therefore has weakened many segments of would-be civil society in their efforts to participate in government. Although not in anyway the goal, Putin's efforts at strengthening the state, including the empowerment of Federal Security Service (one of the successors to the KGB) and the promotion of many individuals from the security services, may inadvertently force environmentalists to be more organized.

Second, the economic crisis in Russia has undermined the environmental movement's public support. Most ordinary citizens who, a dozen or so years ago, might have taken to the streets to protest the construction of a nuclear power plant in Gorky (now Nizhni Novgorod) or a biochemical factory in Kazan, have since become far more concerned with sustaining themselves and their families through an economic depression. The crisis especially affects towns in which a single (often polluting) factory employs the entire population.

Third, the early contributing factor of "movement surrogacy" has vanished. When the environmental cause was considered relatively safe in the late Soviet period, nationalists, democracy and human rights advocates, and others often folded their antistate activities into the environmental protest movement. Since 1992, however, with the breakup of the Soviet Union, nationalists and democracy advocates either achieved their goals or no longer need the cover of the environmental movement.[25] Thus the environmental movement in Russia today has been greatly weakened by abandonment.

Fourth, the movement has suffered what has been called both "decapitation through success" or "the green lift."[26] Many leaders of the environmental movement who rose to prominence in the 1980s left to run for office or were appointed to executive positions in regional or national administrations. A notable example is Boris Nemtsov, who was an environmental activist and later became the governor of Nizhni Novgorod oblast, then a deputy prime minister under Boris Yeltsin, and now is a Duma deputy and party leader. The loss of such activists deprived the movement of some of its most charismatic organizers.

These factors affect not only indigenous environmental advocacy groups in Russia but Western assistance efforts as well. While external actors cannot readily address movement surrogacy and decapitation by success, they can address, if not solve, the weak state and the economic crisis. Some Western groups seeking to assist the development of Russian environmental advocacy groups do take such broad-based issues into consideration, but many do not. Assistance programs that do not explicitly consider these overarching political and economic factors may be helping third-sector groups, but their influence, and that of the third-sector groups they assist, is inherently limited.

INFLUENCE

All the Western NGOs under consideration, no matter which strategies they used, helped to develop environmental NGOs in Russia. Whether they funded projects, built capacity, provided training, dropped equipment, or engaged in a cooperative activity, foreign donors greatly aided Russian environmental NGOs to become more strategic, professional, and embedded in a network, both national and transnational. Without computers and communications equipment from the West, for example, Russian environmental NGOs would continue to work in isolation. Given that the vast territory of Russia stretches over eleven time zones, the transportation and communications infrastructures are of poor quality, and money for equipment is simply nonexistent, Russian environmental groups would still be working in a virtual vacuum were it not for foreign assistance.[27] While NGOs in other postcommunist countries also lack a good communications system, the sheer magnitude of the Russian landmass, as well as the historical emphasis on vertical communication between center and region at the expense of horizontal communication among regions, considerably magnifies the problem.

In the post-Soviet period interactive strategies have had the most influence on both third-sector development and the environment by emphasizing strategy and professionalism, coalition building among all sectors, and an overt environmental agenda. Less important is whether the recipient groups are grassroots or (nonstate) elite. An interactive, explicitly environmental strategy with imported ideas affects both the development of third-sector groups and multisectoral environmental coalitions and environmental policies more directly than does a general strategy of funding the projects of third-sector groups, including environmental ones.

When asked to consider the counterfactual—what would be the shape of the Russian environmental NGO community today without foreign assistance?—representatives of several different Russian groups said that while the number of indigenous NGOs would be much smaller, and their range of activity much narrower, the absence of foreign aid would also eliminate the so-called grant junkies or fictitious organizations.[28] Such groups exist for the sole purpose of receiving foreign grants in order to carry out some minimal level of work that appears to justify their continued survival. The problem of the grant junkies is one encountered mainly by foreign foundations engaged in project funding rather than interactive cooperation. Western groups that team up with Russian NGOs obviously have a much closer relationship with the indigenous groups and can evaluate their utility and level of effort more critically and accurately.

Interactive cooperation also provides a more direct mechanism for transferring Western ideas, specifically the key concepts of strategic professionalism and multisectoral coalition building. While funding noninteractive projects may also encourage the transfer of such ideas into practice, a group that receives money may give only lip service to such ideas in order to receive the grant. In an interactive environment, on the other hand, the Western group is working alongside and influencing the practices and ideas of the recipient group.

When Ecologia, for example, first introduced to its Russian recipient groups the concept of building coalitions—among NGOs, local or regional government organs, industrial enterprises, and others—the groups treated it as an alien idea, preferring instead to work almost exclusively either with other NGOs or with like-minded intellectuals and scientists. After several years of cooperative activity, however, plus Ecologia's practice of having its Moscow office work only with NGOs willing to engage in such coalition building, the recipient NGOs now treat regional coalition building as standard operating procedure. In contrast, large-scale noninteractive grant programs, while typically able to distribute aid to many more organizations, have less direct influence over the recipient groups' ideas and operations.

Coalition building begins to address some problems associated with the political and economic transformations occurring in post-Soviet Russia. Of the four factors that limit the influence of Western NGOs on the environment in

Russia, coalition building addresses three: the weakness of the state with respect to industrial and commercial interests, the autonomy of the state with respect to its citizenry, and the link between economic and environmental problems. To some degree each Western NGO engaged in a specifically environmental agenda espoused a coalition-building approach, with the exception of protest-oriented groups such as Greenpeace or the Rainbow Keepers. Foreign funders with agendas oriented toward the third sector in general tended not to stress the importance of coalition building to the same degree as those with environmental agendas. This may be a result of the less targeted, more diffuse goal orientation of organizations assisting third-sector development versus the more targeted and specific orientation of organizations assisting the environment.

A representative of the World Wide Fund for Nature, for instance, explained that the WWF is trying to change the overall attitude toward environmental protection in Russia. Instead of treating the environment as a set of discrete issues solvable on a technical level by a single responsible actor (such as a polluting factory or a regional environment department), the WWF is promoting "ecoregion-based conservation," a more holistic approach in which all sectors— state, industry, media, the public—cooperatively engage in environmental strategizing and problem solving. Thus WWF strongly encourages the local NGOs with which it works, usually in an interactive way, to adopt such a holistic, coalition-building approach.

Similarly, the Green Cross promotes the idea of "cooperation, not confrontation." The executive director of Green Cross Russia noted that this is an international idea. Originating at Green Cross International headquarters in Switzerland, the concept has filtered into Green Cross Russia through interactive cooperation and even out into the hinterland of Russia to affect the behavior of other Russian environmental NGOs.[29] Green Cross Russia thinks of itself as an intermediary between public and state and thus as a spearhead of the so-called pale green movement in Russia. Its cooperation with the authorities does not go uncriticized, however. Some environmental groups that prefer protest to forming multisectoral alliances have branded the Green Cross and other coalition-building groups "collaborators."

Coalition building is being promoted at the local, regional, and national level. Regionally, for example, Ecologia's Volga River monitoring network links six or seven areas along the Volga. In each area Ecologia has given NGOs portable water-monitoring equipment that provides immediate in-field results. It has required the recipient NGOs to work collaboratively with local municipalities, local enterprises, and each other. The Green Cross and the WWF also engage in coalition building at the national level. For example, representatives of the Green Cross and WWF are key participants in a series of regular roundtable meetings in Moscow on environmental and political issues. High-level state decision makers, such as the head of the former Goskomekologia, Viktor

Danilov-Danilyan, and members of the Duma ecology committee, frequently attend these meetings. Such participation involves the Green Cross and the WWF in the national and even international policy-making process.

The concept of strategic professionalism is another key imported idea and one that practically every training program sows in the third sector. Because this concept affects the operation of indigenous NGOs at the most minute as well as the broadest level, its successful adoption requires specific training. Western groups involved exclusively in project financing have little or no influence on the strategic thinking or professionalism of recipient groups, beyond perhaps favoring proposals from organizations that appear to be more strategic or professional. While such a preference may, over time, make itself known to the grant-seeking NGO community and may therefore encourage NGOs to become more strategic and professional, a more direct and influential way to foster strategic professionalism is through interactive training programs or internships at the foreign funders.

LIMITATIONS AND
UNINTENDED CONSEQUENCES

The most important limitations on the success of Western NGOs with respect to environmental issues in Russia derive from the weakness of the state, citizen participation channels that remain unstable and unestablished, and economic and environmental problems that are bound together. If assistance to indigenous environmental NGOs is understood to comprise two separate but related goals—the development of postcommunist third-sector groups and the progressive resolution of environmental issues—it is manifestly clear that greater progress has been achieved on the first front than on the second.

Western assistance has had many unintended consequences, some of which are unique to the environmental community (or even unique to the environmental community in Russia) and some of which all advocacy communities presumably share.

Among the unintended consequences that most assistance programs share, regardless of issue orientation, is that of resentment of recipient groups when aid programs do not consider local realities. This reflects the shortcomings of importing a single blueprint from abroad. An example of such a blueprint was the Regional Environment Center (REC), established in Budapest in the early 1990s with money from the European Union, foreign governments, and private foundations. The REC is an information clearinghouse and central organizing point for environmental advocacy groups and citizens' initiatives throughout Central and Eastern Europe. While not without its critics, the REC has become a key actor in regional environmental politics.

In 1995–1996 Western donors, led by the European Union, began to talk about establishing a REC-like organization in Moscow that would coordinate nonstate environmental activities in the former Soviet Union. The idea of a Russian REC provoked considerable resistance from the Russian environmental NGO community. Several well-known representatives of the Russian environmental NGO community explained that simply importing an idea that worked in Budapest in the early 1990s to Russia in the late 1990s would not work. The two settings, they argued, were different; whereas the Central and Eastern European societies of the early 1990s embraced the organizing ability of the REC (as well as that of the international community in general), the Russian environmental community of the late 1990s was already quite established and organized and did not feel the need for a centrally controlled external organizer. For instance, it already had the Socio-Ecological Union, an indigenously established umbrella group for citizens' environmental initiatives throughout the former Soviet Union. In addition, Russian environmentalists strongly opposed the design proposed for the Russian REC: It was to be partially administered by Goskomekologia, which many Russian NGOs thought was not NGO friendly and was far from being a neutral arbiter. The former chairman of the board of the nongovernmental Biodiversity Conservation Center in Moscow noted, "The REC was a good idea ten years ago in Eastern Europe, because the third sector there was still in the early stages of development, but this is no longer the case in Russia. Establishment of a Russian REC is a matter of contention, fiefdoms, and overlapping activities now . . . . It would be better to use already existing organizations rather than to create a new semi-governmental bureaucracy."[30]

Another common unintended consequence arises from a paradox associated with using indigenous expertise. Representatives of nearly every Western NGO as well as government aid programs spoke of the necessity, often learned the hard way, of using local experts in their in-country activities. Russian NGO representatives too noted that all too often well-paid Western consultants, flown in to administer programs in regions they knew little or nothing about, spent the vast majority of their time learning the local realities, writing reports, and sending information back to the home office, meanwhile contributing nothing of significance to the actual project or the region.

Given the necessity of using indigenous expertise, it was therefore striking that many indigenous NGO representatives also sounded bells of caution when asked about the way in which Western groups used local expertise. Sometimes this vitiates the local experts' intellectual independence: Local experts may be so happy to be paid for their labor that they may say precisely what their foreign funders want to hear. Even the possibility of this may lead local state or industrial organizations to distrust Western-funded indigenous experts, thereby depriving them of the very influence that they seek to develop.

More frequent is a problem encountered by Western groups that use local experts on their grant-making boards. Local experts who are called upon to make decisions on grants and awards are generally well connected to the local advocacy community and may be biased. Such partisanship may lead to resentment and splits within the grant-seeking NGO community. Foreign funders encountering this problem of peer review have had to find ways of stemming partisanship while still drawing on local expertise. For example, ISAR has five to eleven local members on the boards of each of its regional offices but rotates board membership regularly to avoid cliques and bias.

Among the unintended consequences unique to the environmental community is the problem of science-oriented environmentalists who are opposed to using the approach of strategic professionalism. In the perestroika era many environmentalists were affiliated with Academy of Sciences institutes, industrial branch ministry institutes, or universities that stressed scientific, not political, orientations to environmental problem solving. In the 1990s, however, when many Western NGOs were training Russian environmental NGOs to become more professional, politically strategic, and organized, a subset of the environmental movement opposed what it perceived as the abandonment of traditional scientific approaches to environmental protection. Because the Western groups were the most visible and active trainers in Western management techniques, this subset of the environmental movement began to view much of the contact and assistance from the West as superficial and ill spent. The rift in these two sets of groups has, however, more recently diminished, as communications have expanded and those on both sides have learned from each other.

Another common unintended consequence arises where regional or territorial systems of administering assistance inhibit environmental effectiveness. Many environmental issues are by their very nature transboundary. Thus many NGO representatives noted that establishing horizontal communications networks is critical and that NGOs in different locales must work together. Western NGOs, as part of a transnational network, have been successful at fostering horizontal communications networks by donating computers and communications equipment to groups all over Eurasia. However, indigenous NGOs feel that the administration of foreign aid programs by region or territory may inhibit interregional and even international cooperation. For example, USAID gave ISAR two separate grants for its Seeds of Democracy program, one for the Moscow office and one for the Vladivostok office. Each office administered its own grant program in its own region and received its own funding. Though both offices have since become legally independent not only from ISAR headquarters in Washington, D.C., but from each other, some grant recipients expressed concern that the territorial divisions of the grant administration system encourages groups to be active and collaborative only within their own region.

The same logic holds for funding programs that are administered according to country borders. To skirt this problem an active transboundary environmental association has formed in the Leningrad and Karelia regions of the Russian northwest, incorporating participant groups from Scandinavia, the Baltic countries, and neighboring regions within Russia. Transboundary associations can compete for funds from a growing number of sources, pool their resources, and work more effectively on environmental problems that ignore borders.

HOW WESTERN NGOS EVALUATE
THEIR OWN ACTIVITIES

Asked how Western NGOs evaluate their own assistance programs, nearly every respondent noted the extreme difficulty of evaluation. It tends to be performed along two axes: according to the terms of the original project proposal itself and according to the broader criteria set by the funding organization. The first sort of evaluation is more straightforward. Western groups engaged in noninteractive project financing have required funding recipients to submit reports upon completion of their projects or at the end of the funding cycle, for instance.

What is more difficult is taking account of the broader concerns of each organization. For example, Charities Aid Foundation tries to analyze each project's influence on its region. ISAR looks for indications of information sharing across groups and the creation of linkages among groups. Ecologia analyzes the level of influence on public participation and decision making in the regions in which it works. While all the organizations also evaluate projects strictly according to the terms of the original project proposal, these broader concerns reach closer to the core of the Western groups' raison d'être. Yet they are often too intangible to evaluate at such close range, and several respondents argued that even a decade in the field is not enough time for evaluation.

Evaluation of noninteractive project-financing programs by their funders tends to be more formal than evaluation of interactive projects. Recipients generally submit reports, and the Western group's board or staff meets regularly to review the reports and discuss evaluation criteria. Interactive activity tends to be evaluated more informally and irregularly. The head of an NGO using interactive strategies (Ecologia) noted that, since concrete results often appear well *after* submission of the final project report, evaluation has to be flexible and long term. Any evaluation in search of tangible short-term results is an exercise in futility. This is partly a result of the nature of the activity being funded (environmental advocacy), partly a result of the transitional political and economic context in which Russian NGOs work, and partly because of the short amount of time that these assistance programs have been running.

Short-term evaluation in search of concrete tangible results was not common; I did not find a single pure example of such thinking among the organizations that I researched. All the Western groups that I considered sought some evidence of concrete results and incorporated their own broader social or political concerns into assessment. Donors' self-evaluations could be more useful if they factored in considerations of more holistic, coalition-building strategies of benefit to both environmental and sociopolitical objectives. In other words, current self-evaluation systems work as well as possible, given current strategies. However, were strategies changed to incorporate the suggestions made in this chapter, evaluation systems would benefit from criteria for measuring successful coalition building and the influence of such coalition building on both environmental and sociopolitical issues.

LESSONS

One of the clearest lessons from the environmental movement in Russia is that citizen initiatives that promote the onset of democratization do not necessarily promote the consolidation of democracy. A common pair of objectives of Western NGOs (excluding those organizations that are purely protest groups) is, first, to help indigenous NGOs to develop into well-managed organizations in their own right and, second, to help them forge new, stable channels for citizen participation in the political system, thereby helping to consolidate the new Russian democracy.

These intertwined objectives, especially the first, have met with some degree of success in Russia. Russian environmental groups in the first years of the twenty-first century are far more strategic, professional, networked, and sophisticated than they were just a few years earlier, and foreign aid in multiple forms and from multiple sources is partly responsible for the transformation.[31] Observers interested in the future of the Russian environmental NGO community will have to wait and watch, however, given the relatively more repressive atmosphere of the early Putin era. Notwithstanding the recent acquittal of military-officer-turned-environmentalist Alexander Nikitin, who was charged with espionage for publicizing the environmental hazards associated with Russia's decommissioned nuclear submarines around the Kola Peninsula, an apparently increasing suspicion of environmentalists may be the wave of the future in Russia. An inauspicious sign may be the rule announced in May 2001 by the Russian Academy of Sciences that Russian scientists must report to academy officials all contact with foreigners.

It remains unclear whether Russians really have established new stable channels of citizen participation and to what degree foreign aid is responsible. Because most Western NGOs have been active in a substantial way in Russia only since 1993, evaluation of their influence on the political process is difficult because it is better measured in decades or even generations. The future of Russian democracy is by no means a given. Despite Putin's high popularity ratings, the ordinary Russian citizen still greatly mistrusts the government regardless of who is in power and has suffered harsh economic consequences as a result of the quasi transition to market capitalism that is associated with the quasi transition to democracy.

Despite these inhibiting factors, citizen participation channels are being forged at both regional and national levels. Western groups have been at least partly responsible, particularly those engaged in interactive programs of coalition building and working to achieve their goals within the political system itself, rather than resorting to protest from outside. One of the most promising citizen initiatives is a Russian nonprofit environmental law group called Ecojuris, which in 1998 celebrated the first-ever supreme court victory for public ecological interests over an organ of the Russian state that was violating its own laws (the Federal Forest Service). The success of such legitimate means for citizens to express their interest demonstrates that channels for participation are taking root. However, the process of establishing such channels is still in the early stages.

The obvious objective of helping to improve Russia's environment has met with far less success. The weakness and corruption of the state with respect to powerful industrial and commercial lobbies, the continual instability and flux of state institutions and elites, and the link between environmental and economic issues all constrain the influence of Western groups seeking to affect environmental conditions in Russia. Aid programs that explicitly factor these issues into program design are more likely, in the long term, to have a direct effect on improving the environment in Russia.

EPILOGUE

The evolving realities of the Putin era serve to underscore precisely why the strategies identified here as the most effective—in particular, multisectoral coalition building, especially at the regional level—will continue to be so; indeed, they are perhaps even more crucial now than during the Yeltsin era. Many observers note that Putin has presided over an increasingly illiberal regime. Indeed, in a recent survey two-thirds of all Russians interviewed had difficulty labeling their society democratic.[32] Crackdowns on NGOs of all types, as well as the independent media, are increasingly common.

Since Putin's ascendance, many advocacy groups have reported being harassed by police, security, and tax agents, some of whom have been known to barge unannounced into NGO offices and confiscate files while dressed in ski masks and bearing assault weapons. In late 1999 authorities detained several environmentalists for questioning in connection with the bombings of Moscow apartment buildings; these people reported being "interrogated for hours and urged to 'confess' links to terrorists."[33] Though environmental activists had been a target of systematic, but usually low-level, harassment for several years before the Putin era, the pattern has become clearer and more common since he took office. Most observers, both inside and outside the country, believe that this is occurring not because Russian officials necessarily think that environmental advocates are terrorist bombers or foreign spies but because they "see the strengthening of *civil society* as a security threat" more generally.[34]

Bureaucratic obstacles have also increased for Russian NGOs. According to Russian law, all NGOs, charities, religious organizations, and other societal associations must register with the Ministry of Justice, and they must re-register periodically. In the late 1990s, during a phase of re-registration representatives of these civil society organizations lodged numerous complaints with the Ministry of Justice and in the media regarding the near impossibility or even the outright impossibility of complying with the onerous re-registration requirements. By some estimates fewer than half of all national organizations were able to re-register with federal authorities, and the widespread perception is that the process is designed to weed out groups critical of the government.[35]

If this pattern of harassment continues for the foreseeable future, or gets worse, the future of Russia's third sector may be in jeopardy, but the authorities would have to significantly step up the harassment to squelch the third sector as thoroughly as in Soviet times. It is worth noting that the number of third-sector organizations has continued to grow, their international and domestic connections have continued to thrive, and the many cases of groups unable to re-register with the Ministry of Justice do not seem to have seriously repressed the functioning of the sector as a whole. In other words, while government harassment of the third sector has probably slowed the growth of the sector or minimally curtailed its activities, it does not seem to have arrested its growth altogether or put a stop to its activities. So despite the obstacles, and in the absence of a complete reversal of the laws allowing Russian citizens to engage freely in societal associations, the third sector indeed seems to be holding its own. Perhaps it would be stronger and more effective were the state supportive and mobilizing, but even in the face of adversity it has not vanished.

Parts of the third sector have perhaps grown even more determined. In the fall of 2000 Russian environmental NGOs, assisted by several Western NGOs, organized the largest, most widespread, and most visible action since the antinuclear protests of a decade earlier. In response both to Putin's abolishment in May 2000 of the State Committee on the Environment and to the Ministry of Atomic Energy (MinAtom) plan to import as many as twenty tons of nuclear waste from around the world in order to finance the construction of new nuclear power stations, environmental and public health advocates, along with Yabloko Party activists and numerous schoolteachers from across Russia collected 2.5 million signatures in more than sixty regions to force the Russian government to hold a referendum. Importing nuclear waste required a change in Russian law by the Duma. The activists concerned about the poor safety record of and history of obfuscation by the Russian nuclear energy sector believed they had collected more than enough signatures to comply with the 1995 Law on Referendum, which requires at least two million. Numerous regional and

Central Election Commission officials, however, upon reviewing the petition and signatures in November 2000, invalidated more than 600,000 of them, thereby reducing the number of valid signatures to 1.9 million, just short of the number required to get a referendum on the ballot.

As of mid-2001 there were no indications that Putin would reinstate the State Committee on the Environment, and the Duma had approved MinAtom's plan to import nuclear waste, which Putin ultimately supported.However, approval by the Duma was difficult—its second reading was postponed twice—in part because of the public's evident and vocal objections. In addition, Putin sacked his minister of atomic energy, Yevgeny Adamov, who was under a cloud of corruption allegations.

Did the activists win? From a policy perspective, clearly not. But from a longer-term perspective, one could argue that the Russian people are more aware of the proximate environmental issues; that environmental NGOs all over Russia joined forces for a common cause, thereby enhancing their levels of communication and cooperation; that a news story that the domestic and foreign press might once have largely overlooked received more coverage than it would have otherwise; and that the public sent a message to decision makers in Moscow, whether they chose to heed it or not. Indeed, by postponing the second reading of the bill, the Duma unexpectedly acknowledged that it had heard the message, even if it eventually ignored it. Several Western NGOs contributed to this effort, and while the outcome was surely not the one desired, Western assistance nonetheless contributed to the long-term factors just mentioned. While the realities of the Putin era clearly make successful assistance by Western NGOs more difficult, those that engage in multisectoral coalition building and that emphasize strategic professionalism are less likely than others to see their efforts marginalized.

NOTES

1. U.S. Agency for International Development, "Foreign Donor Assistance for Environmental Protection and Natural Resource Management in the Russian Federation," report available from USAID, Moscow, January 1988, p. 1.

2. D. J. Peterson, "Institutions and the Environment in Transition-Era Russia" (Ph.D. diss., University of California, Los Angeles, 1996), p. 164.

3. See Peter Burnell, *Foreign Aid in a Changing World* (Philadelphia: Open University Press, 1997), esp. chap. 11, "To Russia with Love," pp. 212–30.

4. For a discussion of the strength of the environmental movement during the perestroika period, see Jane I. Dawson, *Econationalism, Antinuclear Activism, and National Identity in Russia, Lithuania, and Ukraine* (Durham: Duke University Press, 1996). See also Charles E. Ziegler, "Environmental Politics and Policy Under Perestroika," in Judith B. Sedaitis and Jim Butterfield, eds., *Perestroika from Below*, pp. 113–31 (Boulder, Colo.: Westview, 1991).

5. In pre-Soviet times Russian writers sometimes reflected the reverence for nature often attributed to the Russian *narod* (people or nation). Those with Slavophile tendencies, such as Lev Tolstoi, wrote of a "naturalist attachment to the land" (Charles E. Ziegler, *Environmental Policy in the USSR* [Amherst: University of Massachusetts Press, 1987], p. 7). In the early part of the twentieth century, scientists and engineers, even some working on the early Soviet industrialization projects, demonstrated great concern for the social and ecological consequences of industry. By about 1930, however, most of these nontechnocrats had been silenced in one way or another. In an insightful account of an important and vocal engineer who was executed in 1929 by order of the party, Loren Graham shows how Soviet technology and industry became fatally flawed when the social-minded criticism of engineers such as Peter Palchinsky went unheeded. See Loren R. Graham, *The Ghost of the Executed Engineer* (Cambridge, Mass.: Harvard University Press, 1993). Even into the 1930s, when Stalin's terror began, some Russian scientists and philosophers, such as the Reverend Pavel Florensky, publicized ecological problems arising from heavy industrialization campaigns. See Ruben A. Mnatsakanian, *Environmental Legacy of the Former Soviet Republics* (Edinburgh, Scotland: Center for Human Ecology, Institute of Ecology & Resource Management, University of Edinburgh, 1992).

6. The activist S. R. Fomichev describes the ecopress during Soviet times: "There were practically no critical materials on global ecological issues (unless directly about capitalist nature and useful as propaganda). Demographics, public health issues, industrial influences on nature and man were not allowed." From S. R. Fomichev, introduction to I. Yu. Belov and S. R. Fomichev, eds., *Zelenaya Bibliografia, Pereodicheskie ekologischeskie izdaniya Severnoi Yevrazii* (Green Bibliography, Periodic Ecological Publications of Northern Eurasia) (Moscow: Tsentr okhrany dikoi prirody, 1996), p. 8.

7. The president of VOOP for many years was Nikolai Ovsyannikov, who was also the first deputy minister for land reclamation and water management for the Soviet Russian republic. This ministry was known to be a blatant and major disrupter of the ecological balance in many regions. See John Massey Stewart, ed., *The Soviet Environment: Problems, Policies, and Politics* (Cambridge: Cambridge University Press, 1992), p. 3.

8. D. J. Peterson, *Troubled Lands: The Legacy of Soviet Environmental Destruction* (Boulder, Colo.: Westview, 1993), p. 160.

9. Oksana Yu. Tsitzer, "History and Perspective of Shaping Federal Environmental Policy in the Russian Federation," *Toward a Sustainable Russia*, Bulletin of the Center for Russian Environmental Policy, Moscow, June 1996, p. 10.

10. See Peterson, "Institutions and the Environment," pp. 67–72.

11. The state committees were hydrometeorology, water resources, forestry, geodesy and cartography, geology and mineral resources, and the Arctic and Antarctica.

12. Tsitzer, "History and Perspective," pp. 10–11.

13. Irina Khalyi, Institute of Sociology, Russian Academy of Sciences, interview by author, Moscow, July 1998.

14. Peterson, "Institutions and the Environment," pp. 63–64.

15. Interview of Olga Yakovleva and Vera Mischenko of Ecojuris, *Russian Conservation News*, spring 1998, p. 13.

16. Ibid., pp. 13–14.

17. Randy Kritkausky, Ecologia, telephone interview by author, August 1998.

18. Yakovleva and Mischenko interview, pp. 13–14.

19. Inna Gritsevich, CENEF, interview by author, Moscow, June 1998.

20. Irina Khalyi et al., eds., *Aktsii ekologicheskogo dvizhenia, Rukovodstvo k deistviyu* (Actions of the Ecological Movement, Leadership to Action). Moscow: Programma Maatschappelijke Transformatie, Ministry of Foreign Affairs of the Netherlands, 1996.

21. For an extended discussion see Dawson, *Econationalism.*

22. Peterson, *Troubled Lands,* p. 207.

23. Aleksandr Gamov and Yevgenia Uspenskogo, "Vladimir Putin: Gosudarstvennii perevorot Rossii ne grozit" (Vladimir Putin: No Threat of a Government Revolution in Russia), *Komsomolskaya Pravda,* July 8, 1999, pp. 8–9. See also Julie Corwin, "Environmentalists Fear More Pressure from Federal Authorities," pt. 1, *RFE/RL* March 2, 2000, http://www.rferl.org/newsline/2000/03/020300.html (November 9, 2001).

24. Several cases of severe harassment of environmentalists are well known. See, for example, Thomas Nilsen and Jon Gauslaa, "How the KGB Violates Citizens' Rights: The Case of Alexander Nikitin," *Demokratizatsiya* 5, no. 3 (Summer 1997): 407–21.

25. For more on this see Dawson, *Econationalism.*

26. Michael Bernhard uses the phrase "decapitation through success" in "Civil Society After the First Transition," *Communist and Postcommunist Studies* 29, no. 3 (September 1996): 309–30. Sergei Baranovsky of Green Cross Russia introduced me to the term "green lift" when I interviewed him in Moscow in June 1998.

27. Isolation still persists for many groups. As of the late 1990s, only ten of Green Cross Russia's twenty-three branch organizations in Russia had telephones and e-mail.

28. Ivan Timofeev of Golubka introduced me to the term "grant junky" when I interviewed him in Moscow in July 1998.

29. Baranovsky interview.

30. Evgeny Shvarts, Biodiversity Conservation Center, interview by author, Moscow, June 1998.

31. Tatiana Zhdanova of the MacArthur Foundation made this argument when I interviewed her in Moscow in July 1998. See also Initiative for Social Action and Renewal in Eurasia, "A Brief Overview of the Environmental Movement in the Newly Independent States" (report prepared for the NGO/Donor Workshop, Szentendre, Hungary, May 12–14, 1997), pp. 8–9; Institute of Natural Resource Management, "Evaluation of the Impact Made by the USAID Assistance Program on Environmental Activism and the Non-Governmental Organization Movement," report for USAID, Moscow, 1997, p. 8.

32. The All-Russian Center of Public Opinion Studies (VTsIOM) conducted this survey in October 2000. See Vladimir Shlapentokh, "Putin's Uniqueness in Russian History: The Prospects for Prolonged Corruption in a Nondemocratic Society," January 9, 2001, David Johnson's *Russia List,* http://www.cdi.org/russia/johnson/5017.html##9 (November 9, 2001).

33. Sarah E. Mendelson, "The Putin Path: Are Human Rights in Retreat?" testimony prepared for hearings before the Commission on Security and Cooperation in

Europe, U.S. Congress, 106th Cong., 2d sess., May 23, 2000; see also Sarah E. Mendelson, "The Putin Path: Civil Liberties and Human Rights in Retreat," *Problems of Postcommunism* 47, no. 5 (September–October 2000): 3–12.

34. Ibid.

35. Ibid. Some estimates have put the number of successfully re-registered groups far lower. See, for example, "Briefing Report: Russian Democracy Under Threat," *RFE/RL*, October 24, 2000, http://www.rferl.org/welcome/english/releases/2000/10 /6-241000.html (November 12, 2001).

Chapter 6

ENVIRONMENTAL NGOS IN KAZAKHSTAN: DEMOCRATIC GOALS AND NONDEMOCRATIC OUTCOMES

Erika Weinthal and Pauline Jones Luong

International democracy-building efforts have increasingly focused on promoting local nongovernmental organizations (NGOs) in the successor states of the Soviet Union and Eastern Europe and have done so by orchestrating the active involvement of Western nongovernmental organizations. As part of the democratization process, Western liberal democracies perceive that local NGOs can serve as building blocks of a civil society. This raises two sets of questions that we seek to address in this chapter. First, what is the nature of these efforts? More specifically, what strategies do Western NGOs use to help develop local NGOs in particular and promote democratization in general? Second, and more important, what are the net results of these efforts thus far? To what extent can we say that, several years into the transition from state-sponsored socialism and Communist Party rule, local NGOs are evidence of an emerging "democratic culture"? Are they indeed contributing to the wider process of democratization in the former Soviet Union?

We shed light on these issues by examining the strategies and activities of environmental Western NGOs and local NGOs in Kazakhstan, with a specific

We wish to thank Mike Biddison, Megan Falvey, and Eric Sievers for comments and assistance and the National Research Council for helping to fund our research.

focus on the energy sector. The environment is an appropriate vantage point from which to investigate the status of local NGOs since independence for two reasons. The first is its legacy as a "safe," and therefore particularly salient, issue area for political mobilization in the last few years of the Soviet Union.[1] Second, a variety of Western NGOs—including ISAR (Initiative for Social Action and Renewal in Eurasia)—have actively supported the development of local environmental NGOs in Kazakhstan since the breakup of the Soviet Union.[2]

The proven resources of the Caspian Sea may rival those of the North Sea, with additional reserves that remain unexplored offshore. The Caspian Sea holds 18 to 34 billion barrels of proven oil reserves with the potential to yield another 235 billion barrels. Significant gas reserves—243 to 248 trillion cubic feet—also exist within the Caspian basin, with the potential of 328 trillion cubic feet more, making the Central Asian states some of the largest gas producers in the world.[3] This is a situation ripe for the emergence (or reemergence) of local NGOs in support of environmental protection in Kazakhstan. The public already is widely aware of the environmental risks to the especially fragile ecosystems of the Caspian. And energy exploration elsewhere, in countries as diverse as Nigeria, Ecuador, and the United States, has been a rallying point for local environmental and political activism. Since independence in 1991, Kazakhstan has invited a large number of foreign companies to help develop new and existing oil and gas fields. A few existing projects are joint ventures, such as the TengizChevroil project. Other exploratory projects such as OKIOC (Offshore Kazakhstan International Operating Company) involve a broader consortium of foreign companies, including Agip, Total, British Petroleum/Statoil, and Mobil.[4] We therefore would expect to see the greatest development of local NGOs in relation to offshore oil and gas exploration in the Caspian basin.

However, we found that both local NGOs and Western NGOs deliberately ignored the energy sector immediately after independence and opted instead for small-scale environmental education programs on global topics such as biodiversity and desertification. While the government of Kazakhstan considers environmental regulations pertaining to offshore drilling, and its contracts with foreign firms specify liability for any losses to the "natural surroundings and habitats" in the area under exploration, it is not clear whether, to what extent, or in what form Western NGOs and local NGOs have played a role in establishing regulations and assigning liabilities in Kazakhstan. If Western NGOs and local NGOs are not pushing for environmental protection, what is the origin of such initiatives?

We also inquire into the role of local NGOs in Kazakhstan more generally. Our chief concern is whether environmental organizations are simply part of an "associational culture" that has developed in response to foreign aid or are actually an indication of democratization and the creation of a viable civil society.[5]

We found that local NGOs have played a declining role in environmental policy making since independence. We argue that this is a result of the failure of the Western NGOs to address a set of domestic and international constraints under which both Western NGOs and local NGOs must operate in post-Soviet Kazakhstan. At the domestic level local NGOs face institutional obstacles in a political system that has become more restrictive since 1994, and they lack access to organizational resources because of the continued decline in economic growth. At the international level the interests and strategies of the multiple international actors involved—including Western NGOs, international donor organizations, foreign oil companies, and foreign governments—often hinder local NGOs in promoting environmental protection in the energy sector. The strategies of Western NGOs thus far have reinforced rather than alleviated the effects of these domestic and international constraints on local NGOs, by encouraging their atomization and depoliticization. As a result, while the number of local environmental NGOs in Kazakhstan has grown because of the financial encouragement of Western NGOs, their size and political influence have declined. Western NGO strategies for developing local environmental NGOs have in fact, if inadvertently, hindered the development of a civil society in Kazakhstan.

We base our findings and conclusions upon extensive research in Central Asia. Both of us have spent a decade studying Central Asian politics, history, and languages and conducting fieldwork throughout the region. In this chapter we draw upon research that we carried out in the energy sector in Kazakhstan in March 1997 and December 1997, and it is informed by several trips to the region since that time. Erika Weinthal has examined questions of environmental security and natural resource management in the Aral Sea basin, and Pauline Jones Luong has studied ethnic relations, regionalism, and institutional design in Central Asia.

To explain the ways in which Western NGOs' efforts at strengthening local NGOs and building democracy in Kazakhstan were ineffectual immediately after independence, we proceed as follows. First, we establish that environmental NGOs in general, and the energy sector in particular, are an especially appropriate window into the role of local NGOs and their contribution to the process of democratization in Kazakhstan. Then we outline the goals and strategies of both local NGOs and Western NGOs in Kazakhstan in order to illustrate the overall shift away from pursuing overt policy advocacy and toward an emphasis on more apolitical endeavors. Next we analyze the extent to which Western NGOs have contributed to democracy-building efforts through the development of a civil society. Then we explore the causes of the declining role and effectiveness of local environmental NGOs in Kazakhstan's "post-Soviet transition." Finally, we conclude by offering several policy recommendations for Western NGOs operating within Kazakhstan.

ORIGINS AND SIGNIFICANCE OF
ENVIRONMENTAL NGOS IN KAZAKHSTAN

We have focused on environmental movements in Kazakhstan because they provide a useful gauge for measuring the progress of both local NGO development and democratization in Kazakhstan since independence. Environmental movements were among the first nongovernmental or independent organizations to emerge throughout the Soviet Union as a consequence of opening up political life under Mikhail Gorbachev's liberalization policy known as glasnost.[6] In Kazakhstan environmental activism centered on protest movements against nuclear weapons testing. Since August 29, 1949, the Soviet government has conducted more than four hundred nuclear explosions at the Semipalatinsk test site (*polygon*) in Kazakhstan. Before 1963 many of these tests were conducted above ground. In response to these tests and the environmental damage that they caused, the well-known Kazakh poet Olzhas Suleimenov helped to spearhead an antinuclear movement in the 1980s similar to several other antinuclear movements in Russia, Lithuania, and Ukraine that arose during the glasnost period.[7] In Kazakhstan this movement, known as Nevada-Semipalatinsk, gathered thousands of signatures and organized demonstrations in numerous cities with the goal of halting nuclear testing. In August 1991 public pressure was strong enough to force the closure of the Semipalatinsk test site.[8]

During the glasnost period the environment offered a politically safe and effective issue through which intellectuals could criticize the Soviet regime as a whole and ambitious republican leaders could launch drives for greater sovereignty. Because Soviet policy makers viewed the environment as apolitical, elites with nationalist aspirations could use environmental issues as cover for promoting a political agenda without seeming overtly threatening to the Soviet regime.[9] Nursultan Nazarbaev, then the republican head of Kazakhstan, was able to safely lend his support to the growing numbers within his republic that were demanding compensation from Moscow for nuclear testing.[10]

Following the breakup of the Soviet Union, it seemed reasonable to expect that environmental movements with a strong grassroots base would persist and even strengthen their activities in post-Soviet Kazakhstan. The political climate relaxed considerably in the first few years of independence. Kazakhstan witnessed a proliferation of independent organizations in various issue areas, including human rights organizations such as the Kazakh-America Bureau on Human Rights, as well as the active mobilization of Soviet-era organizations, such as the revitalized trade unions led by Leonid Soloman. However, the environmental concerns that initially mobilized a large proportion of Kazakhstan's population actually became more acute after independence. The government had yet to effectively address the known environmental problems, and new threats emerged as a result of its drive to develop its vast energy reserves in the

Caspian Sea basin. By the early 1990s oil pollution—from transportation of oil and dumping by the oil-processing industry—was already a serious problem near the Ural River delta in Kazakhstan and along its coast.[11] Another indicator of environmental degradation of the Caspian is the noticeable decline in sturgeon stocks. The Caspian contains 90 percent of the world's sturgeon, and seismic exploration for offshore oil reserves in the Caspian poses a direct threat to the fish harvest.[12]

During the Soviet period scientists and policy makers alike had discovered that the northeast Caspian contained fragile ecosystems. At that time the government declared this area a protected zone in which the only economic activities allowed were fishing and shipping/boating; no offshore oil exploration was conducted in Kazakhstan before independence. Despite the public and scientific awareness of the environmental sensitivity of the Caspian, at independence Kazakhstan had no environmental legislation or regulations that would both protect the ecosystem and allow for oil exploration.[13] This, in and of itself, created a need as well as an opportunity for environmental activists to become engaged in drafting regulations for the energy sector.

The energy sector is an appropriate focus of investigation because it is the most important sector for Kazakhstan's future economic and political development. Issues of the environment, economic development, and state security are closely intertwined. According to the ISAR representative for Central Asia from 1996 to 1998, "Considering issues of development and democratization, the environment is the most significant [in Kazakhstan] because it affects everyone."[14] If the environment is misused, the health and economic viability of local populations are likely to suffer. Under such circumstances local groups may mobilize in response to state-sponsored oil and gas exploration, which has the potential to harm local communities in energy-rich regions. This has already occurred in Nigeria, where the indigenous population in Biafra has protested the Nigerian government's energy policies in its territory. Accordingly, we focus on the Caspian Sea region in order to shed light on the overall growth and form of environmental movements in Kazakhstan.

GOALS AND STRATEGIES
OF ENVIRONMENTAL NGOS

When the Soviet Union broke up, Kazakhstan had a fairly well developed local environmental NGO sector with organizations such as Nevada-Semipalatinsk. This sector continued to grow in the first few years of independence. Other local NGOs prominent at that time included Green Salvation in Almaty, Green Cross and Crescent International, and the Association for Ecological Enlightenment. Following independence, Western NGOs with an interest in the environment became active in Kazakhstan.

Independence removed obstacles that had prevented Western NGOs from actively cooperating with local NGOs during the Soviet period. During glasnost some Western NGOs had made inroads into the Soviet Union, but most of their activities had involved establishing initial contacts with local NGOs and organizing conferences. After the collapse of the Soviet Union, Western NGOs—including ISAR, Counterpart Consortium, and American Legal Consortium (run by a for-profit consulting firm)—were able to assume a more direct and active role by channeling financial and informational resources to nascent local NGOs in Kazakhstan. These groups, all of which received funding through the U.S. Agency for International Development (USAID), sought to enhance the local NGO sector at large by targeting the environmental sector for NGO development.[15]

Although local NGOs and Western NGOs have embarked upon cooperative endeavors that are unprecedented in Kazakhstan, each has its own assortment of goals and strategies with respect to the environment and vis-à-vis each another. In general local NGOs want to receive short-term Western financial and technical assistance so they can implement small-scale projects without direct interference from the international community. But as part of the Western NGOs' broader efforts to develop civil society and build democracy over the long term, they seek instead to create local environmental NGOs that will ultimately be self-sufficient.

LOCAL NGOS IN KAZAKHSTAN

Two important trends have occurred in Kazakhstan's NGO sector since independence. The sheer number of local NGOs has increased, while their size has declined—although these organizations have proliferated, their base of support has contracted. Large-scale populist movements such as Nevada-Semipalatinsk have essentially disappeared. The memberships of most local NGOs are in the low double digits or smaller. Also, in devising their goals and strategies, many local NGOs have become increasingly disengaged from Kazakhstani politics, focusing on global rather than local issues. Rather than promoting certain policies, for example, the majority of local NGOs have chosen to concentrate their efforts on providing environmental information and education and promoting awareness. Local NGOs have turned their attention toward environmental issues with high visibility internationally, such as biodiversity and desertification, rather than those that are local.[16] Thus while many local environmental NGOs agree that the development of the Caspian poses a great danger to local populations and ecosystems, most are not actively involved in either opposing this development or advocating strict environmental regulations to govern it. In December 1997 several Western oil company representatives who had been working along Kazakhstan's Caspian coastline and in nearby oil fields since independence remarked that they had not yet witnessed any activism on the part of local NGOs around the Caspian. (They, as well as a number of USAID contractors and gas company representatives in Kazakhstan, agreed to speak with us only on condition of anonymity.)[17]

The majority of local NGOs in Kazakhstan see as their main objective the raising of environmental awareness among the general population in regard to local and international environmental issues. Ecocenter in Karaganda focuses on biodiversity issues; Central Asian Sustainable Development and Information Network's Center supports sustainable development; and Greenspace in Temirtau aims to increase awareness of pollution, especially industrial pollution. Their second, related goal is to prevent further environmental degradation in Kazakhstan and to clean up environmentally damaged sites. Third, a few groups, such as Green Salvation in Almaty, say that their primary goals are to place environmental issues on the policy agenda and to encourage the government to promulgate environmental protection legislation.[18] Fourth, with the loss of funding from the center in Moscow and the state of impoverishment in the country, a universal goal among local NGOs in Kazakhstan is to gain access to Western funding as a means of ensuring their survival.

Local NGOs are following certain general strategies for carrying out these goals. Since 1992 most small groups have become engaged primarily in activities that promote general awareness about the environment and provide some form of environmental education. Many local NGOs have produced children's books, pamphlets, and newsletters. The East Kazakhstan Green Party has established its own environmental information center to disseminate materials and to reprint important environmental laws and regulations.[19] At the international level some local NGOs have contributed to electronic mail publications. The Law and Environment Eurasia Partnership publishes a monthly journal, *Ecostan News*, in both Russian and English in order to reach both a local and international population.

To prevent further environmental degradation and to clean up existing problems, some groups have focused their efforts on data collection to monitor changes in the natural environment. For example, Ecocenter in Karaganda has undertaken a comprehensive assessment of environmental, social, and health effects in rural areas near the Semipalatinsk nuclear test site.[20] A few have engaged in more direct forms of environmental activism. For example, the local NGO Green Cross and Crescent International in Kazakhstan's new capital city, Astana (formerly known as Tselinograd and more recently called Akmola), has sought to improve the water quality in the River Nur in the Temirtau region.[21]

Whereas Nevada-Semipalatinsk organized mass rallies in opposition to nuclear testing, in the post-Soviet period most local NGOs have pulled back from tactics that involve popular mobilization and political confrontation. Except for Green Salvation, few politically motivated groups have attempted to influence legislation. The latter lobbied members of the Kazakhstani parliament (the Majlis) elected in March 1994 (and dissolved in March 1995) to be able to participate in the drafting and review of legislation related to the environment. And Green Salvation is really the only organization that still engages in some form of political activism that is directly aimed at government policy or practice.

In order to raise money from Western NGOs, all local NGOs undertake various activities aimed at improving their grant-writing skills and networking opportunities. Chief among these is active participation in special seminars and conferences organized by Western NGOs. These groups also expend an increasing amount of time and energy developing special relationships with particular international organizations. The Kokjiek Society for Aral Sea Problems, for example, works closely with the United Nations Development Program (UNDP) to develop grant-worthy projects and raise money from donors.[22] Another strategy aimed at attracting Western support is the adoption of Western language and buzz words such as *biodiversity* and *sustainable development,* even if they are detached from local circumstances.[23]

WESTERN NGOS IN KAZAKHSTAN

Like local NGOs, the main goal of Western NGOs with respect to Kazakhstan's environment is to promote environmental awareness among the public and government officials and in the private sector. Western NGOs such as ISAR also seek to encourage environmental protection, which they consider to be an integral part of their larger goal of "sustainable development." Western NGOs want to help local NGOs solve environmental problems in their own communities, and Western NGOs strive to foster a viable environmental movement as a way of promoting democratization in Kazakhstan. They see the creation of local NGOs in the short term as a tool for developing a viable civil society in the long term. The American Legal Consortium sought to develop a legal sector that would be conducive to the growth and expansion of local NGOs. Fostering a healthy NGO sector in Kazakhstan is part of its overarching goal "to strengthen legal knowledge, resources, and institutions in order to help the rule of law function as an effective framework and foundation for democratic, market, and social transitions."[24]

Western NGOs use several different strategies to cultivate a viable local NGO sector. They promote infrastructural development by providing local NGOs with small grants and technical support, often acting as the distributor of money that they have received from USAID or other government development agencies. For example, between 1994 and 1996, the American Legal Consortium awarded $1.1 million (from USAID) in small grants to fifty-four NGOs across Central Asia.[25] ISAR directed the Seeds of Democracy program from 1993 to 1997, which primarily entailed holding a series of competitions for grants to provide assistance to either individuals or groups working on environmental issues. ISAR's Almaty office awarded $480,000 in grants of as much as $3,000 each to more than 360 NGO projects in Central Asia.

Western NGOs also help local NGOs to collect information and disseminate it. Many grants have been used to buy computers and establish Internet access for local NGOs. Because travel costs are often prohibitive, e-mail connections have provided a useful alternative for maintaining contacts across political borders. Other Western NGOs, such as the Netherlands Organisation for International Development Cooperation, have helped organize conferences in which representatives from local NGOs throughout Central Asia can exchange ideas and information about environmental issues and discuss the political and organizational problems that they face. In practice, however, the conferences rarely foster solutions to these problems.

To empower local actors and communities to address their own environmental problems, Western NGOs also teach local NGOs decision-making techniques. This is of particular concern in Central Asia where local actors and communities have little experience in this regard; during the Soviet period they often relied upon the republican leaderships and Moscow for tentative solutions to environmental problems. Thus ISAR seeks to target small-scale projects that emphasize community participation. ISAR has attempted to achieve both goals by creating a board of directors made up of representatives of local environmental groups to help run Seeds of Democracy; the board decides which groups receive grants. ISAR has also used this method to teach local actors how to evaluate projects as they award grants. In contrast to the Soviet-era practice of relying upon personal networks, ISAR deliberately has attempted to teach local NGOs to award grants on the basis of merit. Although local NGOs have learned how to make collective decisions, the program has not been able to get rid of the old Soviet practice of relying on patronage ties.

Western NGOs also have pursued strategies to strengthen human capital. They conduct seminars and hold conferences to teach local NGOs in Central Asia grant-writing skills while developing informational networks among them. Both tasks are designed to help local NGOs continue to achieve international recognition and to acquire international support. Because most local NGOs are dependent upon international sources of funding to carry out their programs, it has become crucial for them to learn how Western foundations and grant-giving organizations work. They have also needed to learn and adopt the environmental discourse of Western NGOs. Many international actors, for example, such as the World Bank and the UNDP, target biodiversity and sustainable development for grants. As a result, Western NGOs like the American Legal Consortium eventually turned away from legal advocacy and toward organizing training seminars "to help [local] NGOs gain knowledge and skills to attract the necessary [international] attention" to allow them to survive.[26]

Most Western NGOs, then, focus on working at the grassroots level and creating links to local NGOs. By emphasizing global issues, Western NGOs are exporting new ideas and salient issues for local NGOs to work on without coming into conflict with government authorities in Kazakhstan. Topics such as biodiversity and deforestation are less politically sensitive than nuclear testing and oil exploration. Yet this strategy neglects local NGOs' need to build relationships with local and national officials as well as with their own communities. Western NGOs have also dissuaded local NGOs from choosing those domestic issues with the greatest potential environmental impact, such as the development of the energy sector in general and the Caspian Sea in particular. The Western NGOs have thus forged a strong connection between the local and global levels in Kazakhstan while engendering a sharp disconnect between grassroots organizations, the local community, and government officials at all levels. Moreover, by not encouraging local NGOs to address the energy sector, Western NGOs have discounted a key environmental issue with local, regional, national, and international ramifications.

THE EFFECTS OF ENVIRONMENTAL NGOS: NONDEMOCRATIC OUTCOMES

Although local NGOs' initial goals and strategies were generally inconsistent and potentially in conflict, this has changed as they have adapted to the Western NGOs' goals and strategies. Local NGOs have become engaged in more education and outreach to the international community and less political activism and confrontation with local authorities and the central government. They have deliberately turned their attention away from local and politically sensitive issues and their efforts away from lobbying the government. Instead, they focus on promoting issues such as biodiversity through educational projects so they can avoid confrontation with government elites and instead attract attention as well as support from international donor organizations. This is not to say that they do not criticize government policy but that they do so primarily in newsletters directed at the international community rather than through activities directed at government officials.[27]

The question, then, is to what extent these strategies are effective. In other words, are local NGOs and Western NGOs able to meet their respective goals? Are they contributing to the development of a civil society and therefore to the broader process of democratization? We contend that these strategies are not consistent with their original goals. Local NGOs and Western NGOs are not solving local environmental problems or serving domestic needs. While they provide general information about the importance of biodiversity and sustainable development, these are really long-term goals achieved through local activism and government participation. The NGOs could immediately address more direct dangers to human health that affect peoples' daily lives, such as water and soil contamination. Yet they are not mobilizing the population to demand that these local environmental issues receive greater government attention.

Most important, grants from Western NGOs do not appear to have fostered democracy or other forms of civic activism that could signal progress toward building civil society. These NGOs can be described and/or understood as a form of "associational culture." According to the ISAR representative Megan Falvey, "One of the greatest weaknesses of NGOs in Kazakhstan is that they have no direct link or contact with the local population. They do not function as [NGOs do] in the West, as a mediator between the government and the people. They function independently from both government and the people."[28]

Many local NGOs were begun by a group of close friends, colleagues, and family members and never developed a real support base in the population. Some have even fewer members now than when they started. This increases their drive for international recognition because it increases their dependence upon international sources of funding. Without expanding their membership local NGOs cannot rely on local dues to support their programs. Instead, they have turned to the foreign donor community for money. Ironically, this is mutually reinforcing, because the perception is that if the local NGOs were to grow, the money and equipment from Western NGOs would be divided among a greater number of members.

The disconnect between local NGOs and the local population has had two concrete effects: It has produced what we call "spin-off NGOs" and NGIs, or "nongovernmental individuals." Local NGOs in Kazakhstan often splinter into several smaller NGOs. This especially popular tactic has been highly successful in both implementing local NGOs' programs and procuring foreign donor assistance. By forming several spin-offs, more individuals become eligible to obtain grants. For example, the leader of Ecocenter in Karaganda encouraged and helped scientists closely affiliated with Ecocenter to form the Karaganda Eco-Museum.[29] In other cases a popular and experienced NGO leader can use his or her influence to enable friends to secure a grant for a project and thereby encourage the formation of a yet another small NGO. This has occurred, for example, among those serving on the board of directors of ISAR.

Thus many NGOs are shrinking rather than growing. In many cases they are run by a single individual. It appears that these two effects are integrally related. The spinning-off of new NGOs, combined with the general resistance to increasing membership or expanding their support base, has kept the composition of local NGOs in the hands of a few local activists who are closely connected. There is a disincentive to increase membership because it dilutes resources. Moreover, the existence of resources spurs the creation of new groups whose founders hope to get start-up money, rather than encouraging older groups to build upon and strengthen their base. For example, ISAR board members cannot participate in ISAR's grant competition or receive grants but can help to ensure that friends or relatives are eligible for the grant competition. This legacy of helping "friends of friends" impedes ISAR's objective of helping to strengthen social capital.

In some ways, then, local environmental NGOs in Kazakhstan have become the equivalent of small business enterprises or corner grocery stores. They organize for profit and are willing to supply what is in demand. In particular, they supply what the international community demands, which is in part the creation of more local NGOs. They quickly learn and adopt the issues and tactics that the foreign donor organizations favor. As in the Soviet period, the environment remains a safe issue for political mobilization. However, the environment no longer serves as a vehicle for protesting against the government or as a means for undertaking real public advocacy. Rather, it serves as a vehicle for individual profit. Perhaps, then, such local NGOs are a better source of entrepreneurism from which to breed capitalism than they are a source for greater democratization.

THE SOURCES OF NONDEMOCRATIC OUTCOMES: STRUCTURAL CONSTRAINTS AND WESTERN NGO STRATEGIES

Why have local environmental NGOs in Kazakhstan chosen strategies that seem to undermine rather than promote their own domestic strength and political importance, and why have Western NGOs chosen strategies that undermine the development of civil society and democratization? The explanation, we argue, stems from a set of structural constraints in post-Soviet Kazakhstan at both the domestic and international levels. Rather than addressing these constraints, Western NGOs' strategies have tended to exacerbate them. As a result, local environmental NGOs have developed much more slowly and in a different form than initially anticipated. In particular, these constraints and the failure of Western NGOs to overcome them illuminate why local NGOs have not focused on energy issues, even though these are crucial issues for the economic development and political stability of Kazakhstan.

DOMESTIC CONSTRAINTS

In Kazakhstan both local NGOs and Western NGOs must operate under essentially the same set of domestic legal and political constraints, which limits the range of strategies that both local NGOs and Western NGOs can pursue. The most striking example is Kazakhstan's civil code, which restricts NGOs from pursuing political goals by defining nonprofits as organizations that are engaged purely in social and philanthropic activities.[30] This stipulation also prevents Western NGOs from promoting politically active local NGOs.[31]

The political climate is also unfavorable to the development of an active NGO sector. Overall, NGOs face significant difficulties in Kazakhstan because of the limited degree of democratization that has taken place in the system as a whole since independence and the country's general retreat from democracy since the end of 1994. The resulting structural constraints for NGOs include restrictions on press freedom, political mobilization, and access to government officials, although these constraints are not as severe as under the Soviet system. A concrete example of this change in the political climate is the nature of the parliament elected in December 1995. According to Green Salvation, some deputies in the parliament elected in March 1994 (and dissolved by President Nazarbaev in March 1995) were sympathetic to environmental issues and willing to work with local organizations.[32] Several had ties with ecological groups and supported their interests in drafting and adopting legislation. Even so, the parliament has operated thus far as a rubber stamp for Nazarbaev's policies, leaving these environmental groups without any effective representation of their interests. Thus NGOs' goals and strategies are constrained by the very government that they are trying to influence.

By deliberately weakening the national legislature and delegating political and economic authority to the regional administrations, Nazarbaev inadvertently strengthened the regional *akims* (governors). Michael Boyd, an environmental consultant with the Harvard Institute for International Development in Kazakhstan, noted that "what the center decides is not clearly meaningful in the regions unless it is what the *akim* wants to support."[33] Thus it is not surprising that the former minister of ecology Nikolai Ivanovich Baev preferred to be appointed *akim* of the Mangistau oblast, an oil-rich region in western Kazakhstan, rather than retain a ministerial post.[34]

This decentralized political atmosphere has reinforced local NGOs' dependence upon the international community and their attempts to foster ties abroad rather than at home. For example, local NGOs feel a need to talk about biodiversity and other high-profile international environmental issues both because they are less politically sensitive and because the Kazakhstani government tolerates organizations such as the UNDP and the World Bank that support such programs. Local NGOs orient themselves toward projects that the international community is willing to fund. This gives them a means of participation that the government regards as legitimate. Western NGOs have encouraged this response by local NGOs because they too are reluctant to overtly challenge the Kazakhstani government. Because of their reluctance they have reduced their support for local environmental NGOs that push causes that could threaten domestic political and social stability; the Western NGOs instead have advocated causes of global concern.

Another set of domestic constraints stems directly from the Soviet legacy. Soviet-style communism precluded the development of a civil society; most local NGOs that appeared after the USSR's collapse lacked experience in forming autonomous and self-sufficient organizations. Even the local NGOs that arose under glasnost were, at least initially, unfamiliar with Western methods. For example, we found no local NGOs in Kazakhstan that follow common Western strategies for increasing membership or winning support for a particular cause, such as by canvassing door to door. This is exacerbated by a general unwillingness by post-Soviet citizens, who were compelled to join public organizations under the Soviet system, to voluntarily join social and political groups. Local NGOs lack the social capital necessary to foster cooperation among their communities.[35]

One element of social capital that is crucial for community building is a sense of trust among members of society. Part of the Soviet legacy, however, is distrust between the government and its citizenry, because the Soviet government was usually unresponsive to the needs of its populations. In Kazakhstan, for example, the Soviet government overlooked the environmental and health consequences of nuclear testing for decades. This legacy of distrust continues as more and more environmental ills are revealed to the general population and remain unresolved. Thus, not surprisingly, many Kazakhstanis are skeptical that the current leadership will address their environmental problems. Because of the history of censorship and secrecy, individuals are suspicious of most information that they receive, even if it is from the international community. Individuals do not trust their representatives in government, and the representatives do not seek to establish ties with their constituencies, even those that want to participate in formulating legislation. Interviews with members of Green Salvation confirm this observation. At the end of glasnost this organization sought to influence legislation through the Kazakhstani parliament. Although it was permitted to comment on the 1991 environmental bill, its recommendations were not included in the final draft.[36]

Another Soviet legacy is the way in which the Soviet government viewed the environment and is reflected in the legislation that regulated the use and allocation of environmental resources. Soviet planners promulgated environmental legislation not to protect the environment but to ensure its exploitation to generate income. The environment was a resource to be used for economic production, without regard for long-term effects on human health and safety or the protection of species and natural habitats. The governments of Western democracies in the 1970s responded to the demands of citizens by instituting environmental regulations that made polluting costly. In contrast, in the Soviet Union it was less expensive to pollute than to introduce more environmentally friendly technologies. Like other post-Soviet states, Kazakhstan did not inherit a strong regulatory and legal culture in regard to the environment.

Local NGOs and Western NGOs also are limited by the deteriorating economic situation. Local NGOs must rely upon international funding sources to survive. Internal sources of funding are largely nonexistent because the general population is unaccustomed to paying membership dues and lacks the money to do so. This is compounded by the local NGOs' loss of their tax-exempt status. Moreover, many local NGOs are comprised of former scientists (e.g., biologists, chemists, and zoologists) who can no longer survive on their salaries and whose survival depends on international funding of NGOs.

Local NGOs' dependence on Western NGOs and foundations for financial support has induced them to adapt their goals and strategies to these Western NGOs' goals and strategies. This is how international organizations such as the UNDP and World Bank transfer their ideas of environmentalism, which are tied directly to financial backing. The proliferation of environmental NGOs since Kazakhstan's independence is probably more the result of the availability of environmental grants than the safe haven that the environment offered for political mobilization.

Finally, the energy sector itself has a crucial role in Kazakhstan's future economic growth, and it acts as an important domestic constraint. Unlike other parts of the world, where indigenous people have mobilized to halt oil drilling for environmental and economic reasons, in Kazakhstan local populations and the local and regional *akims* generally view the exploitation of the Caspian basin favorably because they expect to benefit financially. Thus they also have a favorable view of the international oil companies that are directly contributing to this development.[37] According to Oleg Starukhin, a local safety and health expert for Kazakhstan CaspiShelf, a consortium of foreign companies that undertook seismic exploration in the northern Caspian, Nevada-Semipalatinsk was the exception among local NGOs in Kazakhstan.[38] Environmental damage in eastern Kazakhstan had a direct effect on the local population, and local residents viewed nuclear testing as a policy that promoted only outside interests (Moscow's). The issue of nuclear testing thus provoked the emergence of a powerful local NGO with strong ties to the population. This differs dramatically from the situation surrounding the Caspian Sea, where people are much less concerned with the environmental consequences of developing the oil and gas reserves than they are with the great economic potential. The Caspian, they believe, is their ticket to "health and wealth."[39] Even Western NGOs were reluctant to touch this subject after independence because so many people believed in the promise of Caspian oil.

INTERNATIONAL CONSTRAINTS

International actors bring their own sets of constraints for local NGOs and Western NGOs. One results from Western NGOs' dependence upon external funding sources that have their own particular agenda in Kazakhstan. Another concerns the direct role that international actors such as USAID are playing in Kazakhstan's energy sector. These two constraints have shaped the nature of local NGOs and hindered their development.

By providing information and promoting environmental legislation concerning the development of the Caspian Sea basin, international actors have essentially usurped the traditional function of local NGOs. Western NGOs in Kazakhstan are often compelled to conform to the goals and strategies of their funding sources. For example, USAID heavily underwrote ISAR's activities in Kazakhstan through Seeds of Democracy, a USAID program that provided start-up money to local NGOs to help create a viable civil society in the former Soviet Union. These Western NGOs are also constrained by the timeframe of USAID and other organizations, which tend to target short-term projects. For example, Seeds for Democracy funding was available to local NGOs for a maximum of two years.

In Kazakhstan USAID is one of the key international actors that provides assistance to both the NGO sector and the energy sector. One of USAID's main goals is to promote democratization by fostering the development of civil society, which was largely absent in the former Soviet Union. In this regard, the rule of law is essential to ensure that the government respects basic individual and human rights and guarantees freedom of association and of the press. Another goal of USAID is to encourage the transition to a market-based economy. This requires restructuring an economic system based upon centralized planning and creating a hospitable domestic environment open to foreign investment, especially in the energy sector. The rule of law also plays a crucial role here, serving as the foundation for contractual relations, protection of privately owned assets, and assignment of liability.

To achieve these goals USAID has pursued a multipronged strategy of funding projects at different levels. On one level it is encouraging privatization. For example, it funds organizations such as Winrock International (the Farmer to Farmer program) to teach farmers in Kazakhstan how to organize and manage a profitable private farm. On another level USAID is funding NGOs such as the U.S.-based National Democratic Institute (NDI) to assist with elections throughout the former Soviet Union. In regard to legal and regulatory reform in the energy sector, USAID has contracted with Hagler Bailly (a U.S.-based consulting firm) to help draft new environmental, safety, health, and technology laws to govern oil and gas development in the Caspian. Hagler Bailly is also helping to draft oil and gas laws to promote and sustain foreign investment in the energy sector as a whole. In addition, USAID has provided funding to the American Legal Consortium, ISAR, and Counterpart Consortium to help create a civil society by helping local NGOs.

USAID's goals and strategies hinder local NGOs and Western NGOs in related ways. First, these goals and strategies often conflict with and undermine one another, and many of their funding strategies are therefore counterproductive. While USAID is funding NGOs in the hope that they will produce a healthy civil society, the agency is usurping the role of NGOs by sending in consultants to draft legislation and advocate regulatory regimes in the energy sector without NGO involvement. Consider the Hagler Bailly project to create environmental, health, safety, and technical regulations for the Caspian Sea basin. This is a natural opportunity to include NGOs in the legislative process as representatives of local interests. Instead, USAID has emphasized the role of foreign consultants, who work only with local industry and their counterparts in government ministries and do not invite local environmental NGOs to participate in drafting laws or even consult them.[40]

Before foreign companies could start exploration studies and drilling in the northeastern part of the Caspian, an environmentally sensitive region, the government had to pass a new law to override the Soviet one that had declared it a protected zone.[41] Subsequently, foreign oil companies and the Kazakhstan state oil company formed the consortium known as OKIOC to study the environmental effects of undertaking a seismic study in this part of the Caspian and to examine the effect of oil exploration upon the sturgeon stocks, seal population, and flora.[42] Contrast this with what happens in the United States when oil companies push for the right to drill off the coast of Alaska. Fearing oil spills and contamination, local NGOs organize a campaign to lobby Congress to prevent the opening of Alaska's pristine wildlife to oil exploration. Such an action was unilaterally preempted in the case of the Caspian by the foreign oil companies and governments. Moreover, even the most active local NGOs (e.g., Green Salvation) have little influence because the political and legal climates do not tolerate litigation and political activism. Without such a climate local NGOs cannot play the role that, for example, a Natural Resources Defense Council or Environmental Defense Fund plays in the United States.

In short, because both the Kazakhstani government and Western governments view oil development in the Caspian basin as essential for economic development and to secure the international energy supply, they have essentially excluded local NGOs from the legislative and regulatory process. Rather, oil companies and ministries appear to be regulating themselves. Since 1994 the foreign oil and gas companies working in Kazakhstan have formed the Kazakhstan Petroleum Association. As of December 1997, the association had thirty-two member companies. They formed a subcommittee on the environment to negotiate directly with the Kazakhstani government on all new environmental regulations for the Caspian basin.[43]

Also, USAID has increasingly stressed economic development over democracy building. The unequal weight given to these two goals has indirectly resulted in the weakening of the nascent local NGO sector that was emerging after the breakup of the Soviet Union. During the first few years of independence, USAID concentrated on helping to establish democratic regimes in Central Asia. Elections and human rights, for example, were high-priority issues. Yet over time USAID has shifted its focus away from democracy building and toward economic issues surrounding the Caspian basin. This change seems to have coincided with Nazarbaev's own shift away from democratization in order to push through market-based reforms that were unpopular in the first elected parliament.[44] As it became clear that the Kazakhstani government was less interested in building democracy than in revitalizing its economy through foreign investment, USAID became a more overt advocate of "economics first," particularly in the energy sector. Because the Caspian basin is considered both a crucial future source of economic growth for Kazakhstan and an alternative energy supply for the West, it has become the primary focus of international attention and activity.[45]

Western NGOs reacted to these changes by slowing their efforts at so-called democracy-building programs. Following the disbanding of parliament in March 1995, for example, the American Legal Consortium pulled out and the National Democratic Institute limited the scope of its activities. ISAR continued to stress educational activities among local NGOs. In effect, Western NGOs accepted the contracted domestic political situation instead of working with international actors, the national government, and local NGOs to overcome these political obstacles.

Another significant international constraint is the other international actors that are playing a direct role in the environmental and energy sectors. The extensive role of the oil companies in the local communities with oil and gas resources has decreased the demand for and appeal of environmental activism in post-Soviet Kazakhstan. For example, early on, foreign oil companies as well as Kazakh CaspiShelf have held town meetings to promote support for the development of the Caspian. At the end of the first phase of the exploration in the Caspian in May 1995, OKIOC held a public meeting to explain and present the results of its work and to discuss prospects for the future. Both the general public and the press attended the meeting. Perhaps not unsurprisingly, the oil companies have not sought to engage local NGOs or Western NGOs in discussing oil exploration in the Caspian but to circumvent them. According to one company that belongs to the consortium, it received no negative feedback from the local communities.[46] Overall, because the oil companies have pursued a strategy of engaging the local population directly, rather than through local NGOs, they have lessened the role of local activists. The companies have instead attempted to give the local population a perceived stake in order to prevent mobilization of opposition later.

The foreign oil and gas companies are also popular among the local population because they are seen as solving acute economic and social problems; they are not seen as creating potential environmental problems. This defuses any potential support that local NGOs might have in opposing the development of the energy sector in general and the activities of the oil companies in particular. The representative of only one local NGO (Green Salvation) with whom we spoke commented that Chevron was destroying the environment through its production of the Tengiz oil fields. However, the news shots of oil spills that Green Salvation used to back up this remark were actually the result of Soviet methods of drilling. Chevron had been asked to clean these spills up as part of its deal with the Kazakhstani government but had refused.[47] Local populations view Chevron and other foreign oil companies such as Hurricane Hydrocarbons as "heroes" because these companies have been channeling substantial amounts of money directly into the regions in which they are operating—so much that the local and regional *akims* have not had to turn to the government for money. For example, in a five-year period Chevron allocated US$10 million each year to support the social sector in the Atyrau oblast—money for improving the local water system and power supply and building schools, hospitals, and housing.[48] In addition, Chevron and other oil and gas companies make direct contributions to the budget through tax payments. Both the local governments and the labor unions have insisted upon higher pay and a lifetime guarantee of employment for their workers. Because the labor unions are among the most important political interest groups in post-Soviet Kazakhstan, the oil companies have had to employ a larger labor force than necessary.[49]

The Kazakhstani government has addressed social and environmental problems in part by selling off oil and gas companies in those regions that have been hit hardest by the Soviet Union's demise. The first Soviet oil and gas company that was sold to foreign buyers, Yuzhneftegas, is located in Kazakhstan's poorest region, the Kyzl-Orda oblast. To buy Yuzhneftegas, Hurricane Hydrocarbons had to agree to pay all the social obligations and economic costs of the company and surrounding area. As a result, Hurricane Hydrocarbons spent US$4 million a month on local labor costs alone, because Yuzhneftegas twice increased the number of employees on its payroll before it was bought. The employees are also better paid than the average Kazakhstani worker, at about US$750 a month, compared to the average of US$150.

Hurricane Hydrocarbons' experience is not unique. An examination of several contracts with foreign companies active in the energy sector reveals a consistent pattern of foreign companies' adopting all the social and economic burdens in the regions, cities, towns, and villages surrounding the fields to which they have bought rights to explore and produce oil and gas. These responsibilities include maintaining full employment and paying back wages and a wide range of social services, such as contributing to pension funds, building schools and hospitals, and supporting local sports teams. In fact, the process for negotiating and winning contracts is, to a large extent, predicated upon the willingness and ability of international companies to provide such services. The oil companies are able to buy off local opposition by providing a broad base of social services to the population at large. In this way the oil companies are able to avoid interacting with local NGOs.

The oil and gas companies' goals and strategies are more compatible with USAID goals and strategies than with the NGOs' goals and strategies. For example, both USAID and the oil companies stress economic development over political development, and both want legal reform to create an appropriate or "safe" atmosphere for foreign investment. Since the dissolution of parliament USAID has pulled back from trying to impose democratic norms and institutions in Kazakhstan. Instead, it has focused on programs that will facilitate social and political stability within Kazakhstan and within Central Asia on the whole. The Kazakhstan government has also made it clear that it prefers economic development to political development in the short run and as a result has sought to curtail local NGO activity that is political.

Western NGOs have not succeeded in their overall goal of building a viable civil society in Kazakhstan because they have not tried to address the structural constraints at both the domestic and international levels by providing appropriate guidance and incentives. Instead, they have encouraged local NGOs to respond to this situation by adopting politically safe or nonthreatening goals and strategies that target international rather than domestic constituencies. As a result, Western NGOs have contributed directly to the atomization and depoliticization of local NGOs in Kazakhstan immediately after independence.

Overall, Western NGOs need to reconcile the contradiction inherent in strategies that focus at the grassroots yet are directed at the interests and concerns of the international community. This can be achieved by encouraging local NGOs to forge links with their national government and local communities as well as to interact more closely with local and regional officials in an effort to increase government responsiveness. In short, Western NGOs should do more to spur political activism among local NGOs. The environment and the energy sector provide a particularly appropriate arena for this change in strategy.

First and foremost, Western NGOs should intensify their efforts at building a civil society in Kazakhstan by promoting local NGO development. Since we did our research in 1997, ISAR has begun to focus its attention on the Caspian region; with financial support from USAID and the UNDP, ISAR initiated a three-year program in April 1999 to strengthen cooperation among NGOs in the Caspian basin countries—Azerbaijan, Georgia, Iran, Kazakhstan, Russia, and Turkmenistan. ISAR has succeeded in forcing the oil and gas companies to deal with local NGOs and not just official government representatives in making decisions. Specifically, in September 2000 ISAR organized a seminar, NGO Interaction with Transnational Corporations, that attracted participation from about forty NGOs and ten companies that operate in the Caspian region in a roundtable discussion of ways to enhance cooperation.[50] Whereas prior NGO activity focused on environmental education, many Caspian programs today are turning toward issues of monitoring. Although this initiative is top-down rather than "bottom up," ISAR has helped to strengthen local NGOs in the Caspian basin, resulting in the creation of environmental watchdogs.[51] ISAR's Caspian program has provided opportunities for local NGOs to monitor the operations of the oil and gas companies and then to publicize environmental violations.

Western NGOs also need to encourage local NGOs to look to their own government officials to respond to environmental problems, particularly at the local and regional levels, because these people have become the real sources of authority over the environment. Local NGOs and their local and regional governments need information and technical support designed to help them build links with one another. Training seminars for local NGOs, for example, could focus on negotiation skills, lobbying, and other forms of policy advocacy. At the same time local and regional officials must be persuaded that they have a stake in local NGOs' efforts to address environmental issues; they should be invited to participate in training seminars that address their concerns.

In addition, Western NGOs should encourage local NGOs to foster links with their local communities. This includes funding local NGO initiatives that focus on issues of local importance and rewarding local NGOs that seek to increase their membership and expand their support base. For example, training seminars could focus on strategies for recruiting new members and finding domestic sources of funding, rather than on how to obtain Western funding. Grants could require matching funds gathered from the local community and could provide support for organizing public hearings and other forms of outreach. Encouraging local NGOs to focus on local issues will build links to their community and eventually to their local and regional governments. Funding should also be directed at programs to build trust among local NGOs, the local community, and government officials by targeting small short-term projects that require local NGOs to orchestrate the participation of the community and local government. This is a concrete way to demonstrate to the local community that both local NGOs and the government can play a positive role in their daily lives. ISAR has established a separate program on environmental and health issues in Atyrau in western Kazakhstan, which is one of the main oil and gas regions in the country.

Finally, Western NGOs should have programs in Kazakhstan that encourage foreign companies and consultants to include local NGOs in the drafting and monitoring of environmental regulations and to use them as an intermediary in the Western NGOs' dealings with the national and regional governments. In addition, Western NGOs could provide training programs to help local NGOs develop the capacity to monitor compliance with environmental regulation, particularly concerning the gas and oil sectors. During glasnost the U.S.-based Natural Resources Defense Council provided legal training seminars in the former Soviet Union to prepare environmental lawyers. The same could be done in Central Asia. Likewise, Kazakhstan needs economists and policy advocates trained in environmental economics. Michael Boyd of the Harvard Institute has a few such programs under way to help Kazakhstan understand the economic implications of the overreliance on oil wealth.

These efforts all would help create a legal culture in which citizens have the opportunity to challenge government policies through institutional channels rather than through street protests alone. The key is to convey to local communities, domestic authorities, and international actors alike that the development of a burgeoning civil society is in their best interest in the long term. This can be conveyed most clearly in the energy sector, wherein the costs of environmental damage can certainly outweigh the expected benefits. Local communities and government officials do not yet seem to understand that a well-developed local environmental NGO sector, particularly around the Caspian Sea, can serve to limit these potential costs by monitoring the activities of foreign companies. At the same time international actors are shortsighted in their attitude toward local NGOs as inimicable to a favorable investment climate in the energy sector. This presents Western NGOs with an overwhelming burden that could be reduced by active and well-funded local NGOs. Moreover, unless local activism is fully encouraged at the earliest stages of Caspian Sea development, the local community is likely to claim at later stages that its interests were never considered or served by foreign companies.

NOTES

1. Jane I. Dawson, *Econationalism: Antinuclear Activism and National Identity in Russia, Lithuania, and Ukraine* (Durham: Duke University Press, 1996).

2. Before the collapse of the Soviet Union, ISAR was known as the Institute for Soviet-American Relations.

3. For detailed information about the proven and suspected reserves of the Caspian, see Energy Information Administration, U.S. Department of Energy, "Caspian Sea Region," July 2001, http://www.eia.doe.gov/emeu/cabs/caspian.html (November 13, 2001).

4. For detailed information about the different oil and gas projects in the Caspian, see Energy Information Administration, "Caspian Sea Region."

5. Michael Bratton, "Beyond the State: Civil Society and Associational Life in Africa," *World Politics* 41, no. 3 (April 1989): 407–30.

6. Although discussion clubs were technically the first NGOs to emerge in the Soviet Union, we are primarily concerned with the role of mass movements in the late 1980s. For an organizational history of NGOs in Kazakhstan before 1991, see Vitalii Ponomarev, *Samodeyatel'nye Obshestvennyi Organizatsii Kazakhstana i Kyrgyzstana,*

1987–1991 (The Independent Social Organizations of Kazakhstan and Krygyzstan, 1987–1991) (Moscow: Institut issledovaniyaekstreenal'nykh professov [SSSR], 1991).

7. Dawson, *Econationalism*.

8. D. J. Peterson, *Troubled Lands: The Legacy of Soviet Environmental Destruction* (Boulder, Colo.: Westview, 1993), pp. 202–6.

9. During the Gorbachev period policy makers supported the emergence of environmental movements because they sought to encourage a more rational use of natural resources as a means of revitalizing the stagnate economy.

10. Peterson, *Troubled Lands*.

11. Tatyana A. Saiko, "Environmental Problems of the Caspian Sea Region and the Conflict of National Priorities," in Michael H. Glantz and Igor S. Zonn, eds., *Scientific, Environmental, and Political Issues in the Circum-Caspian Region*, pp. 41–52 (Dordrecht, Netherlands: Kluwer Academic, 1996).

12. Ibid.

13. Yuri Eidinov, "Ecological Aspects of Offshore Operations," *Oil and Gas of Kazakhstan*, no. 6 (November 1997): 23–27, and Oleg Starukhin, a local safety and health expert for Kazakhstan CaspiShelf, interview by authors, Almaty, Kazakhstan, December 1997.

14. Megan Falvey, ISAR, interview by authors, Almaty, Kazakhstan, December 6, 1997.

15. See, for example, Anne Garbutt, "NGO Support Organizations in Central Asia," paper prepared for the International NGO Training and Research Centre, Oxford, October 1997, p. 4.

16. Falvey interview. See also various issues of *Ecostan News*, http://www.ecostan .org/Ecostan/enindex.html (November 12, 2001).

17. Oil company representatives, interviews by authors, Almaty, Kazakhstan, December 1997.

18. Sergei Kuratov, founder and chief coordinator of Green Salvation, interview by authors, Almaty, Kazakhstan, December 1997.

19. American Legal Consortium, "Innovations and Impacts: Success Stories of Central Asian NGOs," report available from Chemonics International Consulting, Washington, D.C., 1996, p. 24. Despite the name, the East Kazakhstan Green Party is not a political party.

20. Initiative for Social Action and Renewal in Eurasia, "Internal Final Report on Kazakhstan Environmental NGOs," Almaty, Kazakhstan, 1997.

21. Ibid.

22. Ibid.

23. Falvey interview; Michael Boyd, Harvard Institute for International Development in Kazakhstan, interview by authors, Almaty, December 1997.

24. American Legal Consortium, "Innovations and Impacts," p. 1.

25. American Legal Consortium grants were awarded to facilitate the establishment of rule of law in Central Asia and covered such fields as human rights, women's issues, children's rights, environment, business development, rights of the disabled, the elderly, consumer rights, culture, NGO development, legal education, conflict resolution, veterans' rights, media, and farmers' cooperatives. Grants were used to fund edu-

cation, publishing, research, equipment, legal consulting, conferences, and travel. See *Ecostan News* 4, no. 4 (April 1, 1996), http://www.ecostan.org/Ecostan/enindex.html (November 12, 2001).

26. Lowry Wyman, American Legal Consortium, interview by authors, Kazakhstan, March 1995.

27. For examples, see *Ecostan News*, http://www.ecostan.org/Ecostan/enindex.html (November 12, 2001).

28. Falvey interview.

29. ISAR, "Internal Final Report."

30. Grazhdanskii kodeks Respublika Kazakhstana (Civil Code of the Republic of Kazakhstan) (Almaty: December 27, 1994). See also Sarah Prosser, "Reform Within and Without the Law: Further Challenges for Central Asian Nongovernmental Organizations," *Harvard Asia Quarterly* 4, no. 3 (Summer 2000): 4–16, available at http://www.fas.harvard.edu/asiactr/haq/200003/0003a001.htm (November 12, 2001).

31. Falvey interview.

32. Kuratov interview.

33. Boyd interview.

34. Baev was the minister of ecology from 1995 to 1997.

35. On social capital see Michael Taylor, *The Possibility of Cooperation* (Cambridge: Cambridge University Press, 1987); and Elinor Ostrom, *Governing the Commons: The Evolution of Institutions for Collective Action* (Cambridge: Cambridge University Press, 1990).

36. Kuratov interview. Members of Green Salvation argue that the 1996 draft version of the law was substantially worse than the original 1991 legislation. The "draft legislation is aimed not at protecting nature and is not founded upon a model of sustainable development; rather, it seeks to ensure the continued utilization of natural resources." See L. N. Semyenova, S. B. Svitelman, and S. G. Kuratov, "Environmental Rule of Law," *Ecostan News* 5 (1997), http://www.ecostan.org/Ecostan/enindex.html (November 12, 2001).

37. For an article that suggests that the local population should be more skeptical, see Seymour Hersh, "The Price of Oil: What Was Mobil up to in Kazakhstan and Russia?" *New Yorker*, July 9, 2001, pp. 48–65.

38. Starukhin interview.

39. Ibid.

40. Various USAID contractors, interviews by authors, Almaty, Kazakhstan, March and December 1997.

41. Eidinov, "Ecological Aspects of Offshore Operations."

42. Ibid.

43. Representatives of oil and gas companies operating in Kazakhstan, interviews by authors, Almaty, Kazakhstan, December 1997.

44. Nazarbaev dissolved this parliament in March 1995, largely for this reason.

45. Janet Bogne, deputy chief of mission, U.S. Embassy, interview by authors, Almaty, Kazakhstan, March 1997.

46. Oil and gas representatives' interviews.

47. Ibid.

48. Ibid.

49. Representatives of oil and gas companies working in Kazakhstan, interview by authors, Almaty, Kazakhstan, March and December 1997.

50. For details see "NGOs Face Off with Corporations and Find Potential for Cooperation," *Give & Take*, Winter 2001, pp. 22–27.

51. Readers who wish to acquaint themselves with recent developments in this area should consult Erika Weinthal, "State Capacity and the Internationalization of Environmental Protection in Central Asia" (paper presented at the Olin Seminar Series on Reconceptualizing Central Asia: States and Societies in Formation, May 17, 2001), which is set to appear in the forthcoming Pauline Jones Luong and John Schoeberlein, eds., *Reconceptualizing Central Asia: States and Societies in Formation* (Boulder, Colo.: Westview).

Chapter 7

INTERNATIONAL DEMOCRACY ASSISTANCE
IN UZBEKISTAN AND KYRGYZSTAN:
BUILDING CIVIL SOCIETY FROM THE OUTSIDE?

Fiona B. Adamson

Since the Central Asian republics gained independence from the Soviet Union in 1991, foreign governments and Western NGOs have spent tens of millions of dollars to promote democratization in the region. In 1998 alone the U.S. Agency for International Development (USAID) spent more than $11 million on democratic transition programs in Uzbekistan and Kyrgyzstan.[1] In addition, international organizations, Western European governments, and private organizations, such as the Soros foundations, have all been involved in promoting democracy in the region. Much of the money finances strategies and programs that are designed to strengthen civil society, particularly the creation of an independent third sector in the region, composed of local advocacy NGOs such as professional organizations, women's organizations, and environmental groups. The logic behind these assistance efforts is that funding local and independent

An earlier version of this chapter was presented at the annual convention of the International Studies Association, Los Angeles, March 14–18, 2000. The findings are based on field research, including more than sixty interviews, that I conducted in Uzbekistan and Kyrgyzstan in September and October 1998. The names of my sources appear in the original report, "Building Civil Society from the Outside: An Evaluation of International Democracy Assistance Strategies in Uzbekistan and Kyrgyzstan," which I will make available upon request.

advocacy NGOs helps to build independent interest groups in civil society that in turn can provide the impetus for democratic reforms or transition.

In Central Asia these democracy assistance programs have produced a number of notable achievements. Both the government and the population now increasingly recognize a burgeoning third sector in the region as a legitimate political player, and many NGOs supported by democracy assistance programs have attained a high degree of success. Democracy assistance programs have empowered local women's groups, such as the Women's Resource Center in Tashkent, Uzbekistan, to engage in community organizing and to publish original research.[2] Democracy assistance programs also provide computers, Internet access, and other infrastructural improvements in the region and sponsor education, training, and exchange programs that are producing a new Westernized elite. Independent local NGOs, such as the International Center Interbilim clearinghouse in Bishkek, Kyrgyzstan, act as hubs for grassroots organizing on a variety of issues, such as legal reform. And a number of independent international NGOs such as the Soros Foundation and the Christian organization Central Asia Free Exchange (CAFE) provide education, training, and skill development to sectors of the youth population.

Democracy assistance programs, however, have not been as successful in effecting large-scale structural changes in the region or strengthening grassroots democracy beyond individual local successes. It is increasingly clear that Central Asian states are not on a track toward anything resembling liberal democracy. Instead, the trend is toward consolidation of authoritarian or semiauthoritarian rule in the region, coupled with the strategic incorporation of some institutional features and discursive trappings of democracy, resulting in little change in the overall structure of power relations within society and continued economic stagnation and underdevelopment.[3] Despite attempts by international actors to strengthen civil society in Uzbekistan and Kyrgyzstan by supporting the development of a third sector and independent civic advocacy groups, popular opposition to authoritarian regimes in the region comes not from a vibrant Western-style NGO sector but from religious movements or ethnic mobilization. Islamist movements in particular have gained strength as expressions of popular opposition to existing regimes, and Central Asian state elites view these movements as posing a threat to existing power configurations in the region.[4]

Why have international democracy assistance strategies generally been so ineffective in building a working and politically engaged civil society in Central Asia? One reason is certainly the challenging economic and political conditions under which international actors operate in Uzbekistan and Kyrgyzstan. Given the concrete challenges that local field offices face in implementing programs there, the success rate of the individual programs supported by democracy assistance efforts in the region is surprisingly high. This attests to the dedication and persistence of many international actors. At the same time, however, the ideal end points that many of these programs and strategies are designed to achieve stand in severe contrast to the reality in which international actors carry out their programs. In part, this may indeed be due to a failure by some international assistance organizations to incorporate an understanding of variations in regional conditions into the design of their strategies. As Sarah E. Mendelson and John K. Glenn point out in the first chapter of this book, democratization strategies designed to be applied to "thickly integrating" states are unlikely to have the same effect in "unintegrated states."

At the same time, however, Mendelson and Glenn's discussion of levels of integration into the international community implies but does not address a deeper issue that is at stake here. They define integration as embracing "norms, ideas, and practices common to the democratic states of Western Europe and North America."[5] The norms and practices that democracy assistance programs are promoting have developed within specific cultural and institutional contexts. It is therefore necessary to address not only the relationship that exists between strategies and ideal results but also between the ideal results and local conditions. In other words, evaluations of democracy assistance programs must move beyond an approach that adjusts strategies to fit local conditions and instead incorporates a more fundamental and open discussion regarding the preconditions and assumptions inherent in the notion that exporting a stylized version of liberal democracy to diverse local settings is either possible or desirable. Are the seeds of liberal democracy likely to spawn the same offspring under all conditions? This question suggests that more attention needs to be paid to the interaction between institutions and political culture or, more specifically, the relationship between transplanted and indigenous political institutions.[6]

In this chapter I discuss some challenges facing democracy promotion in Central Asia and suggest reasons why such a gap exists between the vision of democracy that international actors are promoting and the actual results that democracy assistance programs in the region produce. To do this I draw attention to microlevel processes and dilemmas that shape interactions between international assistance organizations and local actors, and I juxtapose the macrolevel goals that shape democracy assistance programs with the microlevel political conditions that local field offices of democracy-promoting agencies and international NGOs encounter. International democracy assistance programs, however well intended, have not reached broad segments of society in Central Asia and have not resulted in macrolevel democratic outcomes in Central Asian states. In fact, many programs have interacted with the local environment in ways that unintentionally aggravate a number of conditions, such as corruption, income inequality, and dependence on foreign aid. These results, however, should not be taken merely as a sign that the strategies that actors use to promote democratization in the region have failed—because many individual success stories indeed exist at the local level. Rather, they should serve as a reminder that democracy promotion activities, despite great imbalances in power between international and local actors, do not occur within an institutional or cultural vacuum at the local level but are characterized by two-way interactions between international and local actors. The outcome is shaped as much by the local environment into which democracy assistance programs are inserted as it is by the strategies that international actors use to promote democratization.

Local actors draw upon international democracy assistance programs to pursue their own interests, just as international actors in the region represent a certain set of interests to which they are implicitly or explicitly bound. When these interests coincide or can be coordinated, individual programs are likely to be successful. The majority of international assistance organizations have their headquarters in advanced industrial democracies; their overall organizational structure, mission, macrolevel strategies, and programs reflect this context.[7] The goals of international assistance organizations operating in Central Asia reflect the larger geopolitical context within which they operate. Democracy promotion is a key component of U.S. foreign policy, and a large number of democracy assistance organizations in the region are funded by USAID or other government agencies and international organizations.[8] A number of independent international NGOs operate in the region and do not receive government funding, yet the majority of democracy promotion activities in the region are ultimately government funded. There are thus clear limits to the extent to which democracy promotion activities by government-funded international NGOs can be directly compared to the activities of transnational advocacy networks and issue networks that originate predominately from nonstate societal interests rather than the policy interests of powerful states.[9]

Much of the ineffectiveness of democracy assistance strategies in post-Soviet Central Asia is attributable to the challenges that international assistance organizations face as they attempt to operate simultaneously in two or more different institutional environments. Many strategies and programs carried out by international NGOs and other assistance organizations are designed at their headquarters and applied to a variety of local settings. Local branches of international assistance organizations must operate under different conditions in Central Asia and must adapt to these conditions in order to survive. This results in internal incoherence and inefficiency in organizations, as international actors cope with and try to reconcile the contradictory demands of the different environments in which they are embedded. Indeed, the most effective international NGOs are those that operate independently, are flexible, and are able to develop reactive strategies based on local needs, as opposed to proactively implementing strategies imported from abroad. In the former case small international NGOs engaged in grassroots work attempt to meet and articulate local interests. In the latter case international actors arrive with their own interests and goals and attempt to shape local society to fit these end points. In practice, of course, international actors apply a mix of proactive and reactive strategies in their interactions with the local environment. In principle, however, democracy promotion and the building of civil society are to some extent inherently proactive strategies.

The concept of international actors who promote "grassroots" civil society and democratization in Central Asia is therefore filled with practical and, indeed, philosophical contradictions. To what extent can projects that are run, funded, and administered by international actors really bring about local forms of democratic participation? What is the version of democracy that such actors are promoting? Is this vision appropriate to local conditions? What is the relationship between international democracy assistance and the larger international geopolitical context, and how does this play out at the local level? In countries such as Uzbekistan and Kyrgyzstan, what should be the balance between basic economic development programs and programs that are designed to promote democratization and civil society? In this chapter my purpose is to provide a context for thinking about the larger issues raised by these questions, as they relate to international democracy assistance in the region.

First, I examine the political context of democracy assistance in Uzbekistan and Kyrgyzstan. Despite their differences, the two countries share a number of characteristics as "unintegrated states" that provide similar challenges to international actors in designing effective democracy assistance strategies. Second, I present an overview of the international actors, strategies, and programs in the sector of civil society development in Central Asia. I focus primarily on the activities of U.S.-based international donor NGOs, many of which are largely government funded, and I pay particular attention to the ways in which the strategies of international actors have adapted to local conditions. The empirical examples in the chapter are designed to give the reader a sense of what democracy assistance activities look like in Central Asia, how they relate to the local environment, and the inherent dilemmas that local field offices face when they are caught between the conflicting interests of democracy promoters in industrialized states and local actors who are pursuing their own interests. In the conclusion I address what the successes and failures of democracy assistance in Central Asia imply for the overall project of democracy promotion in the region and the power and limits of NGOs that are engaged in this project.

THE POLITICAL CONTEXT OF DEMOCRACY ASSISTANCE IN UZBEKISTAN AND KYRGYZSTAN

The post-Soviet republics of Central Asia can be described as "unintegrated states," given that these states are far from adopting the institutional practices and political cultures that define Western European and transatlantic political communities. This should not be surprising, given the states' geographical location, historical legacies, cultural orientations, and low levels of economic development. Indeed, state elites in the region look only partially to the West as a model for political development. Turkey, Iran, Russia, Saudi Arabia, China, and other East Asian states have all shown interest in the region, and various parties in Central Asia have held many of these countries up as appropriate role models for Uzbekistan and Kyrgyzstan.[10]

Within the Central Asian context Uzbekistan and Kyrgyzstan appear to provide examples of two contrasting types of political environments that have attracted democracy assistance. Uzbekistan has an authoritarian regime, a largely state-controlled economy, and severe restrictions on freedom of expression and association, while Kyrgyzstan has institutionalized many of the formal institutions of democracy, adopted a policy of economic liberalization, tolerated a relatively independent press, and generally places fewer restrictions on freedoms of expression and association. While these differences do matter for understanding the effect of democracy assistance, more significant are the shared characteristics of the two countries. In addition to their common Soviet institutional legacies, the two countries have similarly high levels of corruption; both are marked by a disjunction between formal and informal political and economic institutions; both have low levels of economic development, accompanied by an uneven distribution of wealth; and both are characterized by a weakened public sector infrastructure, especially in realms such as education, health, and social security.

UZBEKISTAN: AUTHORITARIANISM AND STATE-RUN ECONOMY

Uzbekistan is in many respects less democratic today than during the glasnost period of the late 1980s. During the 1988–1989 period of liberalization in Moscow, widespread political opposition movements such as Birlik (Unity) and Erk (Will, or Freedom) were allowed to operate and hold mass demonstrations. Following Uzbekistan's independence in August 1991, however, President Islam Karimov increasingly strengthened his grip on power and ensured state penetration into almost all areas of social, political, and economic life. The political context of democracy assistance in Uzbekistan cannot be understood without taking into account the sweeping powers of Karimov and the cult of personality that surrounds him and his office.

Karimov has advocated a gradual, rather than rapid, transition to a market economy, arguing that rapid economic transition would be too disruptive. He makes a similar argument with respect to transformation in the political realm. As justification for his political and economic policies, Karimov has in the past pointed to the relative stability in contemporary Uzbek society, especially when compared to the economic collapse in Russia and the civil wars in the bordering countries of Tajikistan and Afghanistan. Indeed, despite the February 1999 bombings in Tashkent, Uzbek society still has a level of stability that gives Karimov's policies a strong measure of legitimacy with the population, which appears to place greater value on economic and political stability than on increased democratization.[11] At the same time, however, evidence exists that the increasingly repressive policies that Karimov's regime has been using to deter the rise of political Islam in the region may be creating conditions that breed the very instability that they are supposedly designed to curtail.[12]

While the pace of political and economic reform has been slow, the implementation of nationalizing policies such as language reform have been fast. Uzbekistan quickly made Uzbek its single official language and is well on its way to the adoption of a Latin alphabet. The country eliminated Soviet symbols in the space of a few months, when in 1996 Karimov ordered the renaming of "administrative-territorial and other objects," arguing that "the names of objects that serve the old order and communist ideology deflect the people from the concept of independence."[13] Uzbekistan has consistently been the most anti-Russian of the Central Asian republics, and it has almost eliminated the Russian language from public view. The state has shut down most Russian cultural groups, with the result that there is little overt opposition to Uzbekification policies. Despite this process, however, Russian still remains the lingua franca among elites.

On paper Uzbekistan has some formal institutions of democracy. Indeed, the constitution, official government documents, and speeches by Karimov are often full of the terminology of liberal democracy. The constitution, for example, guarantees a number of civil and political rights, including freedom of the press and freedom of association. These rights are not, however, recognized in practice. The government owns most printing presses and can easily withhold printing supplies and time slots. Bureaucratic red tape and loopholes can impede registration of nongovernmental organizations within the state. Nominally, Uzbekistan has held parliamentary and presidential elections, but restrictions on political party formation and bureaucratic impediments have prevented open and democratic multiparty elections.[14]

KYRGYZSTAN: ECONOMIC AND POLITICAL LIBERALIZATION

In contrast to Karimov in Uzbekistan, President Askar Akaev of Kyrgyzstan embraced policies of economic and political liberalization immediately after independence. Determined to win favor with the international community, he began to promote a nominally free press, private political associations, and a market economy. Kyrgyzstan quickly gained recognition in the West as an "oasis of democracy" in Central Asia, and by the end of 1993 Western donors had pledged almost half a billion dollars in foreign assistance to the tiny republic.[15] Kyrgyzstan's acceptance into the World Trade Organization (WTO) in 1998—the first newly independent state of the former Soviet Union to gain admittance—demonstrates the extent to which Kyrgyzstan has made neoliberal economic reforms.[16]

Kyrgyzstan has been less insistent than Uzbekistan on ridding itself of the symbols of the Soviet past. Kyrgyzstan's laws give Russian the status of language of "inter-ethnic communication" and make it an official language in some areas.[17] Kyrgyzstan still universally uses the Cyrillic alphabet, and no one has torn down or replaced Soviet monuments, as in Uzbekistan. Ethnic minorities have been generally free to organize and form associations, although, as in the rest of Central Asia, repression of Islamist organizations has increased since the late 1990s.

The differences between the official policies of Karimov and Akaev are striking. Yet while economic and political reforms have gone further in Kyrgyzstan than any other Central Asian republic, it was clear by the mid-1990s that any transition to democracy and a market economy was not to be a linear process. Kyrgyzstan was plagued with problems of corruption, an inefficient bureaucracy, economic decline, and increasing social divisions. In the first four years of independence productivity fell by an average of 18.5 percent per year, and unemployment soared. The industrial sector virtually collapsed under the pressure of market reforms, and it is estimated that the country's 1995 national income was only 25.9 percent of what it was in 1990.[18] By 2001 the country was in an economic crisis and straddled with a foreign debt that is one-third higher than the annual gross domestic product and requires monthly service payments of $12 million to $15 million, leaving only $3 million per month for socioeconomic expenditures by the government.[19]

In 1994 Akaev began to take antidemocratic measures such as closing down newspapers and shutting down parliament. In the 1995 parliamentary elections "fraud, corruption, and public anomie reigned."[20] Since 1995 Akaev has taken steps to consolidate power in the executive branch of government. More recently, the upsurge in popular support for the Communist Party, intensified crackdowns on independent media outlets by the state, and the emergence of Islamist insurgency groups in parts of the country have called into question the image of Kyrgyzstan as a bastion of liberalization in Central Asia.[21] Kyrgyzstan faces numerous obstacles to a transition to a Western-style liberal democratic system and indeed *transitional* may be too optimistic a description of the current situation. Alexander Cooley has observed that "what is currently transpiring in . . . Kyrgyzstan is less institutional transformation, and more the creation of dual or hybrid institutions, where old established practices tend to coincide and fuse with, rather than be replaced by, new institutions based on Western models."[22]

POLITICAL CONTEXT AND DEMOCRACY ASSISTANCE STRATEGIES: UZBEKISTAN AND KYRGYZSTAN COMPARED

Important differences between Uzbekistan and Kyrgyzstan affect the work of international actors in the region. For example, repressive government policies in Uzbekistan directly influence the decision of international actors to devote less attention to programs that emphasize human rights or freedom of the press and more attention to programs that are less politically threatening. This has not been as much of a problem in Kyrgyzstan. On the other hand, some international organizations claim that implementing programs in Uzbekistan is often easier than in Kyrgyzstan, because the centralized government functions better. Kyrgyzstan has severe problems of corruption and miscommunication between different levels of government, which may be partially attributed to "democratizing" reforms that have emphasized the devolution of power to local authorities. Apart from these differences, a number of other factors affect international democracy assistance strategies and outcomes in the region. Some factors are specific to one or the other country; many are common to both Uzbekistan and Kyrgyzstan. They include levels of economic development, pervasive corruption, a disjunction between formal and informal institutions, levels of press freedom, societal divisions, and political culture.

The economies of Central Asia are facing not simply problems of "economic transition" but also severe challenges of basic economic development.[23] The low levels of economic development found in both Uzbekistan and Kyrgyzstan affect democracy assistance strategies in a number of ways. Democracy assistance programs that are appropriate for more economically developed societies, including many countries in Eastern Europe, are simply not appropriate for Central Asia.[24] For example, the development of self-sustaining local NGOs with membership fees is not a realistic goal where the average monthly income is approximately $25 to $35.[25] Similarly, many democracy assistance programs do not resonate with the goals of the government or the needs of local people, who are more concerned with economic survival than following an idealized Western model of how to be a good citizen. A 1995 survey published by the United States Institute of Peace showed that building a democratic society was low on Central Asians' priority list, compared to achieving economic growth and maintaining social and political order in the region.[26]

Another problem is that most people view the newly rich sector of the population in Central Asia as corrupt and, in the case of Kyrgyzstan, see the wealth and the corruption as products of democratic reforms (the label "democrats," as applied to them, is meant to be disparaging).[27] "Democratization" is associated with structural changes that have simultaneously led to the destruction of Central Asian economies, the loss of social safety nets, and an increase in economic inequality in the region. This creates a problem for international actors that began to work with newly privileged elites and later tried to expand services to reach a wider spectrum of the population.

Corruption is perhaps the biggest obstacle facing international actors in both Uzbekistan and Kyrgyzstan, and it affects democracy assistance strategies in numerous ways. First, international actors must find a way to operate on an everyday, practical basis in a system in which corruption is the norm. International actors may either not have an official policy for this or may have an official policy that is difficult to adhere to. In either case the de facto policy is likely to be in the hands of the local country director. For example, the director may decide that paying a bribe to get phone lines installed is acceptable, but paying a bribe to get a local NGO registered is not acceptable. Or the director may decide that paying a bribe to get an NGO registered is more reasonable and efficient than going through two years of red tape. Corruption is so entrenched in the region that it is difficult, or maybe even impossible, to operate at the local level without making compromises and arriving at a modus vivendi that straddles the abstract political goals of international actors and the pragmatic means used to promote them. This dilemma is one that is rarely acknowledged or addressed openly by those who are engaged in goal setting and planning at the headquarters of an international assistance organization, leaving the local country directors with almost unresolvable dilemmas that lead to internal contradictions in the implementation of local programs.[28]

In Uzbekistan inconvertibility of Uzbek currency compounds such dilemmas, as do black-market foreign exchange rates that are many times higher than official rates. Some international NGOs prefer to bypass official channels in their financial transactions, arguing that the grassroots organizations that they support can put the money to better use than the government can. Organizations that adhere to a policy of using official channels for financial transactions do so at a high price. The director of one major international NGO estimated that it lost more than $45,000 a year in Uzbekistan by using official financial institutions for currency exchange.[29]

Corruption limits the overall effectiveness of international democracy assistance programs. Grant money donated to local groups may be treated as personal funds; donated equipment might be sold on the black market; and local leaders often insist on skimming money off projects. While an element of mutual exploitation is involved in democracy assistance projects in the region, understanding the dynamics behind corruption is impossible without taking into account the important role that social networks play in all aspects of life in the region.[30] International actors may eventually cancel funding programs, but surviving in Central Asian society without membership in strong reciprocal social networks is impossible. It is thus highly rational for local actors to choose to use external resources to strengthen their indigenous support system and survival networks, rather than put themselves at risk by alienating support networks and playing by rules that are not of their making and are relevant to what may only be short-term transactions. Of course, international actors, at the same time, have to ensure that resources are not misappropriated, yet attempts at doing so have other undesirable consequences, such as creating overwhelming levels of paperwork for local NGOs, limiting the autonomy of groups and impinging upon their ability to make independent decisions, or reinforcing the cultural barriers that exist between local and donor organizations.[31]

Finally, corruption undermines the fundamental logic that informs many democracy assistance strategies. For example, giving professional training to defense lawyers is of little use if the usual way to resolve a case is to bribe the prosecutor or judge. Similarly, educational reform programs, such as instituting competency tests for teachers, do not have the desired effect if bribery pervades all aspects of educational institutions, from admissions procedures to grading to the awarding of degrees. Sending officials on trips abroad may not lead to greater respect for the rule of law but to a heightened desire for expensive Western products that can only be filled by demanding bigger bribes. Democracy assistance programs designed to promote reform must take into account the underlying logic of how local institutions function *in practice*, rather than assume that an idealized version of an institutional arrangement can be transplanted into a new environment without being affected by local realities.

Corruption is a symptom of the disjunction that exists between formal and informal institutions, but other examples exist of discrepancies in how things work on paper or in their formal institutional design and how things work in reality.[32] One example is the discrepancy between written legislation and its actual application. International assistance organizations may take a long time to understand the distinctions between the formal institutions of society and where the real power lies, because informal networks of patronage or personal influence are difficult for outsiders to access. The obvious result is that international actors find it difficult to operate in the local society on an everyday basis: to know which channels to go through for permits and permissions, to know with whom they are really working, or to know how to evaluate the genuineness of grant applications.

In both Uzbekistan and Kyrgyzstan independent NGOs are a relatively new phenomenon and have provoked suspicion on the part of both local and national government officials. Many practitioners in the NGO sector say that officials understand the term *nongovernmental organization* to mean *antigovernment organization*.[33] While this problem is common to both countries, it is more marked in Uzbekistan than in Kyrgyzstan. In Kyrgyzstan establishing good relations between local NGOs and the government has been an ongoing challenge for third-sector actors but has achieved mixed degrees of success.[34] In Uzbekistan government suspicion of NGOs is compounded by its repeated attempts to control the NGO sector by a number of means, including establishing "government NGOs"; attempting to install government personnel as leaders of grassroots NGOs; using threats, sanctions, or bureaucratic red tape to prevent the setting up of local NGOs; and monitoring NGO events.

The Western NGO community in Uzbekistan has engaged in considerable debate about how best to interact with the government and government-organized NGOs (known as "GONGOs" or "quasi NGOs"). Some Western donors have a policy of not providing direct financial assistance to government NGOs, whereas others give assistance to a wide variety of both governmental and nongovernmental organizations.[35] In general, the Western donor community agrees that it must do more to address the issue of relations between international or local NGOs and government officials at the local or national level. But whereas some outside observers view improved NGO-government relations as a much needed step, others are suspicious of what they view as "kowtowing" to government officials.

In both Uzbekistan and Kyrgyzstan the regulatory framework for NGOs provides a number of challenges. In Uzbekistan, for example, "public associations" must register with the Ministry of Justice. This process can be extremely bureaucratic and relatively expensive. Registration fees are the equivalent of twenty monthly salaries for national organizations and ten monthly salaries for local and regional organizations. The organization has to submit its by-laws, which are subject to approval by the ministry. Tax laws in Uzbekistan and Kyrgyzstan make it difficult for local NGOs to finance their activities. For example, NGOs are taxed for any income-generating activities in which they engage, even if these are designed to provide money to underwrite NGO programs. Additionally, contributions to NGOs from private business are not tax exempt.[36]

In Kyrgyzstan relations with government officials have generally improved in the past years, with local governments giving some NGOs land or office space or offering NGOs contracts to perform some social services. However, in some cases problems have arisen, and "the distinction between government and NGOs is blurred."[37] Local governments or parliamentarians have been known to establish NGOs in order to get Western money to carry out local government initiatives and to line their own pockets.

The level of press freedom is considerably different in Uzbekistan and Kyrgyzstan. The press has almost no freedom in Uzbekistan, and finding foreign publications is difficult. Kyrgyzstan has had a fairly high degree of press freedom (with important exceptions), and there are several independent newspapers. In Uzbekistan NGOs have had mixed success in getting into the press, publicizing their events, and publishing their opinions, such as critiques of new legislation.

When they do gain press coverage, it is mostly superficial but not negative. The typical press coverage of international NGOs consists of a story about a ceremony to initiate a new program or a conference that portrays the event as a sign that Uzbekistan is a modern state. Some international NGOs also use the press to promote and announce grant competitions. In Kyrgyzstan both international and local NGOs have less difficulty getting access to the press, but corruption, scandals, and misappropriations of funds have brought them a great deal of negative publicity from both the government and independent press. At times the government press has made a concerted attack on specific NGOs.

In addition to these concerns, numerous societal divisions affect democracy assistance strategies in Central Asia. These include ethnic, linguistic, and clan or tribal divisions, rural versus urban divisions, and intraelite divisions. Distribution of resources such as humanitarian aid, microcredit lending programs, and NGO grants can easily play into ethnic or local divisions. This has occurred repeatedly in southern Kyrgyzstan. In some cases international NGOs have also increased tensions between ethnic groups in the region by hiring staff of only one ethnic group or by working with only one group in the local population. This has usually occurred inadvertently, from a lack of knowledge or sensitivity on the part of external actors regarding salient cleavage lines.

Language divisions also influence the effectiveness of international NGOs. Most local elites in Central Asia are Russified; most foreigners coming to Central Asia are more likely to know Russian than a local Turkic language, and Russian is still the lingua franca in urban areas. This means that much of democracy assistance is conducted in Russian with Russified elites. This is changing, and democracy assistance organizations are making an effort to publish materials in local languages and provide simultaneous translation at conferences, but the gap is still wide: Many programs operate in Russian despite the large percentage of the population that does not know Russian.

The language problem intensifies the effects of rural-urban divisions in the administration of democracy programs. The first wave of democracy assistance in the region was concentrated in the cities of Central Asia; little assistance reached rural areas, where 80 percent of the population live and where it is most needed. This was a result not only of language issues but of other problems in the ability of international actors to distribute information and monitor rural organizations. The situation has improved somewhat since the late 1990s.

A lack of understanding of the local culture or political culture can in many instances undercut the effectiveness of international NGO strategies in Central Asia. One example comes from work with women and women's organizations: Organizing discussion groups will not be an effective strategy in areas where women are unable to leave the home, nor will seminars on birth control options for young women be effective if participants will be ostracized by the community. Home craft production, which might appear to provide an independent source of income to women, will not have the desired result if women must hand over all their earnings to the men in the family. Promoting Western-style women's rights may create a negative reaction in areas where it looks like a continuation of forced Russification/Sovietization or the suppression of local traditions.[38]

DEMOCRACY ASSISTANCE STRATEGIES FOR BUILDING CIVIL SOCIETY IN CENTRAL ASIA

In both Uzbekistan and Kyrgyzstan much of the democracy assistance provided by international actors is designed to strengthen civil society in the region. This has been in response to the limited political openings that exist in the region, as well as a general trend to focus assistance efforts on projects that will promote democracy from the bottom up.[39] A surprisingly wide variety of actors are involved in democracy assistance in Central Asia. In addition to international NGOs, these include international organizations and multilateral assistance efforts such as the United Nations Development Program, the World Bank, and the European Union's Tempus and TACIS (Technical Assistance to the Commonwealth of Independent States) programs; government foreign aid programs such as those run by USAID, the U.S. Information Agency/U.S. Information Service, British Know-How Fund, Swiss Aid; and local NGOs such as the Tashkent Center for Public Education, and International Center Interbilim.[40]

The degree of overlap between the various actors and their strategies is high. For example, distinguishing the interests of a local NGO from the interests of a donor organization is often difficult. Some international NGOs act as contracting organizations for government foreign aid programs, and some local NGOs act as contracting organizations for the development programs of international organizations and international NGOs. A number of different types of actors may work together on specific projects. Actors at all levels can simultaneously pursue a variety of strategies that may at times be contradictory. For example, USAID promotes programs that simultaneously support privatization and democratization—although in some instances these two goals are mutually exclusive.

Table 7.1 provides an overview of the strategies that international actors use to strengthen civil society in the region. Supporting local advocacy groups and an independent third sector is key to their overall strategy. Yet it is only one aspect of the multipronged approach that they pursue in the region. The far left column of table 7.1 suggests the variety of strategies that external actors use to strengthen civil society in Central Asia. The middle column, Methods and Programs, provides a survey of the actual programs that are implemented and funded in the region. The far right column, Actors, lists the organizations engaged in each strategy. In parentheses is the affiliation or funding source of each organization.

TABLE 7.1 Building Civil Society in Central Asia:
Strategies, Methods and Actors

Strategy	Methods and Programs	Actors
Create and support independent advocacy groups; foster the development of a local NGO sector	• Provide seed money to establish civic-oriented NGOs • Provide training to individual NGO leaders • Provide grants to local NGOs for specific projects • Strengthen independent interest groups • Create and work with local NGO support centers.	• Counterpart International (USAID) • Eurasia Foundation (USAID) • Soros • INTRAC • NOVIB (largely Dutch gov't.) • EU's TACIS Program • American Bar Association (USAID) • Aid to Artisans (USAID) • Citizens Network for Foreign Affairs, Inc. (USAID) • Save the Children • Center Interbilim (Local NGO clearinghouse, Bishkek)
Expose elites to Western ideas; educate elites in the practices of democracy	• Fund and organize long-term and short-term academic exchange programs • Fund and organize trips abroad • Organize partnerships between local and Western organizations • Provide seminars and conferences on democratic principles • Provide technical assistance and consulting.	• IREX (USIA/USIS) • ACCELS (USIA/USIS + Central Asian governments) • EU's TACIS and Tempus programs • Soros • Konrad Adenauer Stiftung (German gov't.) • Goethe Institute (German gov't.) • British Council (British gov't.) Civic Education Program (largely Soros)
Increase public access to information and ideas	• Provide computers and internet access • Provide internet training • Provide language training • Sponsor and organize conferences for exchange of information between various sectors • Sponsor regional conferences • Provide journal subscriptions • Establish information centers and libraries.	• IREX (USIA/USIS) • Soros • ACCELS (USIA/USIS) • CAFE • American Bar Association (USAID) • INTRAC

(table continues)

TABLE 7.1 *(continued)*

Strategy	Methods and Programs	Actors
Change the institutional structure within which civil society operates	• Advise government and draft laws in the areas of NGO development, human rights, and other reforms.	• American Bar Association (USAID) • International Center for Not-for-Profit Law (USAID) • NDI (USAID) • UNDP • CAFE
Transform political culture in society	• Provide textbooks and civic education training materials • Provide pedagogical training to teachers • Provide foreign instructors • Fund and organize youth events (e.g., debate camps and mock parliaments) • Support cultural events.	• Soros • NED (U.S. Congress) • CAFE • Peace Corps • Junior Achievement • Tashkent Center for Public Education (local NGO) • Kyrgyzstan Peace Research Center (local NGO)
Promote community development at the grassroots level	• Conduct community needs assessment • Community empowerment projects • Support and organize local development projects.	• Crosslink International • NOVIB • Mercy Corps International • (USAID) • UNDP • Peace Corps • Aid to Artisans (USAID) • Farmer to Farmer (USAID) • CAFE

CREATING INDEPENDENT ADVOCACY GROUPS

The independent NGO sector in Uzbekistan and Kyrgyzstan is an interesting example of both the successes and failures of democracy assistance in Central Asia. The millions of dollars that USAID- sponsored donor organizations, such as Counterpart International and the Eurasia Foundation, have spent on seed money, grants, and training have made a significant difference. Whereas Central Asia had few, if any, independent civic-oriented NGOs when Counterpart began its work, many people in the region now know what an NGO is, and there are hundreds of NGOs, both registered and unregistered. Of these new NGOs, however, only a small percentage are active organizations. The majority are inactive or were set up simply to acquire Western grant money (the so-called BONGOs, or business-oriented NGOs). This means the discrepancy between the "on paper" success story of NGO development in Central Asia and the actual state of the sector is quite big, as I explain later. Two other problems are the donor-driven nature of the sector and a "brain drain" from the public sector to NGOs.

As a measure of its success, USAID counts the number of NGOs created in a year. For example, in 1998 it listed 157 new NGOs created in Kyrgyzstan.[41] What USAID counts as a success, however, others view as problematic: The British International NGO Training and Research Centre asserts that "new NGOs continue to be established at a sometimes alarming rate."[42] Many, or even most, of the new organizations are likely to be BONGOs, which makes the USAID claim to success rather suspect. Quantitative criteria are not the only evaluative criteria that USAID and its NGOs use, but institutional pressure to measure successes largely in quantitative terms—number of NGOs founded, number of grants distributed, number of people trained—is strong.[43] In order to have their USAID funding renewed, international NGOs have an incentive to distribute as much grant money to as many organizations as quickly as possible.

This quantitative approach to NGO development is slowly changing, but its effects on the sector appear to have been lasting. Seed grants for NGOs of $15,000 or more—a considerable sum in the local economy—constitute a large incentive for the misappropriation of funds.[44] Examples abound of what reappears on the black market—everything from computer equipment to school textbooks and donated heating oil. Commented one observer, "Most of the funds from humanitarian organizations that finds its way there [to Kazakhstan] turns into Mercedes, Ford Explorers, and new houses for the rich and politically connected."[45] Stories of NGO leaders who suddenly buy houses after receiving a grant or are spotted flying first class are equally common in Uzbekistan and Kyrgyzstan.

The problem of misappropriation of funds undermines the effectiveness of the whole NGO sector. When individuals first learned that they could obtain seed money and computer equipment after attending an NGO training session, both countries saw a rush to continually establish new NGOs at the expense of undertaking long-term programming work. Many were resentful when the rules of the funding game began to change. Even when donors are aware of problems of misappropriation, they face an organizational imperative to distribute grant money but lack the organizational resources to work closely with every grantee.

Misappropriation of funds also undermines the credibility of the NGO sector as a whole and is an issue that legitimate local NGOs have repeatedly complained about.[46] The local NGO sector, in the words of one observer, is composed of "both efficient energetic activists and lazy, greedy frauds."[47] Not only do legitimate organizations have a more difficult time being taken seriously in society but they may also be forced to pay for the sins of others. They find themselves overwhelmed with paperwork when donors, attempting to prevent misappropriation, increasingly require them to keep close track of finances, go through official banking channels, obtain receipts for all purchases, submit quarterly reports, and the like.[48] On the surface this is a reasonable way of trying to get the misappropriation problem under control. However, what are standard procedures in the West can easily take on burdensome dimensions for small organizations where bureaucracy is relentless and receipts are the exception. Furthermore, paperwork can easily be falsified and does not, in and of itself, prevent misappropriation.

One side-effect of misappropriation is that well-known legitimate local NGOs quickly become overextended. They are overburdened with paperwork and find that every international donor organization wishes to work through them. This is a danger for the best local organizations in both countries. Some successful organizations are able to manage this challenge and either expand slowly or turn down project and grant offers. Others may find that their effectiveness decreases as they become answerable to more and more different international donors.

A further problem with the NGO sector in Central Asia is its donor-driven nature. Local NGOs receive almost 100 percent of their funds from international actors and can easily become almost 100 percent donor driven. A 1997 survey of the third sector in the region acknowledges that "many of the lessons learned in other countries about creating NGO dependency on donor strategies appear not to have been taken account of here in Central Asia."[49] In some cases international donors implicitly or explicitly expect local NGOs to administer programs that do not necessarily match local needs. A common complaint by local NGOs is that donors are more interested in their own agendas than those of the region and that they take an approach of handing out money and then asking for reports from local NGOs, rather than providing core management or organizational support relevant to the local context.[50]

Local NGOs also point to problems with funding cycles. Many local NGOs find it difficult to cover their operating costs, since most grant money available is to support start-up costs or specific projects. Grants rarely cover salaries and overhead. Expenses such as international phone and fax bills can quickly mount as local NGOs become more successful and make contact with overseas organizations. Local NGOs also have a sense of uncertainty because they are aware that they are financially dependent on donors and can never be sure that international NGOs will not pull out of Central Asia and stop funding their projects. This is not a feature unique to Central Asia, but the uncertainty regarding long-term commitments in the region, combined with the larger sense of economic uncertainty produced by rapid transition and economic decline, further contributes to the problem of misappropriation of funds.

One unintended consequence of the emphasis on developing a local NGO sector is the continued brain drain from the public sector to the NGO sector. This is good news in some respects for the NGO sector and bad news for the public sector. Ula Ikramova and Kathryn McConnell write that many women who have started and led Central Asia's NGOs are professionals with experience in problem solving—scientists, physicians, lawyers, engineers, teachers, administrators, artists, museum workers, architects, and advocates.[51] This is a positive aspect of NGO development, as highly qualified people often head the burgeoning sector. The problem is that many of these people may turn to the NGO sector as a means to earn an income that is simply not attainable as, for example, a university professor or high school English teacher. This creates, for the public sector, a serious deficit of qualified professionals. It may also create a problem for the NGO sector, because many may be doing jobs for which they are not ideally suited (e.g., they are academics who would prefer to be doing research but are obligated instead to produce newsletters). Some view NGOs simply as a means to support their own research or their main line of work and may thereby lack a deep commitment to the sector.

EXPOSING ELITES TO WESTERN IDEAS AND MODELS

A second strategy used by international NGOs in Central Asia has been to expose local elites to Western ideas and institutions by bringing Central Asian elites to Western countries on short trips or for academic exchanges and by bringing Western ideas to Central Asian elites via conferences, seminars, technical assistance, and partnership programs.

Academic exchanges were institutionalized in Central Asia before the breakup of the Soviet Union, but since that time they have expanded and attracted more participants. The major challenge for the biggest academic exchange organizations, IREX (International Research and Exchanges Board) and ACCELS (American Council for Collaboration in Education and Language Study), has been to disburse information about exchange programs, attract qualified applicants, and ensure that the selection process is fair and transparent. One notorious problem has been that academic exchanges and trips are viewed as a form of patronage. The long-term effects of academic and professional exchanges are difficult to measure. Most returnees have good English skills and are therefore in high demand in Western firms or international organizations. In theory academic and professional exchanges provide training and open up new possibilities for work or research. However, many participants have a difficult time making use of their training when they return to their home countries and may face challenges in reintegrating into their old work environment, often leaving it soon after to work for a Western organization. Nevertheless, many have gone on to make significant contributions in their fields and are able to act as a bridge between local and Western organizations.

The regime in Uzbekistan routinely uses access to externally funded seminars, conferences, and trips as a form of patronage. A certain number of slots are allotted to government-chosen participants in USAID-funded trips and conferences. Similarly, the attendees of seminars on democracy sponsored by groups such as the Konrad Adenauer Stiftung are almost wholly apparatchiks. A similar problem exists with the European Union's Tempus programs, which pair local and Western educational institutions. Trips abroad may increase not only professional aspirations but also consumer appetites. One critic argues that trips abroad for government officials lead to greater corruption, because they develop new consumer tastes that their civil servant salaries cannot support, and this increases the incentives for corruption.[52]

Exchange programs and travel are a crucial aspect of democracy assistance in the region. If political change in the direction of democratization, liberalization, and increased openness is to occur in the region as a whole, it will likely come from a Westernized elite that has participated in exchange programs and established ties with foreign institutions. At the same time, because of the language and other skills required for participation, these are programs geared toward a small percentage of the country's elite, not the general public. Given the severe inequalities that have arisen in the region since independence from the Soviet Union, it is important that programs such as exchanges and trips abroad be balanced with assistance that can strengthen the basic educational infrastructure in the region.[53]

INCREASING PUBLIC ACCESS TO INFORMATION

A third strategy of international actors has been to provide increased access to information and ideas in Central Asia. One popular method for facilitating access to information has been to provide computers, Internet hookups and access, and training. Primarily because of the work of international NGOs and substantial financial support from the U.S. government, Internet access in Central Asia has increased from virtually none in the early 1990s to the current level with several national and local providers; most educational institutes and local NGOs are on line. In addition, public access sites are numerous, although most of the local population does not use them. As of 2001 only a very small portion of the total population (approximately 0.2 percent) used computers and had access to the Internet.[54]

Despite efforts by international actors to promote Internet usage in the region, the five post-Soviet Central Asian republics have earned a reputation for having some of the least connected and tightly controlled areas of Internet access in the world. Together they comprise one-quarter of the world's "enemies of the Internet," according to the 2000 *Annual Report* of Reporters Sans Frontières; three out of five republics require Internet connections to be run through the government.[55] In Uzbekistan the government is attempting to catch up with the implications of Internet access and is now requiring Internet providers to regis-

ter and sign agreements pertaining to the content of information to be distributed. Government concerns about Internet access in Uzbekistan focus on both
political and moral issues. A particular government concern is that the Internet
will become an organizing tool for Islamic fundamentalists and other opposition groups. While international actors were the first to promote Internet access
in the region, and access has certainly grown since the early 1990s, early predic-
tions that Internet access would lead to greater democratization in Central Asia
have proved to be overly optimistic. Instead, governments in the region are
adapting to the Internet and at times using it to their advantage to monopolize
political control and raise revenue by instituting access fees.[56]

CHANGING THE DOMESTIC
INSTITUTIONAL CONTEXT

Several international organizations are working for legal reform in areas such as
NGO laws, human rights, and women's issues. NGOs have had some success
with legal reform in both Uzbekistan and Kyrgyzstan. The Foundation for International Legal Cooperation, International Center Interbilim, and the Krygyz
Bar Association were all part of an NGO coalition that was influential in developing a new regulatory framework for NGOs in Kyrgyzstan. Some claim that
this "may be the only genuinely successful case of effective legislative lobbying
by domestic NGOs in the region."[57] A consortium of international assistance organizations in Uzbekistan also drafted new NGO laws in 1998. The government
initially rejected them, but several months later President Karimov announced
that Uzbekistan, as a "modern country," needed to revise its laws on associations
to allow for more freedoms for NGOs. He established a working group to draft a
new NGO law, and in late December 1998 the Uzbek parliament unanimously
approved a new NGO law with Karimov's support. In April 1999 Uzbekistan became the first country in the region to adopt a completely new law aimed only
at NGOs; the new law allows for the establishment of philanthropic foundations and simplifies registration procedures.[58]

These examples point to the influence that international and local NGOs
have had in achieving both legal reform and symbolic changes in governments'
attitudes toward NGOs. The extent to which the new law will substantively affect the NGO sector in Uzbekistan remains to be seen. Richard Remias writes,
"Most commentators on the new legislation agree that ultimately the law will
prove itself in the way it's implemented and enforced by the authorities."[59] If
past instances of legal reform provide any indication, only a minimal de facto
change is likely to occur. Legislation that was adopted in the area of women's
rights, for example, was not implemented. This is a problem that affects legal reform in all areas: The process of reform is slow and time consuming, and any
written changes are likely to be open to a broad range of interpretation or even

ignored in practice. Still, legal changes provide symbolic openings that both local and international actors can draw upon to expand the role of nonstate actors in the region.

TRANSFORMING POLITICAL CULTURE

Another broad strategy for building civil society is to promote civic education, educational reforms, and cultural events. Kyrgyzstan has seen much more activity in this area than Uzbekistan has because of the continued government restrictions there. Promoting civic education includes teacher training and providing civics and history textbooks and training materials. In Kyrgyzstan civic education programs have been widespread and successful, but they appear to have been quite divisive because they have been done without the participation of the Ministry of Education. A number of local groups in Kyrgyzstan compete to provide civic education textbooks (and receive grants for the provision of textbooks), leading to confusion about the motives of the different organizations, the content of the different textbooks, and a hostile and less than civil atmosphere surrounding the whole enterprise.

In Uzbekistan civic education programs are at a very early stage of development. The government has tighter control of education and the content of textbooks. The sector is small, with groups working together rather than competing. Providing civics textbooks and training has a limited effect because teachers, especially in rural areas, are surviving on low salaries and therefore have little incentive or motivation to devote time and resources to adding a new field of study to their curricula.

PROMOTING COMMUNITY DEVELOPMENT AT THE GRASSROOTS LEVEL

A number of international actors are engaged in what could be termed "grassroots community development work." Small community development projects appear to be among the most successful forms of democracy assistance in the region. However, few organizations are flexible enough to work at the local level and respond to local needs. Such community development work is labor intensive and will affect only a small number of people initially but may have a more enduring and greater influence than larger projects. Such small-scale projects reach sectors of the population that are difficult to reach in other ways. The most successful projects are run by dedicated volunteers with a strong personal interest in the region and are cemented by personal relationships with members of the community. They do not necessarily include the direct transfer of financial resources or equipment. That personal relationships form the basis of these projects is more in tune with local norms and appears to lead to better results than projects that are run in a more "rational-bureaucratic" style.[60]

The grassroots approach has had mixed results when administered by larger organizations. Observers count the USAID-sponsored Aid to Artisans program as one of the most successful democracy assistance programs in the region and has resulted in the development of strong, independent, and financially self-sustaining regional artisan organizations engaged in making traditional handicrafts. Several artisan organizations have independently contested local government policies by organizing petition campaigns. Artisan organizations have also been successful both at getting grants from outside donors and at collecting membership fees from their constituencies. The reason for this success is that the programs' design gave participants a strong personal financial stake in the success of the organization, and they received tangible economic benefits; for example, association members could participate in local crafts fairs that were targeted at the Western expatriate community in Central Asia. In contrast, another USAID program, which was designed to foster the development of independent farmers' associations, had to shut down after a massive misappropriation of microcredit funds that further entrenched local divisions, inequalities, and corruption. Part of the explanation is that the farmers' associations were not bringing their members direct financial benefits, and the programs were in rural areas, which are more difficult for the central administration to monitor.

My purpose here has been to provide examples of how democracy promotion activities function in "unintegrated states" that are characterized by semiauthoritarian or authoritarian regimes. I discussed features of the Central Asian setting that influence the effectiveness of international democracy assistance programs, and I described and evaluated various strategies that international actors use to build civil society within such an environment. By highlighting both the successes and failures of democracy assistance in the region, I have highlighted the power and limits of international NGOs as actors that can effect significant political changes in the region. Despite many individual success stories, and some promising trends, the overall effect of democracy assistance in the region has been largely limited to the development of an externally funded third sector and has not brought about large-scale political changes leading to greater democratization.

One point that I want to emphasize is the disjunction between visions of democracy as promoted by many international actors in the region and the actual social, political, and economic conditions in Central Asia. This means that local branch offices of international NGOs are involved in a continual struggle to reconcile competing demands from their head office and local constituencies. In the case of democracy assistance to Central Asia, international actors often rely on fixed meanings of democracy, civil society, and NGOs that bear little relation to the realities of the local environment. In addition, local structures constrain international actors in their work—the means of promoting democracy are at times less than democratic—often because of the structural contradictions between the two environments (headquarters and local office).

International actors need to explicitly take into account the effect of informal processes and institutions on their strategies and programs and pay as much attention to these factors as to the formal institutional environment. These include patronage networks, ethnic cleavages, the local political culture, and informal networks. Legal and other reforms will be unsuccessful, and will lead only to the creation of hybrid organizations, such as patronage-based NGOs, if such processes and institutions are not taken fully into account. The best democracy assistance programs can be quickly undermined if they are not designed with an eye for how they will interact with informal processes and local power configurations.[61]

The model of promoting democracy by creating parallel Western-style institutions and organizations, rather than by strengthening and working with existing structures and institutions, has its limits. An internationally funded "democracy sector" that has no deep roots in local society, and interacts little with indigenous institutions and structures, is in danger of exacerbating tensions between the small elite that is able to benefit from international assistance and the majority of the population, which is struggling for economic survival and, increasingly, the right to religious expression. The hostility of the region's governments to most forms of political Islam has contributed to the increased politicization of religion as a form of opposition to authoritarian regimes. At a minimum international actors must be willing to work with a variety of local groups in the region, including religious organizations and institutions, but also extending to government-organized NGOs as well as to traditional local community structures, such as the neighborhoods associations (*mahallas*) in Uzbekistan. The latter have been co-opted by the state but nonetheless still provide the basis for communal life in many areas. If international actors work exclusively with the so-called independent NGO sector—which is largely an artificial creation of foreign assistance organizations—they will continue to reach only a small sector of society, which may be more attuned to international funding trends than local political needs.

Following an early period of enthusiasm and optimism about the prospects for democratic transition in the region, the growing consensus is that the language of transition is increasingly counterproductive for addressing the core problems facing Central Asian states.[62] Moving beyond the language of transition and reevaluating the goals of assistance programs in this light may provide a means for international assistance organizations to reconcile the discrepancies between their mission statements in the region and the political context faced by local field offices. If democracy assistance is to be context specific in Central Asia, this may mean less democracy assistance and a greater emphasis on grassroots economic and local community development projects. Democracy assistance efforts that are appropriate for the level of economic and political development in Eastern Europe and Russia are not necessarily appropriate for Central Asia. While democracy assistance programs geared to NGO development and civic education have had notable successes in the region, they cannot be expected to expand in areas where basic economic and educational opportunities are limited. Any effective strategy of democracy assistance in Central Asia must focus first and foremost on programs that promote human development and redress social and economic inequalities in the region.

NOTES

1. U.S. Agency for International Development, FY1998 presentation to Congress for Uzbekistan and Kyrgyzstan, available at the USAID Web site http://www.usaid.gov /pubs/cp98www.usaid.gov/pubs/cp98 (November 5, 2001).

2. The results of this research appear in Marfua Tokhtakhodjaeva and Elmira Turgumbekova, *The Daughters of Amazons: Voices from Central Asia* (Lahore, Pakistan: Shirkat Gah, 1994) and *Assertions of Self: The Nascent Women's Movement in Central Asia* (Lahore, Pakistan: Shirkat Gah/Women Living Under Muslim Law, 1995).

3. For more about this pattern and the challenges that it poses to the promotion of democracy, see Martha Brill Olcott and Marina Ottaway, *The Challenge of Semiauthoritarianism* (Washington, D.C.: Carnegie Endowment for International Peace, 1999). See also Fareed Zakaria, "The Rise of Illiberal Democracy," *Foreign Affairs* 76, no. 6 (November–December 1997): 22–43.

4. The extent to which Islamist movements have a role to play in the region as indigenous social movements and political opposition parties is subject to debate. States in the region severely repress Islamist activity by groups such as Hizb-ut-Tahrir, and the U.S. State Department has placed the Islamic Movement of Uzbekistan on its list of terrorist organizations. Yet many observers have argued that moderate Islam can play a more prominent role in the development of an independent civil society in the region. Promoting institutional channels that can be used by moderate Islamist movements to participate as legitimate political actors in civil society should be one of the goals of democracy assistance in the region. See, for example, Abumannob Polat, "Can Uzbekistan Build Democracy and Civil Society?" in M. Holt Ruffin and Daniel C. Waugh, eds., *Civil Society in Central Asia*, pp. 135–57 (Seattle: University of Washington Press, 1999); Reuel Hanks, "Civil Society and Identity in Uzbekistan: The Emergent Role of Islam," in Ruffin and Waugh, *Civil Society*, pp. 158–79; and Roger D. Kangas, "The Three Faces of Islam in Uzbekistan," *Transition* 1, no. 24 (December 29, 1995): 17–21. For general discussions of the political dimensions of Islam in the region, see Roald Sagdeev and Susan Eisenhower, eds., *Islam and Central Asia: An Enduring Legacy or an Evolving Threat?* (Washington, D.C.: Center for Political and

Strategic Studies, 2000), and Ahmed Rashid, *The Resurgence of Central Asia: Islam or Nationalism?* (London: Zed, 1994).

5. Sarah E. Mendelson and John K. Glenn, "Introduction: Transnational Networks and NGOs in Postcommunist Societies," p. 10.

6. For an excellent discussion of problems of commensurability between Western notions of democracy and local practices, see Frederic C. Schaffer, *Democracy in Translation: Understanding Politics in an Unfamiliar Culture* (Ithaca: Cornell University Press, 1998). For a discussion of the relationship between international norms and local institutions in democracy promotion activities in Central Asia, see Fiona B. Adamson, "International Norms Meet Local Structures: The Dilemmas of Democracy Promotion in Post-Soviet Central Asia" (paper presented at the annual meeting of the American Political Science Association, Washington, D.C., August 30–September 3, 2000).

7. See Thomas Carothers, "Democracy Assistance: The Question of Strategy," *Democratization* 4, no. 3, (Autumn 1997): 109–32.

8. On the geopolitics of democracy promotion, see William I. Robinson, *Promoting Polyarchy: U.S. Intervention, Globalization, and Hegemony* (New York: Cambridge University Press, 1996). The most comprehensive survey and evaluation of U.S. democracy assistance programs is Thomas Carothers, *Aiding Democracy Abroad: The Learning Curve* (Washington, D.C.: Carnegie Endowment for International Peace, 1999).

9. See Margaret E. Keck and Kathryn Sikkink, *Activists Beyond Borders: Advocacy Networks in International Politics* (Ithaca: Cornell University Press, 1998), for a discussion of transnational advocacy networks.

10. See Ali Banuaziz and Myron Weiner, eds., *The New Geopolitics of Central Asia and its Borderlands* (Bloomington: Indiana University Press, 1994); Alvin Z. Rubinstein and Oles M. Smolansky, eds., *Regional Power Rivalries in the New Eurasia: Russia, Turkey, and Iran* (Armonk, N.Y.: Sharpe, 1995); Michael Mandelbaum, ed., *Central Asia and the World* (New York: Council on Foreign Relations Press, 1994). For an argument that Uzbekistan is "transitioning" from a Soviet-style to East Asian–style autocracy, see William Donald Shingleton, "Uzbek Autocracy in the Central Asian Context" (master's thesis, Harvard University, 2000).

11. In surveys conducted in 1994–1995, less than one-eighth of the respondents said that a "Western-style democracy" was the best political system for Uzbekistan. Within that small group, less than 1 in 4 said that a politician should be "democratic" in order to win votes. Similarly, only 16 percent of respondents felt strongly that a political opposition is a necessary element of a democracy. More than half of respondents felt that limiting political rights and freedoms in order to solve economic problems is appropriate, and half of all respondents were willing to support "any system, as long as there is order." See Nancy Lubin, *Central Asians Take Stock: Reform, Corruption, and Identity* (Washington, D.C.: U.S. Institute of Peace, 1995); Office of Research and Media Reaction, U.S. Information Agency, "Uzbekistanis Broadly Back Karimov," December 27, 1994, and "In Uzbekistan, Checkered Views of Democracy," June 15, 1995; William Fierman, "Political Development in Uzbekistan: Democratization?" in Karen Dawisha and Bruce Parrot, eds., *Conflict, Cleavage, and Change in Central Asia and the Caucasus* (New York: Cambridge University Press, 1997), pp. 396–98.

12. While Karimov increasingly represses almost all forms of pious religious expression, organized underground Islamist opposition groups such as Hizb-ut-Tahrir and the Islamic Movement of Uzbekistan (which has expanded from a national to a pan–Central Asian movement, with ties to the al Queda network) have grown in strength, and the region has been characterized by sporadic insurgencies. Even before U.S. military action in Afghanistan, many experts claimed that Central Asia was on the verge of becoming a region of permanent low-intensity warfare, should political and economic conditions not improve. See, for example, Ahmed Rashid, "Confrontation Brews Among Islamic Militants in Central Asia," *Central Asia–Caucasus Analyst*, November 22, 2000, http://www.cacianalyst.org/Nov_22_2000/Islamic_Militants_in_Central_Asia.htm (November 5, 2001); Stephen Blank, "Rumors of War in Central Asia," *Central Asia–Caucasus Analyst*, May 9, 2001, http://www.cacianalyst.org/May_9_2001/May_9 _2001_RUMORS_OF_WAR.htm (November 5, 2001); Alima Bissenova, "The Latest Hizb-ut-Tahrir Trial Defendants Say They Confessed Under Torture," *Central Asia–Caucasus Analyst*, June 6, 2001, published by the Central Asia-Caucasus Institute, Paul H. Nitze School of Advanced International Studies, Johns Hopkins University, http://www.cacianalyst.org/June_6_2001/June_6_2001_Uzbekistan_Trial.htm (November 5, 2001).

13. Graham Smith et al., *Nation Building in the Post-Soviet Borderlands: The Politics of National Identities* (New York: Cambridge University Press, 1998), pp. 140 and 147.

14. For example, in the 1991 elections the government gave groups one day to collect the sixty thousand signatures required to get on the ballot. In 2000 the Organization for Security and Cooperation in Europe refused to send a delegation of observers to the presidential elections, claiming that it would be pointless because voters had no real choice, thanks to media restrictions in Uzbekistan, the deregistration of candidates and parties, and the politicization of the Central Election Commission. See Fierman, "Political Development," pp. 378–79; Shingleton, "Uzbek Autocracy," pp. 16–17.

15. Eugene Huskey, "Kyrgyzstan: The Fate of Political Liberalization," in Dawisha and Parrot, *Conflict, Cleavage and Change*, p. 242.

16. Kyrgyzstan was also the first of the Central Asian republics to break the ruble zone and win International Monetary Fund approval of its reforms in May 1993. See Richard Pomfret, *The Economies of Central Asia* (Princeton: Princeton University Press, 1995), chaps. 8 and 11.

17. Smith et al., *Nation Building*, p. 201.

18. Turar Koichuev, "Kyrgyzstan: Economic Crisis and Transition Strategy," in Boris Rumer, ed., *Central Asia in Transition: Dilemmas of Political and Economic Development* (Armonk, N.Y.: Sharpe, 1996), p. 170.

19. "Kyrgyzstan's Foreign Debt Hits \$2 Billion," *RFE/RL Newsline*, July 2, 2001.

20. Smith et al., *Nation Building*, p. 201.

21. See Gulsara Osorova, "Communists Win Election in Kyrgyzstan's 'Island of Democracy,'" *Central Asia–Caucasus Analyst*, March 15, 2000, http://www.cacianalyst .org/Mar15/COMMUNISTS_WIN_ELECTION.htm (November 5, 2001); Maria Utyganova, "Crackdown on Independent Media in Kyrgyzstan," *Central Asia–Caucasus Analyst*, April 25, 2001, http://www.cacianalyst.org/April_25_2001/April_25_2001 _Media_Crackdown_Kyrgyzstan.htm (November 5, 2001); "Media Is (Again) 'Under

Press' in Kyrgyzstan," *Central Asia–Caucasus Analyst*, July 18, 2001, http://www.cacian-alyst.org/July_18_2001/July_18_2001_Media_Kyrgyzstan.htm (November 5, 2001); Gulzina Karym Kyzy, "Kyrgyzstan Under the Specter of Islamic Militants," *Central Asia–Caucasus Analyst*, May 23, 2001, http://www.cacianalyst.org/May_23_2001 /May_23_2001_Kyrgyzstan_Islamic_Specter.htm (November 5, 2001).

22. Alexander Cooley, "Evaluating NGO Strategies and the Effectiveness of Democracy Promotion in Central Asia: The Case of Kyrgyzstan" (unpublished manuscript, Columbia University, May 1998), p. 6.

23. Pomfret, *Economies of Central Asia*, and the review essay by Alexander Cooley, "Transitioning Backward: Concepts and Comparison in the Study of Central Asia's Political Economy," *Harriman Review* 11, nos. 1–2 (1998): 1–11.

24. In this respect the Central Asian cases closely resemble that of Romania, which Thomas Carothers analyzes in detail in *Assessing Democracy Assistance: The Case of Romania* (Washington, D.C.: Carnegie Endowment for International Peace, 1996), esp. pp. 66–74.

25. Karimov ordered the monthly minimum wage in Uzbekistan to be raised 40 percent to $9 per month beginning August 1, 2001. See "Uzbek President Decrees Increase in Pensions, Minimum Wage," *RFE/RL Newsline*, July 3, 2001, http://www.rferl .org/newsline/2001/07/030701.html (November 5, 2001).

26. Lubin, *Central Asians Take Stock*, p. 4. The survey sample was drawn from populations in both Uzbekistan and Kazakhstan. Ninety percent of respondents to the survey viewed the need to "strengthen social order and discipline" as the most pressing problem facing Uzbekistan.

27. Jeremy Bransten, "Kyrgyzstan: A Democracy Only for the Rich," *RFE/RL Reports*, October 14, 1997, http://www.rferl.org/nca/features/1997/10/F.RU.971014134805.html (November 5, 2001).

28. Author's interviews in Tashkent, September 1998. One concrete example of this is budget allocation and the question of how local field offices should record expenditures for bribes in accounting procedures.

29. Author's interview, Tashkent, September 1998.

30. David M. Abramson, "Civil Society and the Politics of Foreign Aid in Uzbekistan," *Central Asia Monitor*, no. 6 (1999): 1–12.

31. Author's interviews with local NGO officials in Tashkent and Bishkek, September–October 1998. Several local NGO officials argued that demanding receipts is unrealistic, because official receipts are not readily available for many goods and services. They claimed that filling out paperwork was taking an inordinate amount of time away from programming activities. Many also were resentful that donors did not trust local NGOs to manage their own finances.

32. For a related discussion see Carothers, "Democracy Assistance," pp. 122–24.

33. Author's interviews in Tashkent and Bishkek, September and October 1998.

34. Erkinbek Kasybekov, "Government and Nonprofit Sector Relations in the Kyrgyz Republic," in Ruffin and Waugh, *Civil Society*, pp. 71–84.

35. As of 1998, for example, the Eurasia Foundation provided grants to both independent and government-organized NGOs, whereas Counterpart International al-

lowed government-organized NGOs to use its resource center but funded only independent NGOs.

36. For overviews of the regulatory environment facing NGOs in Central Asia, see Scott Horton and Alla Kazakina, "The Legal Regulation of NGOs: Central Asia at a Crossroads," in Ruffin and Waugh, *Civil Society*, pp. 34–56; Sarah Prosser, "Reform Within and Without the Law: Further Challenges for Central Asia Nongovernmental Organizations," *Harvard Asia Quarterly* 4, no. 3 (Summer 2000): 4–16, available at http://www.fas.harvard.edu/asiactr/haq/200003/0003a001.htm (November 5, 2001); Richard Remias, "The Regulation of the NGO in Central Asia: Current Reforms and Ongoing Problems," *Harvard Asia Quarterly* 4, no. 3 (Summer 2000): 18–26.

37. Anne Garbutt, "NGO Support Organisations in Central Asia," paper prepared for the International NGO Training and Research Centre, Oxford, October 1997, p. 13.

38. I thank Nailya Ablieva for suggesting these examples.

39. See Carothers, *Aiding Democracy Abroad*, pp. 207–51, for a discussion of the "bottom-up" approach to democracy assistance.

40. For an overview of civil society activity in Central Asia, see Ruffin and Waugh, *Civil Society*, which also provides a useful listing of both international and local NGOs in the region. See also Nancy Lubin and Monica Ware, "Aid to the Former Soviet Union: When Less Is More," Project on the Newly Independent States, JNA Associates, New York, March 1996. For a survey of U.S., European Union, and U.N. democracy assistance programs, see, respectively, Carothers, *Aiding Democracy Abroad*; Kepa Sodupe and Eduardo Benito, "The Evolution of the European Union's Tacis Programme, 1991–96," *Journal of Communist Studies and Transition Politics* 14, no. 4 (December 1998): 51–68; Christopher C. Joyner, "The United Nations and Democracy," *Global Governance: A Review of Multilateralism and International Organizations* 5, no. 3 (July–September 1999): 333–57.

41. USAID, presentation to Congress.

42. Garbutt, "NGO Support Organisations," p. 9.

43. USAID "Results Indicators" for the $5 million to be spent on democratization in Uzbekistan in FY1998 were quantitative: for example, to have two hundred advocacy NGOs in Uzbekistan by 1999 (from a baseline of zero in 1992). For Kyrgyzstan the target was four hundred NGOs in 1999 (from a baseline of zero in 1992). See USAID, presentation to Congress.

44. The dollar figure comes from Lubin and Ware, "When Less Is More," p. 27.

45. The observer was James Brainard, founder of the private humanitarian aid organization Cornerstone, quoted in Sharon Taylor, "Melon Diplomacy," *Amador County (California) Ledger Dispatch*, September 25, 1998, p. A3. See also Matt Bivens, "Aboard the Gravy Train," *Harper's*, August 1997, pp. 69–76.

46. See, for example, Garbutt, "NGO Support Organisations," p. 14.

47. Prosser, "Reform Within and Without," p. 7.

48. Author's interviews with local NGOs in Tashkent and Bishkek, September and October 1998.

49. Garbutt, "NGO Support Organisations," p. 3.

50. Ibid., p. 9.

51. Ula Ikramova and Kathryn McConnell, "Women's NGOs in Central Asia's Evolving Societies," in Holt and Waugh, *Civil Society*, pp. 198–213.

52. See also Cooley, "Evaluating NGO Strategies."

53. With regard to education, one of the most successful initiatives in the region has been undertaken not by Western organizations but by a liberal Turkish Islamist organization headed by Fethullah Gülen. It has set up a network of high schools and educational institutions in Central Asia and other parts of the former Soviet Union. These schools have a moderate Islamic orientation that emphasizes individual spiritual development, and they provide excellent training in foreign languages, computer skills, and economics.

54. Eric Johnson, "Left Behind in the Rush to Go Online," *Open Society News*, Spring 2001, http://www.eurasianet.org/osn/Left_Behind.html (November 5, 2001).

55. Ibid.; Bea Hogan, "Internet Latest Battleground for Central Asian Repression." *Central Asia–Caucasus Analyst*, July 19, 2000, http://www.cacianalyst.org/July_19 /INTERNET_LATEST_BATTLEGROUND_TO%20CONTROL_CENTRAL _ASIAN_SOCIETY.htm (November 5, 2001).

56. On the strategies of authoritarian regimes for regulating the Internet, see Shanthi Kalathil and Taylor C. Boas, *The Internet and State Control in Authoritarian Regimes: China, Cuba, and the Counterrevolution* (Washington, D.C.: Carnegie Endowment for International Peace, July 2001).

57. Horton and Kazakina, "Legal Regulation of NGOs," p. 39.

58. Remias, "Regulation of the NGO," p. 20.

59. Ibid.

60. Some of the most effective community development projects are run by independent evangelical Christian organizations, such as Central Asia Free Exchange and Crosslink International, whose volunteers immerse themselves in the local culture. Like the schools run by Turkish Islamists, these associations efficiently provide needed services, which are dispensed by religiously motivated individuals who are interested in developing personal relationships with their constituencies.

61. Cooley, "International Aid."

62. Anthony Richter, "Looking Beyond Transition in Central Asia," *Open Society News*, Spring 2001, http://www.eura_Hlt521312094s_Hlt521312094ianet.org/osn/Looking _Beyond_Transition.html (November 5, 2001).

Chapter 8

INTERNATIONAL NGOS IN BOSNIA-HERZEGOVINA: ATTEMPTING TO BUILD CIVIL SOCIETY

V. P. Gagnon Jr.

Of all the former socialist states of East-Central Europe and Eurasia, Bosnia-Herzegovina has suffered the most in the post–cold war period. The war in Bosnia-Herzegovina, fought from 1992 to 1995, resulted in the deaths of more than 200,000 people; half the population fled or was expelled; the economy collapsed; and power accrued to antidemocratic extremist forces that had actively participated in the violence. Because of the international community's leading role in ending the war and establishing stability in the postwar period, Bosnia-Herzegovina also has more international NGOs—more than 250—than any other country in Eastern Europe.

In addition, numerous international organizations and more than twenty thousand troops from various countries and the North Atlantic Treaty Organization (NATO) are in Bosnia-Herzegovina. The focus of attention of the United States and the major European powers, Bosnia-Herzegovina is in many ways under a kind of protectorate. International actors make crucial decisions, determine electoral laws, run the central bank, sit on the constitutional court, and decide where the money flowing into the country should go.[1] The international community thus has a large stake in rebuilding Bosnia-Herzegovina as a democratic country and preventing the outbreak of conflict, goals shared by the vast majority of Bosnians.

With this kind of attention, and with hundreds of millions of dollars pouring into the country, Bosnia-Herzegovina is in many ways a good test case for the effectiveness of international NGOs. They play key roles in running the programs of the major donors and funders, and their strategies are crucial to the success of the overall goals of the international community. In this chapter I therefore focus on international NGOs whose activities are meant to construct civil society in Bosnia-Herzegovina.

My findings are based on research that I have been doing on the region since the mid-1980s, as well as a visit to Bosnia-Herzegovina and Croatia from May 27 to June 17, 1998, two visits to Bosnia-Herzegovina in 1996, previous fieldwork in the region in 1994–1995, and by my ongoing research on the former Yugoslavia. During the 1998 trip I conducted twenty interviews, whose subjects included representatives of eight international NGOs, four international organizations, and two groups that function as forums for international NGOs and local NGOs.

I discuss in detail five international NGOs that are working toward the broad goal of building civil society. They are pursuing four general kinds of strategies: trying to directly change the political structures and institutions of postwar Bosnia-Herzegovina by building political parties and conducting civic education; building local nonpolitical party NGO capacity; and using reconstruction and development to strengthen community and civil society. These NGOs include those receiving the largest amounts of funding, and they are representative of the range of strategies being used by international NGOs in Bosnia-Herzegovina.

A review of their work suggests that the most effective international NGOs are those that see their work as a two-way process, wherein the international agencies help local NGOs to determine their priorities, and personnel of the international agencies see locals as equal partners. The most effective strategies are those that integrate concrete projects and an inclusive decision-making process to build community and civil society locally, a strategy that allows local actors, communities, and NGOs to determine priorities, projects, and directions. This seems especially important for international NGOs that are seeking to strengthen local actors and networks as participants in civil society.

International NGOs that focus on "nonpolitical" elements such as housing, infrastructure repair, and economic revitalization, rather than on formal politics (the usual target of democratization efforts), help create alternative sources of stable employment and resources, thereby lessening the economic dominance of existing political parties and power structures. Perhaps more important, strategies that combine construction projects and the local community's participation in identifying and executing them contribute in crucial ways to rebuilding communities and civil society. Reconstruction projects undertaken by private international companies—a policy that is increasingly pursued by the United States—do not include this civil society component and thus would not produce the kinds of change that the international community claims to be seeking. In short, donors can get more bang for the buck by funneling reconstruction and development money to international NGOs that are committed to a particular *process*—one that is sensitive to the experiences and needs of the local society, that works with locals as equal partners in determining priorities and strategies. This integration of concrete projects and a focus on rebuilding communities and civil society seems to be the key to success for international NGOs, if their goal is the long-term sustainable development of civil society.

Apart from the difficulties that are inherent in the context in which the international NGOs operate in Bosnia-Herzegovina—in particular the structures of political power that were established during the war and those that were set up by the 1995 Dayton Peace Agreement—a major limitation on the effectiveness of international NGOs is their structural location. The major challenge to their effectiveness is their dependence for funding on institutions and organizations that have specific interests and perceptions unrelated to the local realities or the interests of Bosnia-Herzegovina society. To the extent that funders and donors rather than local needs drive their actions, international NGOs reflect the interests of powerful states in the international system. As such the NGOs act as instruments of power—a way for states to project their power into other societies—rather than as forces working with the interest of the locals as the priority. This situation is manifested in concrete terms when international NGOs operate without a realistic needs assessment based on the complex and long-term strategies that are necessary for rebuilding Bosnian society, and on what locals deem those needs to be, and instead fashion projects based on the goals of the funders, the donors' priorities and interests. According to a number of Bosnians with whom I spoke, too often these latter factors, rather than the local situation, drive funding priorities and thus limit international NGOs.

The most effective international NGOs that I found used a variety of strategies to do their work: relying on in-depth expertise about the region to convince funders to trust their strategies; directly lobbying funders to change or modify their policies and priorities; using funding to achieve not only donor-specified goals but also the mission or goals of the international NGOs.

Also hampering effectiveness is the tendency of donors and some international NGOs to generalize from experience elsewhere; this leads them to overlook the specificities and complexities, both current and historical, of Bosnia-Herzegovina. One example is the assumption that before 1990 Yugoslavia (or other socialist countries, for that matter) was in some kind of totalitarian deep freeze and that now the population must be retrained in democracy. This ignores the kind of grassroots activism seen throughout the region during the Gorbachev period but even earlier. International NGOs that ignore or write off those experiences ignore what should be a solid basis for moving forward. The disconnect between the experiences and needs of society and the interests that drive projects and priorities is the most severe limitation on international NGO effectiveness.

The next section provides the context within which international NGOs in Bosnia-Herzegovina operate. Following that is a summary of the international NGOs that I examine and their strategies, and an analysis of the effects and limitations of these strategies. I conclude the chapter with some observations about the usefulness of these activities for democratization and the development of civil society.

HISTORICAL AND POLITICAL CONTEXT

The war in Bosnia-Herzegovina was imposed from outside, the result of political strategies by conservative elites in Serbia and Croatia. Although much of the Western journalistic and academic work on the war says otherwise, what is quite clear from a close study of events leading up to and during the war is that the violence was imposed on the republic—that the ruling parties in Serbia and Croatia compelled the "nationalist" political parties to install extremists as their leaders and exported arms, paramilitary groups, and armies into Bosnia to destroy the fabric of that country's existing multiethnic communities. This strategy, which traces at least to 1988, was a direct response to trends toward democratization and liberalization within Serbia, Croatia, and Yugoslavia as a whole and had the goal of preventing shifts in the structure of political and economic power within the Yugoslav republics. Because Yugoslavia in the mid-1980s had seemed to have a better chance than any of the other socialist countries of Eastern Europe to make the transition to liberal political and economic systems, its conservative elites were more threatened than in other socialist countries. The wars were, in effect, the conservatives' response to these pressures for democratization.[2]

Indeed, for the purposes of this study it is of great importance to note that Yugoslavia, of all the socialist countries, was the most open to Western ideas and had its own experience with indigenous concepts of grassroots participation in decision making within firms as well as within local communities. One of the most striking things in talking to international NGOs with no previous experience in the region is the degree to which they believe that Bosnians are coming out of a totalitarian experience—one so profound that it is a caricature of even the Soviet system. Representatives of these international NGOs seem all but unaware of the mechanics and realities of the Yugoslav political system under Tito, which, although not the workers' paradise portrayed by some, was much more participatory than the Western stereotypes of communism portray. They also seem unaware of the political ferment, grassroots movement for democracy, and the events of the late 1980s that showed a full awareness of notions of democracy, civil society, independent media, electoral campaigns, and political participation. Indeed, the war in Bosnia-Herzegovina began in April 1992 when people attending a massive multiethnic peace rally were marching through Sarajevo and were fired upon by a handful of Serb nationalist snipers who had the backing of Belgrade. That all these trends developed in the absence of international NGO assistance is an important sign that any problems that Bosnia is facing are due not to the ignorance of Bosnians but to other structural factors that have been reinforced by the war.

The war, which lasted until 1995, changed the face of Bosnia-Herzegovina. It silenced and decimated the prewar democracy and peace movements, including democratic forces within the republic's main political parties, and it devastated civil society. One of the most insidious and destructive effects of the war was the resulting ethnic homogenization: Whereas before the war few areas of the country were ethnically homogeneous, by 1995, when the Belgrade-backed Serbian Democratic Party (SDS) finally agreed to negotiate a settlement to the conflict, the country had effectively been divided into three areas, each controlled by an extremist, ethnically labeled, and antidemocratic political party that commanded structures of power that the war had not changed.[3] The SDS controlled more than half the country—an area where Serbs now make up 95 percent of the population (compared to 50 percent before the war), while the remainder was under the effective control of the Zagreb-backed and -controlled Croatian Democratic Community of Bosnia-Herzegovina (HDZBH) and the Bosnian Muslim Party of Democratic Action. The SDS and the HDZBH in particular pursued policies of "ethnic cleansing"—that is, they murdered or expelled non-Serbs and non-Croats and in both areas razed Muslim cultural monuments, including mosques.[4]

The current role of the international community stems from its major role in bringing the war to an end. Although the United Nations was present in Bosnia-Herzegovina from the beginning of the war, the role of the United Nations Protection Force was restricted to delivering humanitarian aid and protecting that aid. Infamously, U.N. forces were not allowed to protect the civilian population.[5] The United States became directly involved in 1994, as the Clinton administration brought an end to the Zagreb-initiated war against Bosnia's Muslim population. In 1995 the United States effectively supported the army of Croatia and the official Bosnian army in their attacks on Belgrade-backed Serb forces in Croatia and then in Bosnia. With the help of NATO air attacks on the SDS's military communication system and other forms of air cover, the Croatian and Bosnian armies took SDS-held territory and then threatened Banja Luka, the main SDS-held city in Bosnia. At that point the SDS military and political leadership agreed to a cease-fire and to a U.S.-brokered settlement to the war.

The agreement that was reached in November 1995 at an air base outside Dayton, Ohio, established the institutions that still dominate Bosnia-Herzegovina. The Dayton accords, signed by the presidents of Croatia, Serbia, and Bosnia, as well as the leaders of the three nationalist parties, preserved Bosnia-Herzegovina as a single internationally recognized state but divided it into two "entities": a Serb-designated entity, the Republika Srpska, with 49 percent of the country's territory, and the Croat- and Muslim-designated Federation of Bosnia-Herzegovina. The Dayton Peace Agreement called for free and fair elections and specified that refugees had the right to return to their prewar homes. The Republic of Bosnia-Herzegovina is ruled by a three-member presidency—voters from each of the three major ethnic groups elect one member—and by a parliament that is also elected on an ethnic basis. A NATO-led military force that includes troops from thirty-three countries has been present in Bosnia-Herzegovina since January 1996: 60,000 troops in the first year, reduced by early 2001 to about 20,000.[6] The civilian side of implementation falls under the Office of the High Representative (OHR), an autonomous international institution that has the authority to impose decisions on the country if the Bosnia-Herzegovina institutions are unable to come to agreement and even to remove local officials who block implementation of the Dayton accords.[7] The Organization for Security and Cooperation in Europe (OSCE) is responsible for running elections, and the United Nations runs the International Police Task Force, made up of officers from around the world who are unarmed and whose goal is to help restructure the Bosnia-Herzegovina police force.[8]

Postwar Bosnia is thus in many ways an international protectorate, because the main international organizations—OSCE, OHR, the Peace Implementation Council (a group of fifty-five governments and international organizations that sponsor and direct the peace implementation process)—are effectively in charge. The stated goal of the international community is to create a multiethnic, democratic Bosnia as the best way to prevent the outbreak of violent conflict. Bosnia can be viable only if these actors back up their stated goals with actions, in particular by creating an environment that is conducive to democracy and civil society. Only in such an environment can international NGOs conceivably have a positive influence on Bosnian society. To the extent that the nationalist parties continue to use fear and the threat of violence to silence and marginalize dissenters, the ability of international NGOs to help locals rebuild their society is severely circumscribed. While the international community has often shown its willingness to remove actors who actively obstruct the implementation of the Dayton accords, which call for creating space for moderates, the tendency by international NGOs to accept that the cause of the conflict was ethnic animosities tends, perhaps unwittingly, to strengthen the nationalist parties.[9] This is important because a main challenge for those wanting to strengthen democracy and civil society is overcoming the hold of extremists; the key challenges for international NGOs include reconstructing communities not only physically but also in terms of allowing refugees to return to their homes. In many ways resolving this issue of refugee return, justice, and reconciliation is a prerequisite for building sustainable civil society.

While international NGOs, with the right strategies, can help the process of stabilization, there is certainly a limit to the amount of change that they can bring about on their own. While this is true of international NGOs everywhere, the international community's overwhelming and decisive role in Bosnia-Herzegovina, as well as the identical goals of international NGOs and the main international organizations running Bosnia, means that we would expect international NGOs to have significant positive influence in Bosnia-Herzegovina. Thus in theory this area provides an ideal situation for measuring the effectiveness of international NGOs.

STRATEGIES OF WESTERN NGOS

The international NGOs that I chose to study all have the overarching goal of reconstructing civil society in Bosnia-Herzegovina. They use four broad strategies for rebuilding civil society: directly addressing the issues of political structures and power, and in particular the role of the international community, through the International Crisis Group; building political parties and providing civic education through the National Democratic Institute; building local NGO capacity and networks through the Strategies, Training, and Advocacy for Reconciliation Project (STAR); and rebuilding the community through Catholic Relief Services and Mercy Corps International.

INTERNATIONAL CRISIS GROUP: STRUCTURAL REFORM

The International Crisis Group is a private, independent, multinational NGO "committed to strengthening the capacity of the international community to anticipate, understand and act to prevent and contain conflict."[10] Established in 1995 by a group of "prominent international citizens and foreign policy experts," its funding comes from the European Union, individual states (mostly Western European), foundations, and private companies. By 2001 the International Crisis Group had projects in fourteen hot spots around the world. It mainly researches and publishes detailed, high-quality reports that "combine on-the-ground analysis in conflict-threatened countries, with detailed policy prescription and advocacy." In each report the International Crisis Group advocates specific and detailed policies that it has identified as solutions to existing or potential crises, and it actively lobbies state governments and international organizations, both publicly and behind the scenes, to act on its analyses and recommendations.

The International Crisis Group began its activities in Bosnia-Herzegovina in February 1996, shortly after the Dayton Peace Agreement was signed, with the goal of supporting international efforts to implement the agreement. The International Crisis Group explicitly addresses the factors that are most crucial to the viability of Bosnia-Herzegovina as a state and society—the structural and political ones—and targets the most influential actors: the international organizations and states that are effectively running Bosnia-Herzegovina. The International Crisis Group is thus in many ways the international NGO in the best position to have a major effect because it is attempting to influence those actors that have the power to change Bosnia-Herzegovina's political structures and to ensure the stability and peace necessary for civil society to reemerge. Indeed, in many cases the reports by the International Crisis Group were the only reliable information and analysis available to the international community in specific areas or issues.[11]

The International Crisis Group's in-country staff members all are fluent in the local language, and all have an in-depth knowledge of and experience in the country. They work closely with Bosnians as well as international actors. Many members of the organization's board of directors and top representatives are former senior diplomats, so the International Crisis Group is extremely well connected to international actors, including the European Union, the United Nations, and OSCE, as well as individual state governments. Board members use this informal network to influence policy in a way that most international NGOs cannot. In addition, because the International Crisis Group is not particularly dependent on any one international organization or state for funding, it can publish independent analyses that are often highly critical of international actors and policies.

Staff members have also participated in televised debates with Bosnian politicians and have given numerous talks about the organization's proposals to Bosnian political and intellectual circles in both Republika Srpska and the Federation of Bosnia-Herzegovina. The International Crisis Group has a high profile among Bosnians: Local people with no connections to the international or NGO community often spontaneously mentioned the International Crisis Group and described it as having a good understanding of the local situation and good ideas for Bosnia-Herzegovina. The International Crisis Group thus provides information to the Bosnians themselves about issues that international organizations often decide behind closed doors.

The International Crisis group is clearly not a typical international NGO, in large part because it targets the international policy community, states, and international organizations instead of trying to change how local actors think or behave. As such, it seems to turn the usual flow of influence between international NGOs and donors on its head: It is trying to change the priorities and policies of the donors themselves through carefully researched and argued reports, as well as through direct lobbying by influential diplomats. Thus the International Crisis Group is an interesting new kind of strategy for international NGOs.

NATIONAL DEMOCRATIC INSTITUTE: PARTY BUILDING AND CIVIC TRAINING

The National Democratic Institute for International Affairs is a nonprofit that works to "strengthen and expand democracy worldwide."[12] It is funded mostly by the National Endowment for Democracy, an NGO funded by the U.S. Congress, both directly and through the U.S. Agency for International Development (USAID).

The institute has been in Bosnia-Herzegovina since 1996 and is pursuing two kinds of strategies, both of which are typical, traditional "democratization" approaches that focus on formal political institutions and impose preconceived projects and goals on the local society. A program to develop political parties, based in Sarajevo, aims at directly helping parties to strengthen themselves as democratic institutions and teaches them how to be responsive to citizens. A civic education and advocacy program in Tuzla, Banja Luka, and Mostar aims to "convey democratic values and knowledge of Bosnia's emerging political systems to citizens" as a means of mobilizing them to participate in democratic structures. Part of the latter project involves setting up a network for domestic monitoring of elections.

Although the institute recruits young Bosnians to do much of the political party work, its program seems to be very much a cookie-cutter approach that does not take into account local experience or knowledge. Indeed, the heads of the institute's Bosnian offices have no particular regional expertise, nor do they speak the local language. The party-building program is presented to local "leaders, organizers, and activists" in a Bosnian-language publication that is merely a translation into Bosnian of a handbook that the institute uses in its work around the world (its other printed materials in Bosnian, for example, citizen survey forms, are likewise translations of generic materials).[13] Similarly, the institute's representative in Tuzla, who has no regional expertise, said he was strongly pushing the institutes Bosnian employees to do door-to-door canvassing, which he saw as effective because of his own experience as a political activist in Chicago. The local employees of the institute, however, strongly resisted his suggestion. He discounted their resistance as resulting from their ignorance of the effectiveness of such campaigns, rather than accepting it as a reflection of their knowledge of local customs and experience.[14]

According to the institute's Sarajevo office, it measures the effectiveness of the party-building strategy by election results—whether parties with which the institute has worked have made electoral gains—as well as by increases in party membership and more sophisticated campaign literature. The institute's Washington,

D.C., office, however, strongly disavowed the use of electoral success as the measure of effectiveness; instead, it said, the institute looks at whether the parties have achieved the institute's goals through their internal and external activities, such as better public outreach, better organizational structure, and campaign plans. Neither type of evaluation measures whether the institute's efforts are having a real influence on Bosnian society; apparently, the assumption is that if the parties follow the institute's prescriptions, the benefits to Bosnia will automatically accrue.

The institute's civic education project involves advocacy training and encourages and helps locals to form NGOs and to become actors in the political process. To this end the institute in 1996 and 1997 organized twenty discussions in villages around Tuzla in the Federation of Bosnia-Herzegovina and another thirty in Banja Luka in Republika Srpska. Each group was trained in how to hold "democratic meetings," that is, meetings in which all points of view can be put forward, listened to, and respected. Discussion group meetings, attended mainly by intellectuals, old-age pensioners, and community activists, were held once every four to six weeks, focusing on the general topic of learning about the process of transition in Bosnia-Herzegovina.

These groups also organized a candidates' forum before the 1996 elections in Republika Srpska and monitored the elections. The local staffs of the institute in Tuzla and Banja Luka concentrated on bringing together a group of seven core NGOs from both the Federation of Bosnia-Herzegovina and Republika Srpska to monitor the September 1998 national elections. Here the institute was using monitoring as a way of building an election-monitoring infrastructure for the entire country, with the goal of setting up an NGO that would serve all of Bosnia-Herzegovina.

THE STRATEGIES, TRAINING, AND ADVOCACY FOR RECONCILIATION NETWORK FOR WOMEN'S LEADERSHIP: BUILDING LOCAL NGO CAPACITY

The STAR (Strategies, Training, and Advocacy for Reconciliation) Network for Women's Leadership operates exclusively in the former Yugoslav republics (including Kosovo) and is meant to build the capacity of women's leadership and women's NGOs in that region.[15] STAR's specific goal is to build sustainable, non-nationalist, democratic NGOs that advocate social change and to do so by fostering NGO networks that work to influence public policy and by providing training, technical assistance, and development assistance. STAR has also worked to raise awareness of the situation of women and local NGOs among private U.S. donors and has helped to forge links between its local NGO partners and other international NGOs.

The STAR project came out of a meeting of women NGO leaders from the former Yugoslavia in February 1994. It was established in October 1994 with a three-year, US$2.1 million grant from USAID and continues to be funded mainly by USAID. The STAR project is directed by an American who, like all of STAR's international staff members, speaks the local languages and has long experience in the region. STAR runs projects in four program areas throughout the former Yugoslavia: citizen participation, training local NGOs in participatory leadership and advocacy training, organizational development, and conflict resolution; media and communications; advocacy for women's health; and NGO self-financing and small business development. STAR has an advisory board made up of local NGO representatives, and the needs of local groups drive its overall priorities. STAR works with any non-nationalist women's group; by 1997 it had partnered with twenty groups in eleven cities throughout Bosnia-Herzegovina.

STAR's particular focus is on building networks between women's NGOs within Bosnia-Herzegovina and in the wider former Yugoslavia. STAR also seeks to link these NGOs directly with other women's NGOs worldwide. For example, it brought representatives of South African, Israeli, and Palestinian groups to speak on postconflict civil society problems that are common to all these regions, and it was instrumental in making it possible for local women leaders to participate in the 1995 World Conference on Women in Beijing.

The key part of STAR's strategy is to empower local NGOs, to give them the tools and as much control of the process as possible. STAR also is conscious of issues of equality and the way in which money makes true partnership difficult. STAR's approach is based on the view that learning is a two-way process and that STAR is learning from local NGOs as much as they are learning from STAR, in particular in the areas of grassroots organizing and dealing with postwar gender and community issues.[16]

STAR has succeeded in its main goal of building a sustainable network of women's NGOs; according to an internal evaluation, "USAID saw STAR's experiences in Bosnia-Herzegovina as lessons that could be . . . shared by other international organizations."[17] Likewise, the feedback from partner NGOs is positive and consistently and favorably compares their experiences with STAR to experiences with other international NGOs.

Originally a project of Delphi International, a U.S.-based NGO, since October 1999 STAR has been part of another U.S.-based NGO, World Learning.[18] Since 1999 STAR has branched out and now works not only with women's NGOs but with women in all sectors, including business, government, and trade unions, with the goal of developing women's networks in the region. Recent accomplishments include helping local NGOs to organize a women's conference on the economic situation and poverty in Bosnia in June 2001.

CATHOLIC RELIEF SERVICES: RECONSTRUCTION AS A MEANS OF BUILDING COMMUNITY AND CIVIL SOCIETY

Catholic Relief Services is the official international relief and development agency of the U.S. Conference of Catholic Bishops.[19] Catholic Relief operates globally and supports a range of international assistance projects as well as providing emergency relief. The overall goal of Catholic Relief is to lay the groundwork for a transition from relief activities to development activities, with the focus on human development and social justice. Catholic Relief's activities in Bosnia-Herzegovina are funded mostly on a year-to-year basis, 40 percent from the U.S. State Department's Bureau of Population, Refugees, and Migration (BPRM), 45 percent from the U.N. High Commissioner for Refugees, and 15 percent from private donations to Catholic Relief. In 2001 the BPRM was facing funding cuts in its Bosnia programs and seemed to be cutting back its commitment to integrated strategies, focusing specifically instead on rebuilding shelter.

Catholic Relief's staff has a large percentage of locals, with minimal international staffing (in 2001, 110 staff members were nationals and eight were from other countries). From the start Catholic Relief has worked with local NGOs as partners, especially the main NGOs of Bosnia-Herzegovina's four major religious communities: the Catholic group Caritas, the Serbian Orthodox Dobrotvor, the Muslim Merhamet, and the Jewish group La Benevolencija.

Catholic Relief came to Bosnia-Herzegovina in 1993 to do humanitarian work during the war; from the start it was committed to staying on to do postwar reconstruction. Since the end of the war in 1995 Catholic Relief has been working in emergency relief assistance and recovery, enterprise development, and "counterpart strengthening" (strengthening local NGOs). The focus of its activity is rebuilding civil society through the reconstruction of houses and infrastructure in about twelve communities (by 2001 this was up to forty communities), which takes about 80 percent of Catholic Relief's resources in Bosnia-Herzegovina.

Catholic Relief's goal is "the restoration of multiethnic communities on a sustainable basis," allowing people to return to peaceful and productive lives in their home communities and facilitating community reintegration, with peaceful refugee returns without need for international peacekeeper escorts.[20] To achieve this goal Catholic Relief has been working to reward "open communities," that is, those that have officially declared their willingness to allow minorities to return to their homes.

To this end in each community Catholic Relief first established a multiethnic community working group made up of representatives of local interests and chaired by a Catholic Relief field-worker who is a native of Bosnia-Herzegovina. The working group itself takes the lead in decision making, acting as an assessment and planning body for the community's reconstruction and recovery strategy as well as for the design, planning, and management of Catholic Relief's programs. This idea, of integrating community building into the reconstruction efforts, came from Catholic Relief's experience in Bosnia and elsewhere, doing projects with multiethnic groups as implementing partners, and was begun after a self-evaluation in late 1996 during which Catholic Relief decided that the ideal program would focus on the community instead of on the project.

The funding that Catholic Relief receives is specifically for reconstruction, but while private (U.S.) companies also do reconstruction in Bosnia-Herzegovina under contract from USAID, they are not interested in anything beyond the physical rebuilding of houses. Catholic Relief's mandate is to go beyond that; in the course of rebuilding houses Catholic Relief also seeks to rebuild communities as social organizations, resulting, according to one international organization representative in Bosnia-Herzegovina, in better overall outcomes at a lower cost.

The Office of the High Representative defines success for returns as one person staying one night in a rebuilt house. In contrast, Catholic Relief has a two-stage definition: the first is when part of a family is living in a rebuilt house as its principal residence; "real return," however, is when the family has vacated and given up rights to its temporary residence to fully resettle in its original, rebuilt, home. For the purpose of reporting to donors on the goal of returning to productive lives, Catholic Relief uses proxy indicators such as numbers of houses rebuilt or repaired and the number of agreements of intention to return. This fulfills the obligation to donors, but it does not capture some of the more important or long-term elements. Catholic Relief is working on how to evaluate these aspects of its programs and is trying to develop funding instruments that fit local needs, rather than having projects driven by funding requirements.

MERCY CORPS INTERNATIONAL: RECONSTRUCTION AS A MEANS OF BUILDING COMMUNITY AND CIVIL SOCIETY

Mercy Corps International is headquartered in the United States and Scotland and provides emergency relief and sustainable community development and civil society worldwide. Mercy Corps is funded by the United Nations, the European Union, the United States, and Western European governments, and the World Bank. The Bosnia project is funded mostly by the U.N. High Commissioner for Refugees, specifically for reconstruction of housing. It also sells agricultural surplus from the U.S. Department of Agriculture to raise money for other projects. The Bosnian office has more than one hundred employees, more than ninety of whom are locals, and the staff includes civil, construction, and electrical engineers as well as program officers. The goals of the Bosnia project include the return and reintegration of refugees into their prewar communities;

reestablishment of local communities through civil society initiatives; shelter and infrastructure reconstruction; and provision of microcredit.[21]

The current Mercy Corps project in Bosnia-Herzegovina dates to a 1993 effort to run a water system reconstruction project during the war. The infrastructure reconstruction programs focus on water and heating systems, homes, schools, and medical clinics. The civil society element of the program is based on the belief that Mercy Corps could not just go into a community, build houses, and then leave, because people must participate in the reconstruction of their own communities in order to rebuild those communities. The microcredit strategy addresses the communities' need for economic revitalization. In 1998 Mercy Corps was the only international NGO working to localize the process of providing microcredit. Mercy Corps does not work on strengthening local NGOs, because it sees them as tending to be inefficient and costly. Mercy Corps seeks to provide people with information, skills, and ideas so they can build a social infrastructure. These ideas and strategies came out of Mercy Corps's civil society work in other countries and the experiences of people working in Bosnia-Herzegovina.

Although Mercy Corps's funding from the U.N. High Commissioner for Refugees is strictly for reconstruction, it has carried out this mission in a way that also addresses community building. As long as the houses get built, Mercy Corps can use whatever strategy it deems best. While its reports to donors require quantified results, such as the number of houses built, Mercy Corps's own evaluation of success is based on whether the entire community—business, government, and beneficiaries of reconstruction—is involved. But this cannot be quantified, and results may not be obvious for several years.

More recently, Mercy Corps has received an umbrella grant for the reintegration of refugees in Bosnia-Herzegovina and Croatia through active engagement of communities. As of October 2000, Mercy Corps had rehabilitated and reconstructed more than 4,200 houses; reconnected 80 water systems; reconnected electrical supply systems in more than 80 villages, towns, and cities; repaired central heating systems in two cities; and issued almost 7,400 microcredit loans in more than twenty-one municipalities in all regions of the country.

IMPACT

Because of its focus on the political and structural issues, the International Crisis Group's strategy of influencing international actors to change political structures and policies has perhaps the greatest potential as an effective strategy from the macroperspective. It is important too because it casts light upon activities of international organizations that might otherwise go uncriticized and unchecked, thus forcing them to take into account the effect of their activities on Bosnia-Herzegovina society and to consider other perspectives. The International Crisis Group provides something of a check on the other institutional and political factors that, in the absence of criticism, tend to drive these organizations. Given the power of international organizations in Bosnia-Herzegovina, this watchdog function is extremely important. The International Crisis Group and other observers claim that its activities have been quite successful, bringing about concrete changes and rethinking of a number of important structural and political issues.[22] All these changes have contributed to a more stable environment in Bosnia-Herzegovina that is conducive to democratization and the reemergence of civil society.

The most effective strategies for reconstructing and strengthening civil society have been those that focus on rebuilding communities by encouraging people to work together toward a tangible, common goal. Such a strategy facilitates a re-creation of the organic bases on which any community is built and moves the focus of energy away from the national political scene (which was the focus of nationalists before and during the war) and toward the local and regional scene. Thus it appears that potentially the most effective strategy may be an integrated one that uses major projects, such as reconstruction of housing or infrastructure as the focus of a process of rebuilding community or civil society, supplemented by programs (such as microcredits) that create businesses and jobs in the community.

As the projects run by Catholic Relief and Mercy Corps have shown, this strategy effectively empowers locals, bringing major stakeholders in a community together to work out how to reconstruct their societies, independent of state or other institutional actors. Key to the success of such strategies is that these international NGOs base their activities on decisions made by the community, rather than imposing preconceived concepts or strategies from above. Mercy Corps' experiences in using the rebuilding of housing, electrical and water systems, and other infrastructure, and its participation in the community restoration project in Brčko and in other municipalities, are good examples of this. Likewise, Catholic Relief has expanded its reconstruction work from twelve to forty communities, reintegrating these communities in "sustainable ways." An example is the town of Stolac, from which Bosnian Muslims had been expelled by Croat forces. Catholic Relief enabled thousands of refugee families to return by helping to rebuild their destroyed homes and engaging people in the community in order to smooth the return of the Bosnian Muslims to live among their Croat neighbors.

This approach provides a kind of experiential learning, in which participants reconstruct community and civil society in a concrete way. This strategy focuses on communities, especially in sectors ripped apart by war, and gives them a concrete way to rebuild themselves both physically and in spirit. By working together, deciding together, and building together, people involved in these projects rebuild the interpersonal and community ties that the war severed and

222 V. P. GAGNON JR.

provide these communities and thus Bosnia-Herzegovina as a whole with a basis for the future. They also contribute in important ways to democratization by constructing a process of participatory decision making. As Catholic Relief points out, shelter repair is an especially good focus for such a strategy since it reduces stress on local communities: Refugees living in the community can return to their rebuilt homes, freeing up housing and allowing the community to accept back families that fled during the war.

Another effective strategy is the strengthening of existing local NGOs, empowering them to make decisions and set priorities and to make connections with other local and international NGOs. This strategy builds on the remnants of prewar civil society, drawing on the traditions of political activism that were present in Yugoslavia, rather than imposing wholesale models and preconceived notions from outside. A large part of the success of this strategy, seen in the work of STAR and Mercy Corps, is the result of its reliance on those who know best—the locals—what their communities and society need and how best to achieve those goals. Thus in neighboring Croatia, the women's NGO network and STAR successfully pressured the national government to set up a series of women's shelters and address other women's issues; a partner NGO successfully reduced prostitution of minors related to the international peacekeepers' presence in Zenica; partner NGOs organized an international women's conference in Bosnia in 1996; and local NGOs have a "sense of increased ownership of the network," as evidenced by their initiative in organizing such projects as the May 2001 conference on economic reform and poverty in Bosnia-Herzegovina. Likewise, the Bosnian staff of Mercy Corps' microcredit project, the Economic Development Department, has assumed full responsibility for it and is in the process of transforming it into an independent local microcredit organization.

Less effective is an explicit and narrow focus on political party building and civic education. A North American model of political activity ignores the organic society in which and from which political parties and activities grow. It also misses the basic driving force of political power in Bosnia-Herzegovina, where, unlike in the United States, ruling political parties effectively operate as the state—in some ways ruling parties are too strong. The state—and thus the party that controls the state—is the primary allocator of tangible and intangible resources and especially of secure jobs, and the only other source of stable, secure jobs is the international NGOs and other international organizations. Teaching political parties to behave like "democratic parties" does nothing to address this problem. Even when opposition parties have won elections, they are ruling in the same structural environment and thus tend to be drawn into the same kind of patronage logic that the nationalist parties have relied on. Thus focusing on electoral strategies or formal political institutions by itself does little to change this or to build civil society; rather, it tends to give particular parties access to resources that may give them an advantage in domestic political competition.

What is missing is the context of Bosnia-Herzegovina society, its recent history of political and power structures, and a view of the process as two-way learning. The National Democratic Institute's "political party building" efforts do not address the root cause of political conflict in Bosnia-Herzegovina; it seems to focus narrowly and in a preset way on political parties as key actors because it has a narrow view of what "politics" is about. This view apparently ignores both issues of structural power and the organic bases upon which communities and civil society are built. Civic education probably does not hurt, but the rebuilding of communities, the empowerment of society, and the creation of opportunities and incentives for people outside politics are what will make politics and political parties in Bosnia-Herzegovina democratic. It would seem much more useful for discussion groups to focus on community issues at the local level, coming up with ways to empower themselves and their communities, rather than focusing on abstract issues at the national level. In that sense the integrated strategies of Mercy Corps, Catholic Relief, and STAR are much more promising in terms of their long-term effects, because activism at the local level is likely to translate into more interest in and activism at the national level as well.

According to Bosnian NGO observers, the presence of so many international actors and the in-flow of massive amounts of money has major negative effects on Bosnia-Herzegovina society itself. The best and the brightest Bosnians, especially those who know English, are now working for international organizations and international NGOs as staff members, drivers, and interpreters, rather than in Bosnia-Herzegovina society itself or for local NGOs, most of which cannot afford to pay much. Another effect is generational: Older, more experienced and educated Bosnians who do not know English are left out, creating not only a knowledge gap for international NGOs but also resentment. Because of the money that international NGOs are spending in Bosnia-Herzegovina, Bosnians are now also much less willing to work as volunteers than before. I heard a number of stories of Bosnians who were unwilling to take part in conferences, meetings, workshops, or other activities unless they were paid. Likewise, many Bosnians have become extremely cynical and jaded about international NGOs, often seeing their presence more as a result of the NGOs' desire for self-promotion than of any real desire to help Bosnians. This impression is strong exactly because so many international NGOs did not pursue strategies like those of Mercy Corps, Catholic Relief, and STAR, strategies that take Bosnians seriously and that are sensitive to local knowledge, context, and needs. In this way some international NGOs have actually made it less possible and much harder to rebuild civil society because many Bosnians have the impression that civil society projects are really a sham by well-paid internationals. Indeed, with few exceptions, international actors seem to have little awareness of how their control of resources is negatively affecting Bosnia-Herzegovina society.

LIMITATIONS

As I mentioned in the introduction, the major obstacle facing international NGOs is the structural situation in which they are working, in the sense that they do not control the political and economic environment but also in the sense that they are dependent for funding on donors that have their own priorities and interests. Of course, this is true of international NGOs everywhere. But in Bosnia-Herzegovina this structural constraint is especially striking because at a declarative level, the main international actors have the same goals as most of the international NGOs. As such, one would expect Bosnia-Herzegovina to be a best case scenario for the effectiveness of international NGOs. But donor priorities have tended to shift every six months or year—from humanitarian relief to reconstruction to business development to refugee returns to building civil society—reflecting the donors' political interests. As donor priorities shift, so too do those of the international NGOs, most of which are on one-year funding cycles. They therefore face the choice of shifting their activities or losing support. A related problem is donors' focus on short-term results; this often undermines important long-term goals that only strategies that do not have immediate or quantifiable payoffs can achieve, a dilemma underscored by workers affiliated with Catholic Relief.

The negative effect that occurs when donors drive the process was most clearly expressed by a USAID officer in charge of NGO relations.[23] While he praised the humanitarian international NGOs such as Catholic Relief, the International Rescue Committee, and Mercy Corps for their work during the war and for providing invaluable information during the immediate postwar period, he declared that their time was now over. USAID would be shifting its funding, he said, to international NGOs that have experience elsewhere in Central and Eastern Europe and that work specifically on "democracy assistance." This, however, neglects broader strategies and ignores the limits of democracy assistance narrowly defined, especially when applied to the postwar context.

The same USAID officer commented that a major problem for his agency is that other donors may continue to fund projects and international NGOs that USAID does not agree with or that do not fit USAID's priorities.[24] The ability of USAID to selectively fund only those international NGOs that pursue strategies congruent with USAID's (the U.S. government's) priorities and perceptions means that innovative and effective integrated projects such as those pursued by Catholic Relief and Mercy Corps—which do not necessarily provide an immediate tangible result and do not fit into preconceived notions of democracy assistance—may lose out if the United States attempts to pressure other donors to adhere to a limited vision of democracy assistance.

Donors tend to have a specific focus and to fund only projects that are strictly reconstruction or strictly democracy assistance, which ignores the importance of multidimensional programs. A common concern expressed by Bosnians familiar with international NGO activities is that donors also often appear to neglect realistic and localized needs assessment and that locals are often not equal partners in determining needs and priorities. Indeed, most donors will not work directly with local NGOs or do so only if they have an international NGO as a partner. A Bosnian NGO activist observed that many international NGOs have an interest in remaining as the intermediary for local NGOs and the outside and thus do nothing to encourage local NGOs to establish direct links with outside funders.

A 1996 study for CARE Canada by an international NGO consultant gives some idea of the extent of the distrust of locals. The study proposed the establishment of an endowment to provide local NGOs with a stable source of income; it would have been run by a board of local NGO representatives, and funding was to have come from those international organizations and governments that today are the largest donors to Bosnia-Herzegovina.[25] But donors proved unwilling to surrender control of how their monies are spent, and to date the effort has not been successful.

Even where locals are seen as equal colleagues and peers, the disparity of power between local and international NGOs is a further constraint on effectiveness. The STAR project is perhaps the most sensitive to this factor, perhaps because of the background of the project's directors, who had much experience in this region long before the war, speak the language, and are quite aware of the realities within these societies in a way that most international NGO personnel are not. STAR attempts to empower locals, and its regional advisory board, made up of local NGO leaders, determines the organization's priorities, while partner NGOs have undertaken a number of major projects on their own. STAR also seeks to link local NGOs with NGOs in other countries. STAR treats the locals as colleagues and peers and sees their presence in Bosnia-Herzegovina as a two-way learning process while recognizing that the power disparity can never be completely absent.

Another general problem facing international NGOs is the sheer number of them operating in Bosnia-Herzegovina. This brings problems of coordination, including duplication of activities and projects that work at cross-purposes to each other. The intense competition for limited funding distracts from a real assessment of local needs and exacerbates the problem of funders' interests driving the process by rewarding international NGOs that obey them and punishing those who do not. Some international NGOs, in order to maintain funding and their raison d'être, try to keep local NGOs dependent, maintaining a role as intermediary. STAR is a counterexample; it encourages local NGOs to contact foundations and other donors directly for funding and to contact other non-Bosnian NGOs on their own.

In general terms the long-term viability and success of even the best international NGO projects in an international protectorate such as Bosnia-Herzegovina depend almost exclusively on the degree to which the international community continues its commitment to a situation that is conducive to stabilizing communities by rebuilding them. While the best international NGO strategies contribute to creating such a situation at the microlevel, they cannot accomplish this within communities without stability at the macrolevel. Thus without support from the major international actors, strategies that focus on empowering local actors and communities cannot hope to be sustainable over the long term. In this way, the International Crisis Group's strategy, which explicitly targets the international community at that macrolevel, is a crucial factor in continued success.

The case of Bosnia-Herzegovina provides a number of important lessons for international NGOs that operate in other societies with the aim of building civil society.

First, international NGOs should try to seek funding from donors that take the long view and that leave the international NGOs free to let local actors determine priorities and projects. This is a challenge for international NGOs that rely for funding on government agencies and international organizations, because these actors fund projects for political reasons that may have little to do with the interests of the society in question and everything to do with domestic political interests within the donor country, institutional interests of the funding organization, power interests of the state in the international arena, or preconceived notions of how to ensure democratization. This is especially true for funders of "democracy assistance." One way to do this is to diversify funding in a way that does not give any one funder too much leverage; another way is to change the way donors think about projects by citing successful long-term, integrated projects that have made a difference. In both cases, however, international NGOs should examine the motivations and preconceived notions of those who fund such assistance and question the appropriateness and effectiveness of idiosyncratic U.S. concepts and practices for other societies.

Indeed, international NGOs should examine how even admirable goals like democratization can in fact serve the power interests of their funders rather than the interests of the society in which the NGOs are operating. If international NGOs do have some autonomy in deciding what goals to pursue and the strategies they will use to do so, they should be self-critical about whether they are acting on behalf of their own institutional interests and preconceived notions or according to the realities in the host country. They should encourage horizontal networks among local NGOs in all the countries in which they are active; this focus on networking is a key part of STAR's strategy and one reason for its successes. Likewise, international NGOs should see their activities as interactive processes rather than as a kind of transmission belt running from outside to inside.

Third, the focus of international NGO efforts should be on helping communities build themselves into civil society, rather than importing notions of political party work or building civil society based on U.S. experiences and conditions. International NGOs need to have a firm grasp of the existing communities and relationships within those communities. This includes an understanding of how politics fits into the bigger picture. In cases where politics was the center of power (as in most of the formerly socialist countries), it is important to realize that merely teaching political parties to behave democratically, or teaching people the principles of liberal democracy, will not get to the underlying dynamics of power. Politics must come from the realities of power on the ground. For democracy to be successful, it must be grounded in the everyday experience of the population. Otherwise, what exists is the acting out of democracy without its substance. Attempts to build democracy must build on ideas and experiences of the society in question, not simply assume that there is nothing there on which to build. In the case of Bosnia the experiences of grassroots participation in community and enterprise management under the socialist system, while far from perfect, have given people the experience of participation and activism. Likewise, the political ferment and electoral campaigns of the late 1980s and early 1990s, along with the existence of critical and independent media, are bases on which international NGOs should build their activities.

Fourth, a sensitivity to power relations in the country raises the question of funding opposition parties. Indeed, in a country like Bosnia-Herzegovina the goal should be to decrease the importance of politics and of the center(s), rather than focusing upon it. Electoral outcomes do matter, and who controls the state is an important factor, as recent electoral victories of non-nationalist parties in the Federation of Bosnia-Herzegovina, as well as in neighboring Croatia, have shown. The next step needs to be the empowering of local communities, not in the form of political parties or even NGOs but as communities. STAR has more recently moved in that direction through its shift to facilitating networks of women in all sectors of society rather than just among women's NGOs. This is also where the integrated strategies of Mercy Corps and Catholic Relief are crucial. By focusing on these "nonpolitical" projects, international NGOs in fact are facilitating the creation of political communities and activists.

Along these lines the United States—and USAID in particular—has been moving toward giving reconstruction projects to private companies. This is clearly a mistake, because business has little incentive to spend the time, effort, or resources to rebuild community or civil society. Thus the United States in particular should avoid ceding reconstruction projects to U.S. or other international private contractors and should instead focus its reconstruction money on international NGOs that use reconstruction of houses and infrastructure to achieve other, broader goals.

The situation in Bosnia-Herzegovina and the kinds of strategies that international NGOs have developed there provide important lessons. Bosnia-Herzegovina shows the effectiveness of multifaceted integrated strategies that concentrate on local communities and work on the process of building community. Focusing on an overall common goal, such as infrastructure repair or shelter reconstruction, and having all the community's stakeholders involved in making decisions, planning, and implementing the resulting projects is more effective than workshops in "civic education" and "multiparty democracy." Using this kind of project as the focus, and supplementing it with development strategies such as microcredits, conflict resolution, and advocacy, seems to be a most effective way to build civil society and democracy.

Of course, in some ways Bosnia-Herzegovina is a special case. The wartime destruction provides a clear focus for community-building efforts as well as for donor funding. The challenge is to transfer this kind of strategy into societies that do not have such obvious projects for communities to focus on. A parallel challenge is to convince donors that they can achieve the broader goals of democracy and social stability by funding reconstruction, renovations, or other kinds of infrastructure or housing projects in societies that have not just been through a war.

In more general terms Bosnia-Herzegovina shows the importance of involving locals in decision making and implementation and of explicitly facing the question of the power disparity between the international NGOs, which disburse funds, and the society itself, which receives them. Exactly because of this disparity international NGOs must make extra efforts to seek out and encourage alternative or dissenting voices among locals and be models of good NGO behavior by seeing their relationships with locals as a partnership to which both sides contribute.

NOTES

1. According to the Constitution of Bosnia-Herzegovina—which is part of the Dayton Peace Agreement reached in November 1995—the Constitutional Court is to have nine members—"jurists of the highest standing"—three of whom "shall be selected by the President of the European Court of Human Rights . . . [and] shall not be citizens of Bosnia and Herzegovina or of any neighboring state." Likewise, the constitution provides that the governor of the central bank be appointed by the International Monetary Fund and that he or she not be a citizen of Bosnia and Herzegovina or any neigh-

boring state. The Dayton accords' Annex 3 also charges the Organization for Security and Cooperation in Europe (OSCE) with running all elections in the country. For the text of the constitution, see "General Framework Agreement: Annex 4, Constitution of Bosnia-Herzegovina," *Office of the High Representative*, http://www.ohr.int/dpa/default.asp?content_id = 372 (October 10, 2001). The text of the entire agreement can be found at http://www.ohr.int/dpa/default.asp?content_id = 380 (October 10, 2001).

2. See V. P. Gagnon Jr., "Ethnic Nationalism and International Conflict: The Case of Serbia," *International Security* 19, no. 3 (Winter 1994–95): 131–66; Gagnon, "Ethnic Conflict as Demobilizer: The Case of Serbia," Working Paper no. 96-1, Cornell University Institute for European Studies, Ithaca, May 10, 1996, which is also available at the Web site of V. P. Gagnon Jr., http://www.ithaca.edu/gagnon/articles/demob/index.htm (October 10, 2001); Gagnon, "The Yugoslav Wars of the 1990s: A Critical Reexamination of 'Ethnic Conflict': The Case of Croatia" (paper presented at the annual meeting of Association for the Study of Nationalities, Columbia University, New York, April 2001).

3. In 1991 the population of Bosnia-Herzegovina was 43 percent Bosnian Muslim, 31 percent Serb, 18 percent Croat, and 8 percent others.

4. For details see Human Rights Watch, *War Crimes in Bosnia-Hercegovina*, 2 vols. (New York: Human Rights Watch, 1992–93). See also details from prosecutions at the International Criminal Tribunal for the Former Yugoslavia (ICTY) in the Hague in reports at *Tribunal Watch*, http://www.iwpr.net/index.pl?tribunal_index.html (October 10, 2001). The address for the ICTY site is http://www.un.org/icty/ (October 10, 2001).

5. For a critique of U.N. policy see David Rieff, *Slaughterhouse: Bosnia and the Failure of the West* (New York: Simon and Schuster, 1995).

6. For background on the Stabilization Forces, see NATO's Web site at http://www.nato.int/sfor/ (October 10, 2001).

7. The Office of the High Representative has imposed a common currency, passport, national anthem, license plates, and flag on Bosnia-Herzegovina, as well as numerous other laws and regulations. The mandate of the High Representative is set out in Annex 10 of the Dayton Peace Agreement. It declares that the High Representative is "the final authority in theatre to interpret the civilian aspects of the Peace Agreement." The High Representative is nominated by the Steering Board of the Peace Implementation Council (a group of fifty-five governments and international organizations that sponsor and direct the peace implementation process). The U.N. Security Council, which approved the Dayton Peace Agreement as well as the deployment of international troops in Bosnia-Herzegovina, then endorses the nominee. The OHR budget is funded from the following sources: European Union, 53 percent; United States, 22 percent; Japan, 10 percent; Russia, 4 percent; Canada, 3.03 percent; Organization of the Islamic Conference, 2.5 percent; others, 5.47 percent. For more information see the OHR's Web site at http://www.ohr.int (October 10, 2001).

8. For the Web site of the Organization for Security and Cooperation in Europe mission to Bosnia-Herzegovina, see http://www.oscebih.org/oscebih_eng.asp (October 10, 2001). See the International Police Task Force Web site at http://www.unmibh.org/unmibh/iptf/index.htm (October 10, 2001).

9. That said, recent trends in Bosnian elections have shown growing electoral support for nonethnic parties; for example, in the Federation of Bosnia-Herzegovina the

2000 elections brought to power a coalition of non-nationalist parties, while a coalition of non-nationalist parties from both entities now forms the government at the all-Bosnia level. These trends have been strengthened by the recent changes in government in Croatia and in Serbia.

10. "About ICG," *CrisisWeb*, http://www.crisisweb.org/about/program.cfm?typeid = 4 (October 10, 2001). The address of the Web site of the International Crisis Group is http://www.crisisweb.org (October 10, 2001).

11. Examples include the International Crisis Group's report on politics in Republika Srpska in 1996—a time when outsiders had no information on this topic—as well as its critical analyses of the international community's policies on refugee returns, media, and elections. Indeed, as Christopher Bennett, the head of the International Crisis Group's Sarajevo office from 1996 to 1999, put it, the International Crisis Group began to set the agenda via its research "because nobody else was putting out anything comparable" (personal communication, May 2001). He also noted that the International Crisis Group influenced international media coverage of Bosnia-Herzegovina by providing story ideas to visiting journalists and putting the international community's "spin" into context.

12. "The Work of the National Democratic Institute," *National Democratic Institute for International Affairs*, http://www.ndi.org/about/about.asp (October 10, 2001). See the National Democratic Institute's Web site at http://www.ndi.org (October 10, 2001).

13. National Democratic Institute, "Politicke stranke i tranzicija ka demokratija: Prirucnik za jacanje demokratskih stranaka namjenjen liderima, organizatorima i aktivistima" (Political Parties and the Transition to Democracy: Handbook on Strengthening Democratic Parties for Leaders, Organizers, and Activists), September 1997.

14. Nick Green, director of Civic Education Project, National Democratic Institute, interview by author, Tuzla, June 11, 1998.

15. The Web site for the STAR project may be found at http://www.worldlearning .org/star (November 13, 2001).

16. See Jill Benderly, "A Woman's Place Is at the Peace Table," *SAIS Review* 20, no. 2 (Summer–Fall 2000): 79–83. Benderly is cofounder and codirector of the STAR project.

17. From STAR internal self-evaluation, May 1998.

18. The address for the World Learning Web site is http://www.worldlearning.org (October 10, 2001).

19. See the Catholic Relief Web site at http://www.catholicrelief.org (October 10, 2001).

20. "Bosnia-Herzegovina," Summer 2001, *Catholic Relief Services*, http://www .catholicrelief.org/where/bosnia/index.cfm (October 10, 2001).

21. The address of the Mercy Corps Web site is http://www.mercycorps.org/programs /bosnia.shtml (October 10, 2001).

22. Examples of international policies that were formulated in direct response to reports from and advocacy by the International Crisis Group include helping ensure that eleven thousand Serbs remained in Sarajevo when the city was reunited in 1996; winning the delay of the 1996 elections in the divided city of Mostar in order to address serious problems there; turning the divided and disputed region of Brčko into a separate, nonethnically defined district under the central government; causing USAID and

the World Bank to rethink their aid programs; securing reforms of the judicial system to remove individuals who were undermining the system; developing suggestions for ways to ameliorate the tense situation in Mostar; and convincing the international community in 1997 to take tougher action against local actors who were undermining the Dayton agreement.

23. Jim Hope, USAID officer, interview by author, Sarajevo, June 10, 1998.

24. According to Hope, USAID's attempts to use dollars as leverage with international NGOs will not succeed if they have alternate sources of money, and USAID is less effective if others are giving money "at cross-purposes" (Hope interview).

25. Ian Smillie, "Service Delivery or Civil Society? Nongovernmental Organizations in Bosnia and Herzegovina," report prepared for CARE Canada, December 1996.

Chapter 9

CONCLUSION: THE POWER AND LIMITS OF TRANSNATIONAL DEMOCRACY NETWORKS IN POSTCOMMUNIST SOCIETIES

Sarah E. Mendelson

This book has explored Western efforts to support civil society in widely varied settings throughout Eastern Europe and Eurasia during the 1990s. The authors show how the political landscapes across the regions have changed strikingly since 1989. Because institutions associated with liberal democracies have proliferated, many of these societies look as if they are conforming to international norms: One-party rule is no more; citizens regularly turn out for elections; NGOs have mushroomed; the media are no longer exclusively controlled by the state; many constitutions now protect citizens' rights.[1]

The cases show that Western groups have influenced incremental change at the local level. Many examples show how Western groups have been crucial to the existence of local NGOs in terms of funding and training. In 1990 few NGOs existed; by 2000 they were connected to colleagues and activists in other societies. The case studies show how Western groups have affected the form of new institutions. More than other types of assistance—economic, in particular—the strategies of Western NGOs that were working with local NGOs often resulted in the transfer of ideas and practices or helped indigenous cultures evolve in a direction consistent with democratic practice. In contrast to studies of development in other parts of the world, or of economic assistance to Eastern Europe and Russia, we did not find widespread corruption and collusion.[2]

However, our study also reveals a complex picture. While a "third sector" now exists in these societies, in many cases it cannot truly be described as "civil" or "civic" minded. NGOs often are weak factors in their local culture; they focus more on issues of importance to people outside their community than on the needs of those nearest them. Their influence on elites and decision makers is negligible to nonexistent; in many states in these regions power is still centralized.

The evidence suggests that neither assistance nor transnational networks alone make a state democratic. The influence of the transnational networks, and particularly of activist nongovernmental organizations (NGOs) that help to spread norms at the microlevel (that is, within and among specific groups of activists), has been substantial. The macrolevel changes in state behavior that recent studies of norms and networks document, however, appear not to have occurred.[3] Local and Western NGOs have had very little effect on the actual functioning of new fragile institutions. In parts of Eastern Europe and Eurasia, such as Russia and Central Asia, authorities have engaged in abuses, even as networks became more dense. The diffusion of norms and practices associated with democracy has in many cases been affected more by regional norms and practices than by imported international ones.[4] The findings from Eastern Europe and Eurasia suggest that democratic as well as human rights norms and practices are not as robust as the scholarly literature seems to suggest.[5] Western NGOs unfamiliar with the domestic settings and relying on foreign experts and advisers to formulate strategies were hampered in their ability to help make new institutions function. These imported practitioners tended to be good architects, but they did not have the skills to build the structures that they had helped to design.[6]

In this chapter I explore how our findings might alter policy debates about assistance and scholarly debates about the influence of international norms and transnational networks.[7] Although the policy and the scholarly communities rarely speak to one another, the overlap is significant in terms of their concerns and the implications of our findings.[8] At the most fundamental level both are interested in understanding the conditions under which ideas, norms, and practices, such as those inherent in democracy, diffuse inside states.

In this chapter I elaborate on the implications of our findings for NGOs. I then discuss the policy community's analysis of assistance, particularly to Russia, which has been almost devoid of actual empirical evidence and reflects misunderstandings about the exact role that powerful states play in supporting or undermining transnational networks. I note how some of these misunderstandings are shared in the scholarly community. I detail how our findings from Eastern Europe and Eurasia both corroborate and challenge arguments that have focused mainly on the power of norms and networks. The authors in this book find that, although networks influence specific communities of activists, the networks have little power to create fundamental change in the absence of support from the host state and powerful Western states. I conclude by discussing important areas of further investigation suggested by our findings.

THE ROLE OF NGOS

The case studies here highlight many constraints on transnational democracy networks that were at work in Eastern Europe and Eurasia in the 1990s. Western NGOs, central to the advocacy networks, fell prey to significant organizational issues. They relied on young, enthusiastic, but often inexperienced, staff members.[9] They were plagued by overly flat organizational structures, so that no one was entirely sure who was directing the work, which led to inefficiency. Too few people with small budgets worked on enormous issues, such as rebuilding civil society in Bosnia after a war that claimed the lives of more than 200,000 or helping support NGOs in Russia after seventy-five years of authoritarian rule. NGOs that talked only about their successes in order to generate resources raised undue expectations about their effectiveness. They engaged in what the organizational theorist Nils Brunsson describes as the "decoupling" of principle from practice, of "scripts" from behavior.[10] For example, Western groups would talk as if transparent elections had occurred, when in fact the state had greatly manipulated the electoral process. Or groups would emphasize how many local NGOs existed, never mentioning that few, if any, had developed advocacy skills. Western diplomats held fragile and often highly dysfunctional institutions up as shining examples of democracy, and thus these became "rituals that are used for external display."[11] While some NGOs were good at self-promotion, the vast majority were reluctant to be introspective or to learn lessons from their own or others' experience.[12]

When the interests of Western actors dominated transnational networks, such as when Western contexts were the main source of strategies, the networks had unintended negative consequences. For example, the efforts to link local groups to Western networks has come at the cost of ties *between* like-minded groups and has diverted local groups' attention from pressing local needs. Local NGOs that might have campaigned against uranium tailings in the local drinking water flocked instead to biodiversity because donors were more interested in fostering campaigns around transnational environmental issues, while governments and big businesses were pressuring local NGOs to stay away from the uranium issue. Activists might use the discourse of Western-style feminism but fail to mobilize around issues that affect the day-to-day lives of families in postcommunist settings.

In some cases an imbalance in a network has contributed inadvertently to a decline rather than an increase in ideas and practices associated with democracy within the activists' community. It often leads to tremendous competition between groups for funding, as NGOs spring up around issues important to donors, simply to receive money. These observations reveal that networks as such are not inherently balanced entities. Moreover, variations in their structures—for example, how they are weighted, how much financing they have from governments, how local activists are embedded—seem to be related to their efficiency.

The case studies have shown that Western assistance can make a difference if NGO strategies are derived from local ingredients rather than a global cookbook. Western NGOs are, in the second decade after the collapse of communism, just beginning to understand the mix of these ingredients. The practice of applying recipes that worked in Bosnia to Russia or Uzbekistan did not help make new fragile democratic institutions sustainable. Instead, donors and NGOs are having to generate and use as many different strategies and solutions as there are communities engaged in transformation. The reality that strategies and solutions can be developed only in these societies and not in Western capitals poses organizational challenges for NGOs and donors.

Because of the overwhelming reliance on Western practitioners, Western NGOs could not gauge how they should have adapted their strategies to the inherited historical legacies and to the rapidly changing political environment of a country in transition. Often unclear was what the country was moving toward; Russia in 2000 was not the same as Russia in 1992; Slovakia in 1994 and 1999 looked quite different from Czechoslovakia in 1990. Infrastructural assistance and human capital development based on strategies imported from the West may have been appropriate for the early periods when new institutions remained unformed. Later, however, Western NGOs confronted new problems posed by both the transition from communism and the great variation in postcommunist governments.[13] By the late 1990s political parties no longer needed help campaigning; they needed help responding to constituents. Media organizations had been formed, but many were only nominally independent because economic "reform" had created controlling business interests. NGOs existed all across the regions, but some were actually nongovernmental individuals; little, if any, advocacy informed their agenda.

The authors here suggest that when new institutions have emerged and a critical mass of local NGOs and other institutions has developed, reactive strategies that call for local proposals and respond to domestic needs are more likely to be effective in helping to develop sustainable institutions. Regional experts and especially local activists can help devise explicit strategies for reducing the political isolation that this study identifies as widespread among the new local groups that have sprung up since the fall of the Berlin Wall and the collapse of the Soviet Union. Even where local groups' transnational ties are strong, Western NGO strategies should focus more, for example, on incentives for encouraging these groups to develop horizontal (that is, within-country) ties with political parties, trade unions, other local NGOs, and the like. Those Western groups that team regional and local experts with Western practitioners will be better able to read the political and organizational contexts, develop close working relationships with local groups, and implement informed strategies.

Quantitative analysis of programs does not begin to capture the dynamic process of change in diverse groups across the political spectrum in many formerly communist states. Yet both donors and NGOs alike have been reluctant to move away from numbers. This has limited their ability to talk about how ideas and practices actually diffuse. In theory, the spread of ideas beyond activists within a network is a positive outcome. In practice, however, American NGOs and donors alike have feared the congressional response to newspaper headlines claiming that assistance "helped" communists or nationalists; they fear, with some justification, that this would dry up U.S. government funding. Public education about political transitions would help increase the tolerance for NGOs to talk about what really happens, rather than what Congress seems to want to hear.

In this vein it is worth considering, as is sometimes argued, whether the work of Western NGOs and their strategies have contributed to, or resulted in, the rise of "illiberal democracies," countries where rulers hold elections but nevertheless govern in autocratic ways.[14] This book provides much evidence that, for good or ill, assistance to the societies across East-Central Europe and Eurasia tends to influence developments only at the margins. Assistance may have a significant influence within a certain community in these formerly communist states, but it is unlikely that Western NGOs and their local colleagues could in any way alter the internal balance of power within one of these states, either toward or away from democratic rule.

Variations in outcomes across the regions are the result of many factors.[15] Little discussed is that the building blocks of democratic states, whether they are political parties, independent media, or civic groups, are inherently neutral, not exclusively positive organizational structures. As we know from Nazi Germany, they can serve as the building blocks of a fascist state. Elections can lead to bad outcomes for a country in which autocrats rise to power through the ballot box. Nationalist interests can capture the media. Indigenous NGOs can be mobilized to support fascists.[16] Does this mean that NGOs, donors, and policy makers should avoid the promotion of parties, elections, independent media, and civic advocacy groups? Because the results have not been exclusively positive, does that mean all assistance should be stopped?

None of the cases suggests this. Moreover, given the transnational links that already exist between activists in the West and in many formerly communist states, it is too late to turn back the clock. Additionally, local demand drives much of this work. That institutions can be subverted does not mean that activity should stop but that organizations should be more critical and thoughtful about their activity. NGOs, states, and donors must think preventatively to ensure that democracy assistance programs foster democracy and to ensure that their efforts to strengthen transnational democracy networks actually do so.

IMPLICATIONS FOR POLICY DEBATES

Policy makers in the United States and Europe have an interest in understanding how Western efforts to support the development of democratic institutions have affected Eastern Europe and Eurasia. Failed democratization has, at least three times in the last two hundred years, led to overturning the global balance of power.[17] Government officials, particularly in the United States, have tended to exaggerate their own influence on changes in Eastern Europe and Eurasia, but there is no exaggerating the importance of the political transition, nor the hoped-for consolidation of democracy, in these states. The political trajectory of Russia, for example, is key to Europe's stability in the next two decades. It will influence every major security issue of the day, from the proliferation of weapons of mass destruction to crime and corruption to the spread of disease.[18]

Unfortunately, the debate about the effect of assistance has been problematic. Through the 1990s it grew increasingly partisan, parochial, and less empirically based. By 2000 the Republicans in the U.S. Congress were excoriating the Clinton administration for just about everything bad that occurred in Russia, while the Democrats defensively built the "Clinton legacy" on foreign policy.[19] Critics of assistance and crusaders for it have tended to focus mainly on Russia, to the exclusion of other states in the region, and have limited their criticism to the United States, as if no other Western states or organizations were involved. This book shows that U.S. and European groups have worked in many states with mixed results.

The authors here suggest that any critique of assistance should be a fairly focused exploration of a specific type of assistance in a particular place. Blanket statements about U.S. assistance to Russia, for example, usually fail to distinguish meaningfully between economic, democratic, and traditional security programs, such as those funded by the Cooperative Threat Reduction Act.[20] Criticism must focus on specific sectors within each type of assistance. The effect of assistance to political parties and elections is different from the effect of assistance to advocacy groups. The effect of assistance to independent media looks different from the effect of assistance to foster the rule of law.[21] The focus of the analysis should be at the nongovernmental level; governments mainly fund but do not actually carry out the work.

Analysts should also distinguish between the activists targeted by assistance and the policy makers who were not. Democracy assistance is intrinsically limited, as many of the case studies here have shown. Assistance, especially at the nongovernmental level, cannot force decision makers to comply with international norms or practices. It can help transfer or develop skills in people who may, from time to time, work with or serve in government. That Russia's Vladimir Putin or Serbia's Slobodan Milosevic, for example, was outside the scope of democracy assistance is no small detail, yet this is often overlooked in discussions about influence; these men, and others within their countries' governments, have played an enormous role in determining how new political and social institutions actually function in new states.

Western states do have a role to play and thus power to exert. They financed many nongovernmental efforts aimed at supporting the development of institutions commonly associated with democracies, such as civic advocacy groups. The actions of Western decision makers and international organizations have sometimes undermined the work done by the transnational networks—for example, Western support for leaders in Eastern Europe and Eurasia, some of whom are corrupt and ambivalent about democracy.

In both realms, that of funding and that of counterproductive actions, powerful Western states behaved inconsistently throughout the 1990s. The discrepancy in verbal and monetary support, especially by the United States but also by Europe, for the development of democratic institutions in postcommunist states was great. Despite what U.S. policy makers said repeatedly about the importance of developing democratic institutions in Russia, from 1992 to 1996 USAID spent the majority of its Freedom Support Act budget in Russia on market reform while allocating at times as little as 6 percent for democracy assistance. Policy makers offered various explanations for the low amounts of democracy assistance in the early years after the collapse of the Soviet Union (such as Russia had little "capacity" to absorb the funds or the work of Western groups). While these may be correct, they do not account for later figures, which decreased even as capacity increased. They also do not explain why so much more money was allocated to market reform at a time when capacity in the economic sector was perhaps even more limited.[22] In contrast to many pronouncements, particularly in the United States, policies suggested that markets were the first priority and institutions associated with democracy a distant second. This seems to have been a mistake: Economic institutions may have been important to stabilizing the situation in these countries, but political and social institutions play a crucial role in controlling corruption, now rampant in many postcommunist states.

Policy debates about the effect of democracy assistance are incomplete without an understanding of how the larger international environment has affected the transition of states in Eastern Europe and Eurasia. The limits of transnational democracy networks are exacerbated when Western policy makers fail to understand how support for the promotion of democracy is affected by and affects other policies pursued by governments. The actions of the "international community" often have the unintended consequence of undermining the work done at the activist or NGO level. The Euro-Atlantic powers, and institutions such as the Organization for Security and Cooperation in Europe, the Council of Europe, and NATO influence decision makers to comply with or ignore international norms and practices associated with democracy and human rights.

The Euro-Atlantic community of states has been inconsistent in its response to postcommunist states. NATO used force against Serbia for abuses of human rights, but in other cases where the offenses were more widespread and civilian casualties greater, such as in Chechnya, the international community has barely responded.[23] An international environment that permits abuses in some states and punishes them in others makes for a highly fragmented template against which new fragile institutions are developing. The responses of international organizations and governments to leaders such as Vladimir Putin and Boris Yeltsin, who have tolerated enormous abuse of civil and human rights, has isolated democratic activists and undermined the very policies that Western diplomats hoped to be pursuing—the development of democratic institutions.[24]

Many in the West were eager for Russia to be labeled a democracy; they supported Yeltsin because they feared that Communist Party leader Gennady Zyuganov would come to power. The result was that international organizations and powerful Western states evidently set the bar quite low for what is considered democratic. As has been documented many times in places as disparate as the Philippines and Chile, policies based on the fear of communists are not the same thing as supporting democracy. As a result, the Russian leadership appears to have learned the wrong lessons about democracy: The Western, and especially U.S., response to institutional change in Russia suggested that the *form* of institutions was as important as their functioning.[25]

Finally, absent from most policy debates about assistance is the degree to which the state and society in question, whether Poland, Russia, or Uzbekistan, is moving toward or away from integration in the Euro-Atlantic community—not as a product of assistance but as state policy with public support. Perhaps it is not surprising that Western NGO strategies have had the greatest influence in those states where the majority of the population wants to democratize and integrate rapidly into NATO and the European Union. Western NGOs in such contexts provide additional resources in an environment already moving toward democratic governance. Examples include the work of Western NGOs on media in the Czech Republic and women's groups in Poland. In such cases Western NGOs and other outside groups have facilitated the transformation process.

By contrast, the effectiveness of particular strategies in the contested political environments of thinly integrated states such as Russia and unintegrated states such as Uzbekistan has been much more mixed and is much more sensitive to the dynamics of the international environment. In Russia, for example, activists are increasingly isolated from the government that they seek to influence and the citizens whom they hope to represent. At the same time the support for

Russia's president by Western governments such as Great Britain tends to alienate the activists from those governments as well.

In unintegrated states that allow Western NGOs to work, such as in several states in Central Asia, the influence of NGOs and transnational networks is particularly limited. Effective Western NGO strategies in such contexts were those that focused on the periphery of the political sphere, such as working with local cultural organizations and training journalists. Strategies of infrastructural assistance were virtually impossible to implement, given the restrictive nature of the political regimes. Infrastructural assistance to public advocacy groups, with the risks of infighting among recipients and limited influence upon broader goals, was a long-term investment; should the domestic political regimes change, the groups that received funding might one day be in a position to take a leading role in democratization.

IMPLICATIONS FOR SCHOLARLY DEBATES

Transnational democracy networks are a form of transnational advocacy, related to and often overlapping the human rights and environmental networks.[26] International relations scholars have paid increasing attention to the power of these networks, but the cases in this book suggest that the limits of these networks are considerable and need to be better understood.

SIMILARITIES

For more than a decade the networks have engaged in campaigns that "strategically linked activities in which members of a diffuse principled network," in this case centered on the support of democratic institutions in Eastern Europe and Eurasia, "develop[ed] explicit, visible ties and mutually recognized roles in pursuit of a common goal." As described by Margaret Keck and Kathryn Sikkink in *Activists Beyond Borders*, "core network actors mobilize[d] others."[27] Networks developed around issues such as women's rights, environmental degradation, political party formation, free trade unions, and independent media. Environmental networks have campaigned against the dumping of nuclear waste in the Barents Sea. The human rights networks formed under the Helsinki Final Act still exist in Eastern Europe and Eurasia. In Russia, Belarus, and throughout Central Asia they track torture, arbitrary arrest, detention, and disappearances. Other human rights networks formed around issues of conscription, hazing in the military, and the treatment of civilians, refugees, and those who care for the wounded in Chechnya. Some networks intersect at specific events such as elections or the persecution of particular individuals.

Democracy work, like human rights work, is fundamentally a social phenomenon. As Keck and Sikkink argue, personal relationships have a dramatic influence on success or failure. In countries with little or no democratic tradition, democratization appears to be influenced by how people reconcile ideas and practices common in democracies with their long-held domestic beliefs and customs. Personal relationships are central to this process. While new technologies like the Internet and fax machine have facilitated the building of networks, the case studies in this book suggest that ideas spread best through face-to-face contact. Over and over Western NGOs present ideas and practices that derive from norms. Local political activists accept, reject, or adapt these ideas and practices. Which norms and standards of behavior win out over others is the result of human agency; therefore the exploration of advocacy networks must be grounded in the activities of individual actors, both foreign and domestic.

The cases here suggest hypotheses about the conditions under which ideas are likely to spread. These hypotheses should be tested in other cases:

- If new ideas and practices are presented in a way that directly competes with local organizational cultures, local people are likely to reject them.
- If Western NGOs promote ideas and practices that in some way complement local customs, local people tend to adopt and adapt them.
- Central to the diffusion of ideas and practices is the support of local political entrepreneurs; they are the brokers through which the Western NGOs interact with the society.

The power of these groups, like advocacy networks elsewhere, lies not in their access to brute force, funds, or political office but in their ability to spread information. In the post-Soviet context the Western parts of the networks helped level the playing field in terms of information, by getting hardware to groups, helping to set up printing presses, translating texts and mailing newsletters to people, and conducting thousands of hours of training sessions on topics connected with the specific issue around which they were mobilized.[28] "Information politics," this redistribution of knowledge, was particularly important in the post-Soviet context, where the state had monopolized information and kept like-minded groups of people from banding together. It helped empower people whose voices had been muffled by communist authorities for as long as seventy-five years. Networks organized around a specific issue, such as the war in Chechnya or nuclear waste, used information and publicity as a shaming technique against authorities that were perpetrating the crimes.

DIFFERENCES

The case studies from Eastern Europe and Eurasia challenge dominant trends in the literature concerning international norms and transnational advocacy networks. Implicit in much recent work is an idealized picture of a seemingly steady march toward increased compliance, as human rights and democracy norms "cascade" through "the international community." At this moment in "world time" many scholars expect to see such norms grow particularly strong.[29] The post-Soviet cases here challenge this growing conventional wisdom and provide a detailed look at how Western ideas and practices interact with local cultures and norms.[30]

Case selection seems to play a role in the comparative weight that scholars give to the power or to the limits of norms and advocacy networks. Latin Americanists working on human rights and scholars of the antiapartheid movement have evidence that international norms have power. Journalists even write about the "Pinochet effect," referring to efforts in Chile, Argentina, and Uruguay to investigate the human rights abuses of leaders.[31]

However, Eastern Europe, and especially Eurasia, looks quite different. In the states that emerged from the collapse of the Soviet Union, not a single legal case has been brought—never mind one resulting in conviction or other form of accountability—on behalf of the millions of citizens killed under Stalin. Instead, in a 1999 poll that asked Russians to choose the "most outstanding personalities of all times and all nations," Stalin ranked in 1999 in fourth place with 35 percent, up from 11 percent in 1989. More Russians object to people who have gotten rich since the collapse of the Soviet Union than to people carrying portraits of Stalin.[32] President Vladimir Putin was reported to have toasted Stalin on his birthday in December 1999; in May 2000 the Russian state issued commemorative coins in honor of Stalin as a "war hero."[33]

In the mid- to late 1990s Russia and many states in Central Asia experienced significant regression in human rights and democracy, despite the presence of many conditions that scholars have argued caused positive change elsewhere. For example, "principled-issue networks" have existed around many aspects of both democracy and human rights, some as far back as the Helsinki Accords of 1975, and became increasingly dense in the decade since the collapse of the Soviet Union. As the chapters in this book show, the degree to which local activists are connected to these transnational networks varies greatly. Leaders in many of these countries, such as Boris Yeltsin and Vladimir Putin, have shown concern for the opinions of Euro-Atlantic decision makers, expending effort to host and visit European and American leaders, seeking and gaining membership in many Euro-Atlantic "clubs." This variable concerning reputation has been an important one in the literature. The states that emerged from the collapse of the Soviet Union, and especially Russia, have been dependent on and have received billions of dollars in financial assistance. Hundreds of millions of dollars have gone to support democracy work.

Yet even with these conditions, outcomes in postcommunist states, especially Russia, diverge from the expectations generated by much of the literature on the power of norms. Although a few postcommunist states are steadily moving in the direction of democracy (Poland, for example), some have regressed (Russia, Belarus, Ukraine, and Georgia), while others, such as in Central Asia, are experiencing conditions worse than under the Soviets.[34] Wherever we look in Eastern Europe and Eurasia, the transition process looks shaky, and the scope and direction of change within these countries contrasts starkly with the triumphant stories in the international relations literature.

The case of Russia is particularly troubling because of the role that it plays in the region and in international politics. By the late 1990s Russia's federal and local authorities had grown increasingly bold in their threats to civil liberties and human rights. The state especially targeted independent media outlets. In numerous cases environmentalists, human rights activists, and even students and academics — Russians but also Americans and Europeans — were intimidated, interrogated, trailed, jailed, robbed, accused of treason, beaten, and run out of the country.[35] The bloodiest part of the regression was the brutal way that the Russian federal forces prosecuted the second war in Chechnya; troops have routinely violated both the Geneva Convention and the Universal Declaration of Human Rights.[36]

The harassment of activists and the war in Chechnya are not unprecedented in post-Soviet Russia. Activists, however, viewed the regression in the late 1990s as more serious and stark than anything Russia had experienced since before Mikhail Gorbachev came to power in 1985. Nevertheless, Putin enjoyed nights at the opera and pints of beer with Tony Blair, tea with the queen of England, was the toast of the town at the July 2000 G-7 meeting in Okinawa, and was warmly included in the July 2001 meeting in Genoa, although Russia had neither a strong industrialized economy nor a robust democracy.

The Russian and Central Asian cases discussed in this book suggest that the likelihood of successful diffusion of norms may be overstated in the literature. The norms that many scholars presume to be increasingly robust, cascading, and shared, such as human rights and democracy, appear in fact to be rather weak, inconsistently applied by powerful states, and repeatedly overwhelmed by historical legacies. The reasons why so many actors in the international system forgive or overlook significant noncompliance, and thereby help to weaken the norms that they profess to be diffusing, deserves additional attention from scholars.

Whatever the reasons, the consequences are stark. The logic of democratic state behavior is muddled. Because the incentives are ambiguous and contradictory, the diffusion of norms does not occur in the (more or less) linear fashion that the literature often depicts.[37] In contrast to expectations generated by studies on human rights, the way that the Euro-Atlantic states have responded to Russia seems to say that it is perfectly possible to be "norm violating" *and* a member of the "in-group" or at least invited to its functions.[38] Thus punishment for lack of progress is absent.

Moreover, the case of Russia suggests that we need to better identify the precise role of powerful states and decision makers in successful outcomes. Especially when dealing with a state as vast and still relatively powerful as Russia, networks have only a limited ability to bring about change if they do not have the support of states. The fall of the Berlin Wall, for example, had as much, if not more, to do with decisions made by Mikhail Gorbachev than with the work of activists and NGOs. Likewise, the power to keep states like Russia out of the in-group, or to change the policies of other countries that abuse rights and threaten new institutions, resides not with advocacy networks but with states like Great Britain and the United States. Nowhere is this clearer than in the inability of transnational networks to protect local activists.[39]

Finally, the cases here make clear that cultural context and historical legacy matter to transnational advocacy networks. Culture, history, and politics do not determine all outcomes, but contextual factors are necessary to the diffusion of norms inside states. In order to be influential, ideas for encouraging the development of democratic institutions, whether in Bosnia, Russia, or Kyrgyzstan, must be compatible with local organizational cultures. Context matters to local people, and ignoring it in research obscures the dynamic of contestation between international and domestic norms.

AREAS FOR FURTHER RESEARCH

The case studies here suggest many important areas for further research. Scholars and policy makers alike have reason to embark on a definitive study of the effect of Western assistance on political and social institutions in Eastern Europe and Eurasia. Ideally, this project would be revisited in ten or twenty years' time in order to build knowledge longitudinally. Policy and scholarship should also compare findings in Eastern Europe and Eurasia in a systematic fashion with those from Latin America and elsewhere.

Several areas deserve additional inquiry. The size of the target country matters, not simply geographically but in terms of the amount of assistance relative to the economy. The ratio of assistance dollars to the size of the local economy seems to be an indicator of the degree to which external assistance can affect the internal balance of power. For example, in Burundi and Rwanda assistance seems to have played a much more central political role than in, say, Russia.[40] Where development assistance has essentially replaced the state, the correlation with increased dependence and even chaos is high.[41] We need to look at these dynamics, as they may shape politics in Eastern Europe and Eurasia.

The cases in this book show that historical legacy matters too, but scholars need to establish under what conditions is it likely to matter. For example, how is the salience of historical legacy related to economic prosperity? David Conradt criticizes the famous study by Gregory Almond and Sidney Verba on postwar Germany for just this reason:

> In neglecting to examine directly or systematically the effects of history upon political culture, [Almond and Verba] were unable to deal satisfactorily with the problem of change. If there is a relationship between a country's "traumatic history" and its political culture, what happens to political values over time as the traumatic events become increasingly remote to an increasingly large segment of the population?[42]

Conradt found that trauma decreased in salience as the economy in Germany developed. In Russia polling data have suggested that trauma seems to become more salient as the economy falters. This correlation needs to be developed further.

Many of the findings of our study confirm earlier work done by some other observers of democracy assistance.[43] Those studies also stressed the need for increased participation by local citizens and more attention to context. The comparisons of strategies in this book provide a range of case studies to support suggestions about *how* Western donors should adapt to the dynamic conditions of political and social transition. They also highlight how, on occasion, such as in Kazakhstan, policies promoting economic and political developments work at cross-purposes.

Our findings suggest that if Western groups pursue a business-as-usual approach in the coming years, their influence on the development of sustainable democratic institutions in Central and Eastern Europe and Eurasia will diminish dramatically. Given the lack of response by NGOs to earlier studies, however, we have little reason to believe that they will respond to these findings. Why is that? Why have organizations — NGOs but also government groups such as USAID — been generally reluctant to change? What is it about how NGOs are configured that inhibits their changing? This organizational behavior too warrants examination by scholars.

IN CLOSING

This book, like most, reflects the period in which it was written. As a post–cold war study it has focused on the rise of transnational efforts to help build democratic institutions and the difficulties of political and social change in the societies emerging at different rates and with varied burdens from communist, socialist, and Soviet legacies. When the cold war was over, many were inclined to hope or believe that great power politics were finished, the bipolar system shattered, and international norms on the rise: People had triumphed, at the Berlin

Wall, in Prague, in Budapest, and on top of tanks in Moscow rather than under them.

By the new century, however, a close look at the states and societies of Central Europe, Eastern Europe, and Eurasia, and their interaction with the West reveals that all are, in many ways, between eras. We are still crossing from the old world order to something new. The new—particularly as embodied by the transnational, the changed conceptions of sovereignty, the links between populations thousands of miles apart—has power but not all the power. What may have looked like the "road to democracy," like the "path to socialism" in another era, turns out to be circuitous and bumpy, and occasionally it even leads backward. When scholars return in ten or twenty years to review the cases in this book, will they find that the power of transnational democracy networks has increased or diminished? Will the constraints have been overcome or have proved overwhelming? Most important, will the people in these regions have prospered or become more impoverished? Will fragile institutions be robust or will they have collapsed? The cases here will, we hope, have convinced critics and crusaders alike that these issues are crucial as we move into an increasingly interlinked global future.

NOTES

1. On the tendency to conform to international norms, see Martha Finnemore and Kathryn Sikkink, "International Norm Dynamics and Political Change," *International Organization* 52, no. 4 (1998): 903.

2. By 2000 several investigations were pending concerning the abuse of Western economic assistance to Russia from the International Monetary Fund, the World Bank, and USAID. See Janine Wedel, *Collision and Collusion: The Strange Case of Western Aid to Eastern Europe, 1989–1998* (New York: St. Martin's, 1998). For a critique of development assistance in Africa, see Peter Uvin, *Aiding Violence: The Development Enterprise in Rwanda* (West Hartford, Conn.: Kumarian, 1998).

3. On transnational networks see the pioneering work of Margaret E. Keck and Kathryn Sikkink, *Activists Beyond Borders: Advocacy Networks in International Politics* (Ithaca: Cornell University Press, 1998).

4. The dynamic of international versus domestic norms has been effectively highlighted by Jeffrey Legro, "Which Norms Matter: Revising the 'Failure' of Internationalism," *International Organization* 51, no. 1 (Winter 1997): 31–63; Andrew P. Cortell and James W. Davis Jr., "Understanding the Domestic Impact of International Norms: A Research Agenda," *International Studies Review* 2 (2000): 65–87; Amy Gurowitz, "Mobilizing International Norms: Domestic Actors, Immigrants, and the Japanese State," *World Politics* 51, no.3 (1999): 413–45.

5. Thomas Risse, Stephen C. Ropp, and Kathryn Sikkink, eds., *The Power of Human Rights: International Norms and Domestic Change* (Cambridge: Cambridge University

Press, 1999); Keck and Sikkink, *Activists Beyond Borders*; Audie Klotz, *Norms in International Relations: The Struggle Against Apartheid* (Ithaca: Cornell University Press, 1995); Daniel C. Thomas, *The Helsinki Effect: International Norms, Human Rights, and the Demise of Communism* (Princeton: Princeton University, 2001).

6. On this point see also Thomas Carothers, *Aiding Democracy Abroad: The Learning Curve* (Washington, D.C.: Carnegie Endowment for International Peace, 1999); Nancy Lubin, "U.S. Assistance to the NIS," in Karen Dawisha, ed., *The International Dimension of Postcommunist Transitions in Russia and the New States of Eurasia*, pp. 350–78 (Armonk, N.Y.: Sharpe, 1997).

7. I draw not only on the evidence presented in this book but also on my involvement with democracy assistance programs in Russia since the early 1990s, including working from August 1994 to July 1995 in Moscow as a program officer with a U.S.-based NGO that helped support political party activists. This chapter also draws on arguments that I developed in "Democracy Assistance and Russia's Transition: Between Success and Failure," *International Security* 25, no. 4 (Spring 2001): 69–103, and "Russians' Rights Imperiled: Has Anybody Noticed?" *International Security* 26, no. 4 (Spring 2002): 39–69.

8. Gideon Rose, "Democracy Promotion and American Foreign Policy," *International Security* 25, no. 3 (Winter 2000–1): 87–123. Carothers, *Aiding Democracy Abroad*, speaks to both scholars and the policy community, and in that it is rare.

9. One former employee of an NGO referred to "crisis hiring" wherein the NGO quickly sent a staffer overseas to become immediately immersed in the fray (Stephen Biegun, former trainer for the International Republican Institute, interview by author, August 25, 1998).

10. Nils Brunsson, *The Organization of Hypocrisy: Talk, Decisions, and Actions in Organizations* (Chichester, U.K.: Wiley, 1989), as cited in Stephen D. Krasner, *Sovereignty: Organized Hypocrisy* (Princeton: Princeton University Press), p. 65.

11. Ibid. In this case *external* refers to those outside the "democracy assistance" community.

12. This observation comes from my attendance at a series of meetings held in 2000 by USAID's Bureau for Europe and Eurasia, Office of Democracy and Governance, to evaluate lessons from ten years of democracy assistance to Eastern Europe and Eurasia. See Carothers, *Aiding Democracy Abroad*, pp. 8–10, on USAID's failure to learn, adapt, and change.

13. On the variation in outcome and how the term *postcommunism* means little, see Charles King, "Post-postcommunism: Transition, Comparison, and the End of 'Eastern Europe,'" *World Politics* 53, no. 1 (October 2000): 143–72.

14. Fareed Zakaria, "The Rise of Illiberal Democracy," *Foreign Affairs* 76, no. 6 (November–December 1997): 22–43.

15. King, "Post-postcommunism."

16. Sheri Berman, "Civil Society and the Collapse of the Weimar Republic," *World Politics* 49, no. 3 (1997): 401–29. Rwanda is a more recent example of genocide that occurred despite the presence of a large number of NGOs and churches; see Uvin, *Aiding Violence*.

17. Examples of failed democratization that led to shifts in the global balance of power would include France under Napoleon, 1803–1815; Germany under Kaiser Wilhelm, 1914–1918; and Nazi Germany, 1939–1945. See Jack Snyder, *From Voting to Violence: Democratization and National Conflict* (New York: Norton, 2000), 20–21.

18. The U.S. Mission (Russia) Performance Plan for 2000–2002 claims that "the consolidation of democratic institutions and values in Russia over the long term is a vital US national security interest" (as cited in David Cohen, McKinney Russel, and Boris Makarenko, "An Assessment of USAID Political Party Building and Related Activities in Russia," report prepared by Management Systems International for USAID/Moscow, Office of Democracy Initiatives and Human Resources, June 30, 2000, p. 38). The U.S. Embassy Mission Performance Plan for 1999–2001 argues that "a prosperous, democratic, cohesive Russia will promote stability at home and among its neighbors. A weak, divided, conflicted Russia will invite destabilizing, outside interference and project dangerous uncertainty" (U.S. Embassy, "Mission Performance Performance Plan FY1999–2001," n.d., Moscow, p. 4). On the distinction between *transition* and *consolidation*, see Guillermo O'Donnell and Philippe Schmitter, *Transitions from Authoritarian Rule: Tentative Conclusions* (Baltimore, Md.: Johns Hopkins University Press, 1986); Juan Linz and Alfred Stepan, *Problems of Democratic Transition and Consolidation: Southern Europe, South America, and Postcommunist Europe* (Baltimore, Md.: Johns Hopkins University Press, 1996); Larry Diamond, Marc Plattner, Yun-han Chu, and Hung-mao Tien, eds., *Consolidating the Third Wave Democracies: Themes and Perspectives* (Baltimore, Md.: Johns Hopkins University Press, 1997); Larry Diamond, *Developing Democracy: Toward Consolidation* (Baltimore, Md.: Johns Hopkins University Press, 1999).

19. Speaker's Advisory Group on Russia, "Russia's Road to Corruption: How The Clinton Administration Exported Government Instead of Free Enterprise and Failed the Russian People," September 2000, at http://policy.house.gov/russia (November 1, 2001); Samuel R. Berger, "A Foreign Policy for the Global Age," *Foreign Affairs* 70, no. 6, (November–December 2000): 22–39.

20. Examples include Speaker's Advisory Group, "Russia's Road to Corruption"; Berger, "Foreign Policy"; and Stephen F. Cohen, *Failed Crusade: America and the Tragedy of Postcommunist Russia* (New York: Norton, 2000).

21. On the effect of assistance to parties and elections in Russia, see Mendelson, "Democracy Assistance and Russia's Transition"; more generally, see Carothers, *Aiding Democracy Abroad*.

22. The argument that NGOs engaged in democracy assistance are less expensive than the corporations under contract for economic assistance (which were paid more than NGOs) is not a reflection of the marketplace but of the priorities of Western policy makers. The result on the economic side of assistance seems to have been inflated budgets and stays at fancy hotels (Wedel, *Collision and Collusion*).

23. Physicians for Human Rights, *War Crimes in Kosovo: A Population-Based Assessment of Human Rights Violations Against Kosovar Albanians* (Washington, D.C.: 1999); Physicians for Human Rights, "Medical Group Releases Final Data on Russian Atrocities in Chechnya; Calls on Clinton to Take a Stand on War Crimes," press release, June 2, 2000, http://www.phrusa.org (November 1, 2001).

24. Western and Russian organizations tracked human rights abuses during the Yeltsin era and continue to do so in the Putin era. These include "filtration" or concentration camps in the first and second war in Chechnya (Amnesty International and Human Rights Watch); hazing and torture among conscripts in the military (Committee of Soldiers' Mothers); and treatment in prisons and jails (Amnesty International, Human Rights Watch, and Nizhni Novgorod Society for Human Rights). Labor activists argue that the unpaid wages long owed to Russian workers are also a form of human rights abuse (Irene Stevenson, executive director, American Center for International Labor Solidarity, update on labor conditions in Russia after the fall of the ruble, AFL-CIO headquarters, Washington, D.C., September 9, 1998).

25. Perhaps nowhere is this more problematic than in the international stamp of approval issued to elections. A memo written by the the National Democratic Institute's in-house expert on observing international elections notes that "autocrats have become more sophisticated in their attempts at electoral manipulation." He also notes that "autocrats know [that observers tend to focus on election day] and increasingly attempt to manipulate other elements of the electoral process so that election day seems more-or-less normal," prompting observers to release statements just forty-eight to seventy-two hours after polls close (Patrick Merloe, "Lessons Learned and Challenges Facing International Monitoring," in-house memo, National Democratic Institute, Washington, D.C., March 1999, pp. 3, 5).

26. Keck and Sikkink, *Activists Beyond Borders*; Risse, Ropp, and Sikkink, *The Power of Human Rights*.

27. Keck and Sikkink, *Activists Beyond Borders*, p. 6.

28. For example, while working in Russia in 1994 and 1995, I attended numerous meetings on elections and political parties held by the National Democratic Institute. These sessions included information about transparency in elections, such as how to monitor an election, and about all aspects of competitive campaigns, such as getting out the message and the use of polling data.

29. See Finnemore and Sikkink, "International Norm Dynamics"; Keck and Sikkink, *Activists Beyond Borders*; Risse, Ropp, and Sikkink, *The Power of Human Rights*; Klotz, *Norms in International Relations*; Kathryn Sikkink, "Human Rights, Principled Issue-Networks, and Sovereignty in Latin America," *International Organization* 47, no. 3 (Summer 1993): 411–42; Audie Klotz, "Norms Reconstituting Interests: Global Racial Equality and U.S. Sanctions Against South Africa," *International Organization* 49, no. 3 (Summer 1995): 451–78; Richard Price, "Reversing the Gun Sights: Transnational Civil Society Targets Land Mines," *International Organization* 52, no. 3 (Summer 1998): 613–44; Paul Wapner, "Politics Beyond the State: Environmental Activism and World Civic Politics," *World Politics* 47, no. 3 (April 1995): 311–40; Gregory Flynn and Henry Farrell, "Piecing Together the Democratic Peace: The CSCE, Norms, and the 'Construction' of Security in Post–Cold War Europe," *International Organization* 53, no. 3 (1999): 505–35; John Boli and George M. Thomas, eds., *Constructing World Culture: International Nongovernmental Organizations Since 1875* (Stanford, Calif.: Stanford University Press, 1999).

30. On the need to study the interaction see Jeffrey T. Checkel, "The Constructivist Turn in International Relations Theory," *World Politics* 50, no. 2 (January 1998): 324–48; and Cortell and Davis, "Understanding the Domestic Impact."

31. Klotz, "Norms Reconstituting interests"; Sikkink, "Human Rights"; Ellen L. Lutz and Kathryn Sikkink, "International Human Rights Law and Practice in Latin America," *International Organization* 54, no. 3 (2000): 633–59; Anthony Faiola, "Pinochet Effect Spreading," *Washington Post*, August 5, 2000.

32. One survey in 1999 found that 55 percent felt negatively toward people "who got rich in the last ten years" versus 29 percent who felt negatively toward "people carrying portraits of Stalin." Fifty-two percent felt positively toward Stalinists. Figures come from a series of polls conducted by the All-Russian Center for Public Opinion, http://www.RussiaVotes.org (November 1, 2001), as cited in Edward Skidelsky and Yuri Senokosov, *Russia on Russia: Issue Two: The Fate of Homo Sovieticus* (London: Social Market Foundation and the All-Russian Center of Public Opinion Studies, 2000).

33. Ian Traynor, "Russia's New Strongman Puts Stalin Back on a Pedestal," *Guardian* (U.K.), May 13, 2000, as carried on David Johnson's *Russia List*, http://www.cdi.org/russia/johnson (November 1, 2001).

34. Cassandra Cavanaugh, "The Iron Hands of Central Asia," *Washington Post*, August 2, 2000. (Cavanaugh is a researcher for Human Rights Watch.) See also Sophie Lambroschini, "Central Asia: Russia Sanctioning Anti-Islamic Crackdown," *RFE/RL*, August 2, 2000; see also the weekly updates on human rights and democracy in Central Asia in "Voice of Democracy," an e-mail publication by the Kazakhstan 21st Century Foundation; and those from EurasiaNet, http://www.eurasianet.org (November 1, 2001).

35. See "On the Violations Committed in the Course of Registration and Re-Registration of Public Associations in the Russian Federation in 1999" (report prepared by the Information Center of the Human Rights Movement and the Center for the Development of Democracy and Human Rights, Moscow, February 15, 2000); Boris Pustintsev, Citizens' Watch, St. Petersburg, "Russian Authorities Declared War on Human Rights NGOs," courtesy author's e-mail correspondence with Alyson Ewald of the Sacred Earth Network, May 2000; Yuri Dzhibladze, president, Center for the Development of Democracy and Human Rights, interview by author, Moscow, March 24, 2000; Masha Lipman, former deputy editor, *Itogi*, interview by author, Moscow, May 18, 2000. (*Itogi* was taken over by a state-owned company, Gazprom Media, and most of the journalists were fired in April 2001.) For examples of non-Russians being harassed, see Joshua Handler, "Under Suspicion," *IEEE Spectrum* 7, no. 3 (March 2000): 51–53, where he recounts his October 1999 experience when the FSB, a successor to the KGB, confiscated his research materials, and he was expelled from Russia. Handler had been an environmental activist with Greenpeace before enrolling in a doctoral program at Princeton University. The number of foreign missionaries expelled from Russia has increased. A program officer from the National Democratic Institute, a U.S.-based NGO, fled the country in 1999 after repeated harassment and threats from the FSB. The British charity that removes land mines, Halo Trust, was accused of treason and expelled from Russia (Halo Trust program officer who asked to remain anonymous, telephone interview by author, May 31, 2000). For other examples see Masha Gessen, "In Russia, Echoes of the Old KGB: Going After Foreign Aid Workers and Others," *U.S. News and World Report*, July 30, 2001, as carried on Johnson's *Russia List*, http://www.cdi.org/russia/johnson (November 1, 2001).

36. Many groups have gathered testimony on the abuses by federal forces, including Human Rights Watch, Amnesty International, Physicians for Human Rights, the Russian groups Memorial and Committee of Soldiers' Mothers in St. Petersburg, the French group Doctors of the World, and the Nobel Peace Prize recipient Doctors Without Borders. See in particular "Civilian Killings in Staropromyslovski District of Grozny," *Human Rights Watch* 12, no. 2 (February 2000); "No Happiness Remains: Civilian Killings, Pillage, and Rape in Alkhan-Yurt, Chechnya," *Human Rights Watch* 12, no. 5 (April 2000); "February 5: A Day of Slaughter in Novye Aldi," *Human Rights Watch* 12, no. 9 (June 2000); Rachel Denber, deputy director, Europe and Central Asia division, Human Rights Watch, testimony before U.S. House Commission on Security and Cooperation in Europe, May 23, 2000, available at http://www.house .gov/csce/denber.htm (November 1, 2001). Francis Boyle, a University of Illinois law professor who, on behalf of Bosnian Muslims, won a suit against Yugoslavia for committing genocide in Bosnia, filed suit with the International Court in the Hague in July 2000 on behalf of Chechnya, accusing Russia of committing genocide. See "Chechnya Seeks Genocide Finding Against Russia," *RFE/RL Briefing Report*, August 15, 2000, available at http://www.rferl.org/welcome/english/releases/chechnya000815 .html (November 1, 2001).

37. See, for example, Risse, Ropp, and Sikkink, *Power of Human Rights*.

38. Ibid., p. 38. Russia has membership or a special relationship with many international organizations, including NATO, the G-7, the Organization for Security and Cooperation in Europe, and the Council of Europe.

39. Transnational groups have no concrete ability to protect their partners and must rely on policy makers to do so. Several incidents in 1999 and 2000 suggest that even non-Russians who work for Western NGOs are not always safe in Russia, yet Western decision makers have not been willing to do much when representatives of NGOs are kicked out, according to activists from British and American NGOs with whom I spoke. For an alternative argument, see Risse, Ropp, and Sikkink, *Power of Human Rights*.

40. See Michael S. Lund, Barnett R. Rubin, and Fabienne Hara, "Learning from Burundi's Failed Democratic Transition, 1993–1996: Did International Initiatives Match the Problem?" in Barnett R. Rubin, ed., *Cases and Strategies for Preventive Action*, pp. 47–91 (New York: Century Foundation Press, 1998).

41. Uvin, *Aiding Violence*.

42. David P. Conradt, "Changing German Political Culture," in Gabriel A. Almond and Sidney Verba, eds., *The Civic Culture Revisited* (Newbury Park, Calif.: Sage, 1989), p. 225.

43. Carothers, *Aiding Democracy Abroad*; Lubin, "U.S. Assistance to the NIS."

INDEX

Uzbekistan, democracy assistance in
(*continued*) 188; third sector development , 177, 190, 199; women's organizations, 178, 189

Vandenberg, Martina, 65
Velvet Divorce, 14
Velvet Revolution, 95
Verba, Sidney, 245
VOOP (All-Russian Society for the Pro-
tection of Nature), 130
Voronina, Olga, 77

Warsaw Declaration (2000), 7
Weinthal, Erika, 17, 154
Winrock International, 64–65, 67, 167
Women Also, 42
Women for Clear Water, 42
Women, Law, and Development, Inter-
national, 69, 70
Women's Beijing Conference, 35, 217
Women's Chapter of Autonomous Trade
Unions, 42
Women's Club, 42
Women's Information Network, 67
Women's Leadership Program, 65
Women's organizations, 23, 29, 30, 31, 47,
217; charitable, 61–62; coalition build-
ing, 65; competition among, 48; femi-
nist, 13, 14, 60–61, 65, 81; participation

in, 41; political, 60; *see also* Hungary,
women's NGOs in; Poland, women's
NGOs in; Russia, women's Organiza-
tions and Western assistance in
Women's Program, 30
Women's Resource Center, 178
Women's Right Center, 30, 33
Women's World Banking (WWB), 30, 31,
38, 39, 45
Women's World Banks, 31, 36
Women Working with Women Against
Violence, *see* NaNE
World Bank, 135, 160, 164, 166, 190, 219
World Learning, 68, 217
World Wide Fund for Nature (WWF),
128, 133, 140
WWB, *see* Women's World Banking
(WWB)

Yekaterinburg, 56, 78
Yeltsin, Boris, 4, 60, 131, 239
Yeltsin government, 76, 77, 131, 146
Yershova, Yelena, 65, 76
Yugoslavia, 210
Yuzhneftegas, 170

Zagreb, 211
Zakaria, fareed, 4
Zelikova, Julia, 61
Zyuganov, Gennady, 239